The Story of the

Sarah Orne J

THE STORY OF THE NORMANS.

I. THE MEN OF THE DRAGON SHIPS.

"Far as the breeze can bear, the billows foam,

Survey our empire and behold our home." —BYRON.

THE gulf stream flows so near to the southern coast of Norway, and to the Orkneys and Western Islands, that their climate is much less severe than might be supposed. Yet no one can help wondering why they were formerly so much more populous than now, and why the people who came westward even so long ago as the great Aryan migration, did not persist in turning aside to the more fertile countries that lay farther southward. In spite of all their disadvantages, the Scandinavian peninsula, and the sterile islands of the northern seas, were inhabited by men and women whose enterprise and intelligence ranked them above their neighbors.

Now, with the modern ease of travel and transportation, these poorer countries can be supplied from other parts of the world. And though the summers of Norway are misty and dark and short, and it is difficult to raise even a little hay on the bits of meadow among the rocky mountain slopes, commerce can make up for all deficiencies. In early times there was no commerce except that carried on by the pirates—if we may dignify their undertakings by such a respectable name,—and it was hardly possible to make a living from the soil alone. The sand dunes of Denmark and the cliffs of Norway alike gave little encouragement to tillers of the ground, yet, in defiance of all our ideas of successful colonization, when the people of these countries left them, it was at first only to form new settlements in such places as Iceland, or the Faroe or Orkney islands and stormiest Hebrides. But it does not take us long to discover that the ancient Northmen were not farmers, but hunters and fishermen. It had grown more and more difficult to find food along the rivers and broad grassy wastes of inland Europe, and pushing westward they had at last reached the place where they could live beside waters that swarmed with fish and among hills that sheltered plenty of game.

Besides this they had been obliged not only to make the long journey by slow degrees, but to fight their way and to dispossess the people who were already established. There is very little known of these earlier dwellers in the east and north of Europe, except that they were short of stature and dark-skinned, that they were cave dwellers, and, in successive stages of development, used stone and bronze and iron tools and weapons. Many relics of their home-life and of their warfare have been discovered and preserved in museums, and there are evidences of the descent of a small proportion of modern Europeans from that remote ancestry. The Basques of the north of Spain speak a different language and wear a different look from any of the surrounding people, and even in Great Britain there are some survivors of an older race of humanity, which the fairer-haired Celts of Southern Europe and Teutons of Northern Europe have never been able in the great natural war of races to wholly exterminate and supplant. Many changes and minglings of the inhabitants of these countries, long establishment of certain tribes, and favorable or unfavorable conditions of existence have made the nations of Europe differ widely from each other at the present day, but they are believed to have come from a common stock, and certain words of the Sanscrit language can be found repeated not only in Persian and Indian speech to-day, but in English and Greek and Latin and German, and many dialects that have been formed from these.

The tribes that settled in the North grew in time to have many peculiarities of their own, and as their countries grew more and more populous, they needed more things that could not easily be had, and a fashion of plundering their neighbors began to prevail. Men were still more or less beasts of prey. Invaders must be kept out, and at last much of the industry of Scandinavia was connected with the carrying on of an almost universal fighting and marauding. Ships must be built, and there must be endless . supplies of armor and weapons. Stones were easily collected for missiles or made fit for arrows and spear-heads, and metals were worked with great care. In Norway and Sweden were the best places to find all these, and if the Northmen planned to fight a great battle, they had to transport a huge quantity of stones, iron, and bronze. It is easy to see why one day's battle was almost always decisive in ancient times, for supplies could not be quickly forwarded from point to point, and after the arrows were all shot and the conquered were chased off the field, they had no further means of offence except a hand-to-hand fight with those who had won the right to pick up the fallen spears at their leisure. So, too, an unexpected invasion was likely to prove successful; it was a work of time to get ready for a battle, and when the Northmen swooped down upon some shore town of Britain or Gaul, the unlucky citizens were at their mercy. And while the Northmen had fish and game and were mighty hunters, and their rocks and mines helped forward their warlike enterprises, so the forests supplied them with ship timber, and they gained renown as sailors wherever their fame extended.

There was a great difference, however, between the manner of life in Norway and that of England or France. The Norwegian stone, however useful for arrow heads or axes, was not fit for building purposes. There is hardly any clay there, either, to make bricks with, so that wood has usually been the only material for houses. In the Southern countries there had always been rude castles in which the people could shelter themselves, but the Northmen could build no castles that a torch could not destroy. They trusted much more to their ships than to their houses, and some of their great captains disdained to live on shore at all.

There is something refreshing in the stories of old Norse life; of its simplicity and freedom and childish zest. An old writer says that they had "a hankering after pomp and pageantry," and by means of this they came at last to doing things decently and in order, and to setting the fashions for the rest of Europe. There was considerable dignity in the manner of every-day life and housekeeping. Their houses were often very large, even two hundred feet long, with the flaring fires on a pavement in the middle of the floor, and the beds built next the walls on three sides, sometimes hidden by wide tapestries or foreign cloth that had been brought home in the viking ships. In front of the beds were benches where each man had his seat and footstool, with his armor and weapons hung high on the wall above. The master of the house had a high seat on the north side in the middle of a long bench; opposite was another bench for guests and strangers, while the women sat on the third side. The roof was high, there were a few windows in it, and those were covered by thin skins and let in but little light. The smoke escaped through openings in the carved, soot-blackened roof, and though in later times the rich men's houses were more like villages, because they made groups of smaller buildings for storehouses, for guest-rooms, or for workshops all around, still, the idea of this primitive great hall or living-room has not even yet been lost. The later copies of it in England and France that still remain are most interesting; but what a fine sight it must have been at night when the great fires blazed and the warriors sat on their benches in solemn order, and the skalds recited their long sagas, of the host's own bravery or the valiant deeds of his ancestors! Hospitality was almost made chief among the virtues. There was a Norwegian woman named Geirrid who went from Heligoland to Iceland and settled there. She built her house directly across the public road, and used to sit in the doorway on a little bench and invite all travellers to come in and refresh themselves from a table that always stood ready, spread with food. She was not the only one, either, who gave herself up to such an exaggerated idea of the duties of a housekeeper.

When a distinguished company of guests was present, the pleasures of the evening were made more important. Listening to the sagas was the best entertainment that could be offered. "These productions were of very ancient origin and entirely foreign to those countries where the Latin language prevailed. They had little or nothing to do with either chronology or general history; but were limited to the traditions of some heroic families, relating their deeds and adventures in a style that was always simple and sometimes poetic. These compositions, in verse or prose, were the fruit of a wild. Northern genius. They were evolved without models, and disappeared at last without imitations; and it is most remarkable that in the island of Iceland, of which the name alone is sufficient hint of its frightful climate, and where the very name of poet has almost become a wonder,—in this very island the skalds (poets) have produced innumerable sagas and other compositions during a space of time which covers the twelfth, thirteenth, and fourteenth centuries."

The court poets or those attached to great families were most important persons, and were treated with great respect and honor. No doubt, they often fell into the dangers of either flattery or scandal, but they were noted for their simple truthfulness. We cannot help feeling such an atmosphere in those sagas that still exist, but the world has always been very indulgent towards poetry that captivates the imagination. Doubtless, nobody expected that a skald should always limit himself to the part of a literal narrator. They were the makers and keepers of legends and literature in their own peculiar form of history, and as to worldly position, ranked much higher than the later minstrels and troubadours or trouvères who wandered about France.

When we remember the scarcity and value of parchment even in the Christianized countries of the South, it is a great wonder that so many sagas were written down and preserved; while there must have been a vast number of others that existed only in tradition and in the memories of those who learned them in each generation.

If we try to get the story of the Northmen from the French or British chronicler, it is one long, dreary complaint of their barbarous customs and their heathen religion. In England the monks, shut up in their monasteries, could find nothing bad enough to say about the marauders who ravaged the shores of the country and did so much mischief. If we believe them, we shall mistake the Norwegians and their companions for wild beasts and heathen savages. We must read what was written in their own language, and then we shall have more respect for the vikings and sea-kings, always distinguishing between these two; for, while any peasant who wished could be a viking—a sea-robber—a sea-king was a king indeed, and must be connected with the royal race of the country. He received the title of king by right as soon as he took command of a ship's crew, though he need not have any land or kingdom. Vikings were merely pirates; they might be peasants and vikings by turn, and won their name from the inlets, the viks or wicks, where they harbored their ships. A sea-king must be a viking, but naturally very few of the vikings were sea-kings.

When we turn from the monks' records, written in Latin, to the accounts given of themselves by the Northmen, in their own languages, we are surprised enough to find how these ferocious pagans, these merciless men, who burnt the Southern churches and villages, and plundered and killed those of the inhabitants whom they did not drag away into slavery,—how these Northmen really surpassed their enemies in literature, as much as in military achievements. Their laws and government, their history and poetry and social customs, were better than those of the Anglo-Saxons and the Franks.

If we stop to think about this, we see that it would be impossible for a few hundred men to land from their great row-boats and subdue wide tracts of country unless they were superior in mental power, and gifted with astonishing quickness and bravery. The great leaders of armies are not those who can lift the heaviest weights or strike the hardest blow, but those who have the mind to plan and to organize and discipline and, above all, to persevere and be ready to take a dangerous risk. The countries to the southward were tamed and spiritless, and bound down by church influence and superstition until they had lost the energy and even the intellectual power of their ancestors five centuries back. The Roman Empire had helped to change the Englishmen and many of the Frenchmen of that time into a population of slaves and laborers, with no property in the soil, nothing to fight for but their own lives.

The viking had rights in his own country, and knew what it was to enjoy those rights; if he could win more land, he would know how to govern it, and he knew what he was fighting for and meant to win. If we wonder why all this energy was spent on the high seas, and in strange countries, there are two answers: first, that fighting was the natural employment of the men, and that no right could be held that could not be defended; but beside this, one form of their energy was showing itself at home in rude attempts at literature. It is surprising enough to find that both the quality and the quantity of the old sagas far surpass all that can be found of either Latin or English writing of that time in England. These sagas are all in the familiar tongue, so that everybody could understand them, and be amused or taught by them. They were not meant only for the monks and the people who lived in cloisters. The legends of their ancestors' beauty or bravery belonged to every man alike, and that made the Norwegians one nation of men, working and sympathizing with each other—not a mere herd of individuals.

The more that we know of the Northmen, the more we are convinced how superior they were in their knowledge of the useful arts to the people whom they conquered. There is a legend that when Charlemagne, in the ninth century, saw some pirate ships cruising in the Mediterranean, along the shores of which they had at last found their way, he covered his face and burst into tears. He was not so much afraid of their cruelty and barbarism as of their civilization. Nobody knew better that none of the Christian countries under his rule had ships or men that could make such a daring voyage. He knew that they were skilful workers in wood and iron, and had learned to be rope-makers and weavers; that they could make casks for their supply of drinking-water, and understood how to prepare food for their long cruises. All their swords and spears and bow-strings had to be made and kept in good condition, and sheltered from the sea-spray.

It is interesting to remember that the Northmen's fleets were not like a royal navy, though the king could claim the use of all the war-ships when he needed them for the country's service. They were fitted out by anybody who chose, private adventurers and peasants, all along the rocky shores. They were not very grand affairs for the most part, but they were all seaworthy, and must have had a good deal of room for stowing all the things that were to be carried, beside the vikings themselves. Sometimes there were transport vessels to take the arms and the food and bring back the plunder. Perhaps most of the peasants' boats were only thirty or forty feet long, but when we remember how many hundreds used to put to sea after the small crops were planted every summer, we cannot help knowing that there were a great many men who knew how to build strong ships in Norway, and how to fit them out sufficiently well, and man them and fight in them afterward. You never hear of any fleets being fitted out in the French and English harbors equalling these in numbers or efficiency.

When we picture the famous sea-kings' ships to ourselves, we do not wonder that the Northmen were so proud of them, or that the skalds were never tired of recounting their glories. There were two kinds of vessels: the last-ships, that carried cargoes; and the long-ships, or ships-of-war. Listen to the splendors of the "Long Serpent," which was the largest ship ever built in Norway. A dragonship, to begin with, because all the long ships had a dragon for a figure-head, except the smallest of them, which were called cutters, and only carried ten or twenty rowers on a side. The "Long Serpent" had thirty-four rowers' benches on a side, and she was a hundred and eleven feet long. Over the sides were hung the shining red and white shields of the vikings, the gilded dragon's head towered high at the prow, and at the stern a gilded tail went curling off over the head of the steersman. Then, from the long body, the heavy oars swept forward and back through the water, the double thirty-four of them, and as it came down the fiord, the "Long Serpent" must have looked like some enormous centipede creeping out of its den on an awful errand, and heading out across the rough water toward its prey.

The crew used to sleep on the deck, and ship-tents were necessary for shelter. There was no deep hold or comfortable cabin, for the ships were built so that they could be easily hauled up on a sloping beach. They had sails, and these were often made of gay colors, or striped with red and blue and white cloths, and a great many years later than this we hear of a crusader waiting long for a fair wind at the Straits of the Dardanelles, so that he could set all his fine sails, and look splendid as he went by the foreign shores.

To-day in Bergen harbor, in Norway, you are likely to see at least one or two Norland ships that belong to the great fleet that bring down furs and dried fish every year from Hammerfest and Trondhjem and the North Cape. They do not carry the red and white shields, or rows of long oars, but they are built with high prow and stern, and spread a great square brown sail. You are tempted to think that a belated company of vikings has just come into port after a long cruise. These descendants of the long-ships and the last-ships look little like peaceful merchantmen, as they go floating solemnly along the calm waters of the Bergen-fiord.

The voyages were often disastrous in spite of much clever seamanship. They knew nothing of the mariner's compass, and found their way chiefly by the aid of the stars—inconstant pilots enough on such foggy, stormy seas. They carried birds too, oftenest ravens, and used to let them loose and follow them toward the nearest land. The black raven was the vikings' favorite symbol for their flags, and familiar enough it became in other harbors than their own. They were bold, hardy fellows, and held fast to a rude code of honor and rank of knighthood. To join the most renowned company of vikings in Harold Haarfager's time, it was necessary that the champion should lift a great stone that lay before the king's door, as first proof that he was worth initiating. We are gravely told that this stone could not be moved by the strength of twelve ordinary men.

They were obliged to take oath that they would not capture women and children, or seek refuge during a tempest, or stop to dress their wounds before a battle was over. Sometimes they were possessed by a strange madness, caused either by a frenzy of rivalry and the wild excitement of their rude sports or by intoxicating liquors or drugs, when they foamed at the mouth and danced wildly about, swallowing burning coals, uprooting the very rocks and trees, destroying their own property, and striking indiscriminately at friends and foes. This berserker rage seems to have been much applauded, and gained the possessed viking a noble distinction in the eyes of his companions. If a sea-king heard of a fair damsel anywhere along the neighboring coast, he simply took ship in that direction, fought for her, and carried her away in triumph with as many of her goods as he was lucky enough to seize beside. Their very gods were gods of war and destruction, though beside Thor, the thunderer, they worshipped Balder, the fair-faced, the god of gentle speech and purity, with Freyr, who rules over sunshine and growing things. Their hell was a place of cold and darkness, and their heaven was to be a place where righting went on from sunrise until the time came to ride back to Valhalla and feast together in the great hall. Those who died of old age or sickness, instead of in battle, must go to hell. Odin, who was chief of all the gods, made man, and gave him a soul which should never perish, and Frigga, his wife, knew the fate of all men, but never told her secrets.

The Northmen spread themselves at length over a great extent of country. We can only wonder why, after their energy and valor led them to found a thriving colony in Iceland and in Russia, to even venture among the icebergs and perilous dismal coasts of Greenland, and from thence downward to the pleasanter shores of New England, why they did not seize these possessions and keep the credit of discovering and settling America. What a change that would have made in the world's history! Historians have been much perplexed at the fact of Leif Ericson's lack of interest in the fertile Vinland, New England now, which he visited in 986 and praised eloquently when he left it to its fate. Vinland waited hundreds of years after that for the hardy Icelander's kindred to come from old England to build their houses and spend the rest of their lives upon its good corn-land and among the shadows of its great pine-trees. There was room enough for all Greenland, and to spare, but we cannot help suspecting that the Northmen were not very good farmers, that they loved fighting too well, and would rather go a thousand miles across a stormy sea to plunder another man of his crops than to patiently raise their own corn and wool and make an honest living at home. So, instead of understanding what a good fortune it would be for their descendants, if they seized and held the great western continent that stretched westward from Vinland until it met another sea, they kept on with their eastward raids, and the valleys of the Elbe and the Rhine, of the Seine and Loire, made a famous hunting-ground for the dragon ships to seek. The rich seaports and trading towns, the strongly walled Roman cities, the venerated abbeys and cathedrals with their store of wealth and provisions, were all equally exposed to the fury of such attacks, and were soon stunned and desolated. What a horror must have fallen upon a defenceless harbor-side when a fleet of the Northmen's ships was seen sweeping in from sea at daybreak! What a smoke of burning houses and shrieking of frightened people all day long; and as the twilight fell and the few survivors of the assault dared to creep out from their hiding-places to see the ruins of their homes, and the ships putting out to sea again loaded deep with their possessions! we can hardly picture it to ourselves in these quiet days.

The people who lived in France were of another sort, but they often knew how to defend themselves as well as the Northmen knew how to attack. There are few early French records for us to read, for the literature of that early day was almost wholly destroyed in the religious houses and public buildings of France. Here and there a few pages of a poem or of a biography or chronicle have been kept, but from this very fact we can understand the miserable condition of the country.

In the year 810 the Danish Norsemen, under their king, Gottfried, overran Friesland, but the Emperor Charlemagne was too powerful for them and drove them back. After his death they were ready to try again, and because his huge kingdom had been divided under many rulers, who were all fighting among themselves, the Danes were more lucky, and after robbing Hamburg several times they ravaged the coasts and finally settled themselves as comfortably as possible at the mouth of the Loire in France. Soon they were not satisfied with going to and fro along the seaboard, and took their smaller craft and voyaged inland, swarming up the French rivers by hundreds, devastating the country everywhere they went.

In 845 they went up the Seine to Paris, and plundered Paris too, more than once; and forty years later, forty thousand of them, led by a man named Siegfried, went up from Rouen with seven hundred vessels and besieged the poor capital for ten months, until they were bought off at the enormous price of the whole province of Burgundy. See what power that was to put into the hands of the sea-kings' crews! But no price was too dear, the people of Paris must have thought, to get rid of such an army in the heart of Gaul. They could make whatever terms they pleased by this time, and there is a tradition that a few years afterward some bands of Danish rovers, who perhaps had gone to take a look at Burgundy, pushed on farther and settled themselves in Switzerland.

From the settlements they had made in the province of Aquitania, they had long before this gone on to Spain, because the rich Spanish cities were too tempting to be resisted. They had forced their way all along the shore of the sea, and in at the gate of the Mediterranean; they wasted and made havoc as they went, in Spain, Africa, and the Balearic islands, and pushed their way up the Rhone to Valence. We can trace them in Italy, where they burned the cities of Pisa and Lucca, and even in Greece, where at last the pirate ships were turned about, and set their sails for home. Think of those clumsy little ships out on such a journey with their single masts and long oars! Think of the stories that must have been told from town to town after these strange, wild Northern foes had come and gone! They were like hawks that came swooping down out of the sky, and though Spain and Rome and Greece were well enough acquainted with wars, they must have felt when the Northmen came, as we should feel if some wild beast from the heart of the forest came biting and tearing its way through a city street at noontime.

The whole second half of the ninth century is taken up with the histories of these invasions. We must follow for a while the progress of events in Gaul, or France as we call it now though it was made up then of a number of smaller kingdoms. The result of the great siege of Paris was only a settling of affairs with the Northmen for the time being; one part of the country was delivered from them at the expense of another. They could be bought off and bribed for a time, but there was never to be any such thing as their going back to their own country and letting France alone for good and all. But as they gained at length whole tracts of country, instead of the little wealth of a few men to take away in their ships as at first, they began to settle down in their new lands and to become conquerors and colonists instead of mere plunderers. Instead of continually ravaging and attacking the kingdoms, they slowly became the owners and occupiers of the conquered territory; they pushed their way from point to point. At first, as you have seen already, they trusted to their ships, and always left their wives and children at home in the North countries, but as time went on, they brought their families with them and made new homes, for which they would have to fight many a battle yet. It would be no wonder if the women had become possessed by a love for adventure too, and had insisted upon seeing the lands from which the rich booty was brought to them, and that they had been saying for a long time: "Show us the places where the grapes grow and the fruit-trees bloom, where men build great houses and live in them splendidly. We are tired of seeing only the long larchen beams of their high roofs, and the purple and red and gold cloths, and the red wine and yellow wheat that you bring away. Why should we not go to live in that country, instead of your breaking it to pieces, and going there so many of you, every year, only to be slain as its enemies? We are tired of our sterile Norway and our great Danish deserts of sand, of our cold winds and wet weather, and our long winters that pass by so slowly while the fleets are gone. We would rather see Seville and Paris themselves, than only their gold and merchandise and the rafters of their churches that you bring home for ship timber." One of the old ballads of love and valor lingers yet that the women used to sing: "*Myklagard and the land of Spain lie wide away o'er the lee.*" There was room enough in those far countries where the ships went—why then do they stay at home in Friesland and Norway and Denmark, crowded and hungry kingdoms that they were, of the wandering sea-kings?

As the years went on, the Northern lands themselves became more peaceful, and the voyages of the pirates came to an end. Though the Northmen still waged wars enough, they were Danes or Norwegians against England and France, one realm against another, instead of every man plundering for himself.

The kingdoms of France had been divided and weakened, and, while we find a great many fine examples of resistance, and some great victories over the Northmen, they were not pushed out and checked altogether. Instead, they gradually changed into Frenchmen themselves, different from other Frenchmen only in being more spirited, vigorous, and alert. They inspired every new growth of the religion, language, or manners, with their own splendid vitality. They were like plants that have grown in dry, thin soil, transplanted to a richer spot of ground, and sending out fresh shoots in the doubled moisture and sunshine. And presently we shall find the Northman becoming the Norman of history. As the Northman, almost the first thing we admire about him is his character, his glorious energy; as the Norman, we see that energy turned into better channels, and bringing a new element into the progress of civilization.

The Northmen had come in great numbers to settle in Gaul, but they were scattered about, and so it was easier to count themselves into the population, instead of keeping themselves separate. Some of these settlements were a good way inland, and everywhere they mixed their language with the French for a time, but finally dropped it almost altogether. In a very few years, comparatively speaking, they were not Danes or Norwegians at all; they had forgotten their old customs, and even their pagan gods of the Northern countries from which their ancestors had come. At last we come to a time when we begin to distinguish some of the chieftains and other brave men from the crowd of their companions. The old chronicles of Scandinavia and Denmark and Iceland cannot be relied upon like the histories of Greece or Rome. The student who tries to discover when this man was born, and that man died, from a saga, is apt to be disappointed. The more he studies these histories of the sea-kings and their countries, the more distinct picture he gets of a great crowd of men taking their little ships every year and leaving the rocky, barren coasts of their own country to go southward. As we have seen, France and England and Flanders and Spain were all richer and more fruitful, and they would go ashore, now at this harbor, now that, to steal all they could, even the very land they trod upon. Now and then we hear the name of some great man, a stronger and more daring sailor and fighter than the rest. There is a dismal story of a year of famine in France, when the north wind blew all through the weeks of a leafless spring, the roots of the vines were frozen, and the fruit blossoms chilled to the heart. The wild creatures of the forest, crazed with hunger, ventured into the farms and villages, and the monks fasted more than they thought best, and prayed the more heartily for succor in their poverty. But down from the North came Ragnar Lodbrok, the great Danish captain, with his stout-built vessels, "ten times twelve dragons of the sea," and he and his men, in their shaggy fur garments, went crashing through the ice of the French rivers, to make an easy prey of the hungry Frenchmen—to conquer everywhere they went. And for one Ragnar Lodbrok, read fifty or a hundred; for, though there are many stories told about him, just as we think that we can picture him and his black-sailed ships in our minds, we are told that this is only a legend, and that there never was any Ragnar Lodbrok at all who was taken by his enemies and thrown into a horrible dungeon filled with vipers, to sing a gallant saga about his life and misdeeds. But if there were no hero of this name, we put together little by little from one hint and another legend a very good idea of those quarrelsome times, when to be great it was necessary to be a pirate, and to kill as many men and steal as much of their possession as one possibly could These Northmen set as bad an example as any traveller since the world began. More than ninety times we can hear of them in France and Spain and the north of Germany, and always burning and ruining, not only the walled cities, but all the territory round about. Shipload after shipload left their bones on foreign soil; again and again companies of them were pushed out of France and England and defeated, but from generation to generation the quarrels went on, and we begin to wonder why the sea-coasts were not altogether deserted, until we remember that the spirit of those days was warlike, and that, while the people were plundered one year, they succeeded in proving themselves masters the next, and so life was filled with hope of military glory, and the tide of conquest swept now north, and now south.

From the fjords of Norway a splendid, hardy race of young men were pushing their boats to sea every year. Remember that their own country was a very hard one to live in with its long, dark winters, its rainy, short summers when the crops would not ripen, its rocky, mountainous surface, and its natural poverty. Even now if it were not for the fishing the Norwegian peasant people would find great trouble in gaining food enough. In early days, when the tilling of the ground was less understood, it must have been hard work tempting those yellow-haired, eager young adventurers to stay at home, when they could live on the sea in their rude, stanch little ships, as well as on land; when they were told great stories of the sunshiny, fruitful countries that lay to the south, where plenty of food and bright clothes and gold and silver might be bought in the market of war for the blows of their axes and the strength and courage of their right arms. No wonder that it seemed a waste of time to stay at home in Norway!

And as for the old men who had been to the fights and followed the sea-kings and brought home treasures, we are sure that they were always talking over their valiant deeds and successes, and urging their sons and grandsons to go to the South. The women wished their husbands and brothers to be as brave as the rest, while they cared a great deal for the rich booty which was brought back from such expeditions. What a hard thing it must have seemed to the boys who were sick or lame or deformed, but who had all the desire for glory that belonged to any of the vikings, and yet must stay at home with the women!

When we think of all this, of the barren country, and the crowd of people who lived in it, of the natural relish for a life of adventure, and the hope of splendid riches and fame, what wonder that in all these hundreds of years the Northmen followed their barbarous trade and went a-ravaging, and finally took great pieces of the Southern countries for their own and held them fast.

As we go on with this story of the Normans, you will watch these followers of the sea-kings keeping always some trace of their old habits and customs. Indeed you may know them yet. The Northmen were vikings, always restless and on the move, stealing and fighting their way as best they might, daring, adventurous. The Norman of the twelfth century was a crusader. A madness to go crusading against the Saracen possessed him, not alone for religion's sake or for the holy city of Jerusalem, and so in all the ages since one excuse after another has set the same wild blood leaping and made the Northern blue eyes shine. Look where you may, you find Englishmen of the same stamp—Sir Walter Raleigh and Lord Nelson, Stanley and Dr. Livingstone and General Gordon, show the old sea-kings' courage and recklessness. Snorro Sturleson's best saga has been followed by Drayton's "Battle of Agincourt" and Tennyson's "Charge of the Light Brigade" and "Ballad of Sir Richard Grenville." I venture to say that there is not an English-speaking boy or girl who can hear that sea-king's ballad this very day in peaceful England or America without a great thrill of sympathy.

"At Floras in the Azores Sir Richard Grenville lay,
And a pinnace, like a fluttered bird, came flying from far away:
'Spanish ships of war at sea! We have sighted fifty-three.'"—

Go and read that; the whole of the spirited story; but there is one thing I ask you to remember first in all this long story of the Normans:

that however much it seems to you a long chapter of bloody wars and miseries and treacheries that get to be almost tiresome in their folly and brutality; however little profit it may seem sometimes to read about the Norman wars, yet everywhere you will catch a gleam of the glorious courage and steadfastness that have won not only the petty principalities and dukedoms of those early days, but the great English and American discoveries and inventions and noble advancement of all the centuries since.

On the island of Vigr, in the Folden-fiord, the peasants still show some rude hollows in the shore where the ships of Rolf-Ganger were drawn up in winter, and whence he launched them to sail away to the Hebrides and France—the beginning of as great changes as one man's voyage ever wrought.

II. ROLF THE GANGER.

"Far had I wandered from this northern shore,

Far from the bare heights and the wintry seas,

Dreaming of these

No more."   —A. F.

TOWARD the middle of the ninth century Harold Haarfager did great things in Norway. There had always been a great number of petty kings or jarls, who were sometimes at peace with each other, but oftener at war, and at last this Harold was strong enough to conquer all the rest and unite all the kingdoms under his own rule. It was by no means an easy piece of business, for twelve years went by before it was finished, and not only Norway itself, but the Orkneys, and Shetlands, and Hebrides, and Man were conquered too, and the lawless vikings were obliged to keep good order. The story was that the king had loved a fair maiden of the North, called Gyda, but when he asked her to marry him she had answered that she would not marry a jarl; let him make himself a king like Gorm of Denmark! At this proud answer Harold loved her more than ever, and vowed that he would never cut his hair until he had conquered all the jarls and could claim Gyda's hand.

The flourishing shock of his yellow hair became renowned; we can almost see it ourselves waving prosperously through his long series of battles. When he was king at last he chose Jarl Rögnwald of Möre to cut the shining locks because he was the most valiant and best-beloved of all his tributaries.

Jarl Rögnwald had a family of sons who were noted men in their day. One was called Turf-Einar, because he went to the Orkney islands and discovered great deposits of peat of which he taught the forestless people to make use, so that they and their descendants were grateful and made him their chief hero. Another son was named Rolf, and he was lord of three small islands far up toward the North. He followed the respected profession of sea-robber, but though against foreign countries it was the one profession for a jarl to follow, King Harold was very stringent in his laws that no viking should attack any of his own neighbors or do any mischief along the coasts of Norway. These laws Rolf was not careful about keeping.

There was still another brother, who resented Haarfager's tyrannies so much that he gathered a fine heroic company of vikings and more peaceable citizens and went to Iceland and settled there. This company came in time to be renowned as the beginners of one of the most remarkable republics the world has ever known, with a unique government by its aristocracy, and a natural development of literature unsurpassed in any day. There, where there were no foreign customs to influence or pervert, the Norse nature and genius had their perfect flowering.

Rolf is said to have been so tall that he used to march afoot whenever he happened to be ashore, rather than ride the little Norwegian horses. He was nicknamed Gang-Roll (or Rolf), which means Rolf the Walker, or Ganger. There are two legends which give the reason why he came away from Norway—one that he killed his brother in an unfortunate quarrel, and fled away to England, whither he was directed by a vision or dream; that the English helped him to fit out his ships and to sail away again toward France.

The other story, which seems more likely, makes it appear that the king was very angry because Rolf plundered a Norwegian village when he was coming home short of food from a long cruise in the Baltic Sea. The peasants complained to Harold Haarfager, who happened to be near, and he called the great Council of Justice and banished his old favorite for life.

Whether these stories are true or not, at any rate Rolf came southward an outlaw, and presently we hear of him in the Hebrides off the coast of Scotland, where a company of Norwegians had settled after King Harold's conquests. These men were mostly of high birth and great ability, and welcomed the new-comer who had so lately been their enemy. We are not surprised when we find that they banded together as pirates and fitted out a famous expedition. Perhaps they did not find living in the Hebrides very luxurious, and thought it necessary to collect some merchandise and money, or some slaves to serve them, so they fell back upon their familiar customs.

Rolfs vessels and theirs made a formidable fleet, but although they agreed that there should not be any one chosen as captain, or admiral, as we should say nowadays, we do not hear much of any of the confederates except Rolf the Ganger, so we may be sure he was most powerful and took command whether anybody was willing or not.

They came round the coast of Scotland, and made first for Holland, but as all that part of the country had too often been devastated and had become very poor, the ships were soon put to sea again. And next we find them going up the River Seine in France, which was a broader river then than it is now, and the highway toward Paris and other cities, which always seemed to offer great temptations to the vikings. Charles the Simple was king of France by right, but the only likeness to his ancestor Charlemagne was in his name, and to that his subjects had added the Simple, or the Fool, by which we can tell that he was not a very independent or magnificent sort of monarch. The limits of the kingdom of France, at that time, had just been placed between the Loire and the Meuse, after many years of fighting between the territories, and Charles was still contesting his right to the crown. The wide empire of Charlemagne had not been divided at once into distinct smaller kingdoms, but the heirs had each taken what they could hold and fought for much else beside. Each pretended to be the lawful king and was ready to hold all he could win. So there was naturally little good-feeling between them, and not one could feel sure that his neighbor would even help him to fight against a common enemy. It was "Every one for himself, and devil take the hindmost!" to quote the old proverb, which seldom has so literal an application. King Charles the Simple, besides defending himself from his outside enemies, was also much troubled by a pretender to the crown, and was no doubt at his wit's end to know how to manage the province of Neustria, lately so vexed by the foreign element within its borders. It might be easy work for the troop of Northmen that had followed Rolf. Besides the fact that they need not fear any alliance against them, and had only Charles the Simple for their enemy, one of his own enemies was quite likely to form a league with them against him.

The fleet from the Hebrides had come to anchor on its way up the Seine at a town called Jumièges, five leagues from Rouen. There was no army near by to offer any hindrance, and the work of pillaging the country was fairly begun without hindrance when the news of the incursion was told in Rouen. There the people were in despair, for it was useless to think of defending their broken walls; the city was already half ruined from such invasions. At any hour they might find themselves at the mercy of these new pirates. But in such dreadful dismay the archbishop, a man of great courage and good sense, whom we must honor heartily, took upon himself the perilous duty of going to the camp and trying to save the city by making a treaty. He had heard stories enough, we may be sure, of the cruel tortures of Christian priests by these Northern pagans, who still believed in the gods Thor and Odin and in Valhalla, and that the most fortunate thing, for a man's life in the next world, was that he should die in battle in this world.

There was already a great difference in the hopes and plans of the Northmen: they listened to the archbishop instead of killing him at once, and Rolf and his companions treated him and his interpreter with some sort of courtesy. Perhaps the bravery of the good man won their hearts by its kinship to their daring; perhaps they were already planning to seize upon a part of France and to forsake the Hebrides altogether, and Rolf had a secret design of founding a kingdom for himself that should stand steadfast against enemies. When the good priest went back to Rouen, I think the people must have been surprised that he had kept his head upon his shoulders, and still more filled with wonder because he was able to tell them that he had made a truce, that he had guaranteed the assailants admission to the city, but that they had promised not to do any harm whatever. Who knows if there were not many voices that cried out that it was only delivering them to the cruel foe, with their wives and children and all that they had in the world. When the ships came up the river and were anchored before one of the city gates near the Church of St. Morin, and the tall chieftain and his comrades began to come ashore, what beating hearts, what careful peeping out of windows there must have been in Rouen that day!

But the chiefs had given their word of honor, and they kept it well; they walked all about the city, and examined all the ramparts, the wharves, and the supply of water, and gave every thing an unexpectedly kind approval. More than this, they said that Rouen should be their head-quarters and their citadel. This was not very welcome news, but a thousand times better than being sacked and ravaged and burnt, and when the ships had gone by up the river, I dare say that more than one voice spoke up for Rolf the Ganger, and gratefully said that he might not prove the worst of masters after all. Some of the citizens even joined the ranks of the sea-king's followers when they went on in quest of new adventure up the Seine.

Just where the river Eure joins the Seine, on the point between the two streams, the Norwegians built a great camp, and fortified it, and there they waited for the French army. For once King Charles was master of his whole kingdom, and he had made up his mind to resist this determined invasion. Pirates were bad enough, but pirates who were evidently bent upon greater mischief than usual could not be sent away too soon. It was not long before the French troops, under the command of a general called Regnauld, who bore the title of Duke of France, made their appearance opposite the encampment, on the right bank of the Eure.

The French counts had rallied bravely; they made a religious duty of it, for were not these Norwegians pagans? and pagans deserved to be killed, even if they had not come to steal from a Christian country.

There was one count who had been a pagan himself years before, but he had become converted, and was as famous a Christian as he had been sea-king. He had declared that he was tired of leading a life of wild adventure, and had made peace with France twenty years before this time; and the kingdom had given him the county of Chartres—so he must have been a powerful enemy. Naturally he was thought to be the best man to confer with his countrymen. There was a council of war in the French camp, and this Hasting (of whom you will hear again by and by) advised that they should confer with Rolf before they risked a battle with him. Perhaps the old sea-king judged his tall successor by his own experience, and thought he might like to be presented with a county too, as the price of being quiet and letting the frightened Seine cities alone. Some of the other lords of the army were very suspicious and angry about this proposal, but Hasting had his way, and went out with two attendants who could speak Danish.

The three envoys made their short journey to the river-side as quickly as possible, and presently they stood on the bank of the Eure. Across the river were the new fortifications, and some of the sea-kings' men were busy with their armor on the other shore.

"Gallant soldiers!" cries the Count of Chartres; "what is your chieftain's name?"

"We have no lord over us," they shouted back again; "we are all equal."

"For what end have you come to France?"

"To drive out the people who are here, or make them our subjects, and to make ourselves a new country," says the Northman. "Who are you?—How is it that you speak our own tongue?"

"You know the story of Hasting," answers the count, not without pride—"Hasting, the great pirate, who scoured the seas with his crowd of ships, and did so much evil in this kingdom?"

"Aye, we have heard that, but Hasting has made a bad end to so good a beginning"; to which the count had nothing to say; he was Lord of Chartres now, and liked that very well.

"Will you submit to King Charles?" he shouts again, and more men are gathering on the bank to listen. "Will you give your faith and service, and take from him gifts and honor?"

"No, no!" they answer; "we will not submit to King Charles—go back, and tell him so, you messenger, and say that we claim the rule and dominion of what we win by our own strength and our swords."

But the Frenchmen called Hasting a traitor when he brought this answer back to camp, and told his associates not to try to force the pagan entrenchments. A traitor, indeed! That was too much for the old viking's patience. For all that, the accusation may have held a grain of truth. Nobody knows the whole of his story, but he may have felt the old fire and spirit of his youth when he saw the great encampment and heard the familiar tones of his countrymen. It may be wrong to suspect that he went to join them; but, at all events, Count Chartres left the French camp indignantly, and nobody knows where he went, either then or afterward, for he forsook his adopted country and left it to its fate. They found out that he had given good advice to those proud comrades of his, for when they attacked the enemy between the rivers they were cut to pieces; even the duke of France, their bold leader, was killed by a poor fisherman of Rouen who had followed the Northern army.

Now there was nothing to hinder Rolf, who begins to be formally acknowledged as the leader, from going up the Seine as fast or as slow as he pleased, and after a while the army laid siege to Paris, but this was unsuccessful. One of the chiefs was taken prisoner, and to release him they promised a year's truce to King Charles, and after a while we find them back at Rouen again. They had been ravaging the country to the north of Paris, very likely in King Charles's company, for there had been a new division of the kingdom, and the northern provinces no longer called him their sovereign. Poor Charles the Simple! he seems to have had a very hard time of it with his unruly subjects, and his fellow-knights and princes too, who took advantage of him whenever they could find a chance.

By this time we know enough of Rolf and his friends not to expect them to remain quiet very long at Rouen. Away they went to Bayeux, a rich city, and assaulted that and killed Berenger, the Count of Bayeux, and gained a great heap of booty. We learn a great deal of the manners and fashions of that early day when we find out that Berenger had a beautiful daughter, and when the treasure was divided she was considered as part of it and fell to Rolf's lot. He immediately married her with apparent satisfaction and a full performance of Scandinavian rites and ceremonies.

After this the Northmen went on to Evreux and to some other cities, and their dominion was added to, day by day. They began to feel a certain sort of respect and care for the poor provinces now that they belonged to themselves. And they ceased to be cruel to the unresisting people, and only taxed them with a certain yearly tribute. Besides this, they chose Rolf for their king, but this northern title was changed before long for the French one of duke. Rolf must have been very popular with his followers. We cannot help a certain liking for him ourselves or being pleased when we know that his new subjects liked him heartily. They had cursed him very often, to be sure, and feared his power when he was only a pirate, but they were glad enough when they gained so fearless and strong a man for their protector. Whatever he did seemed to be with a far-sightedness and better object than they had been used to in their rulers. He was a man of great gifts and uncommon power, and he laid his plans deeper and was not without a marked knowledge of the rude politics of that time—a good governor, which was beginning to be needed more in France than a good fighter even.

Fighting was still the way of gaining one's ends, and so there was still war, but it was better sustained and more orderly. These Northerners, masters now of a good piece of territory, linked themselves with some of the smaller scattered settlements of Danes at the mouth of the river Loire, and went inland on a great expedition. They could not conquer Paris this time either, nor Dijon nor Chartres. The great walls of these cities and several others were not to be beaten down, but there is a long list of weaker towns that fell into their hands, and at last the French people could bear the sieges no longer, and not only the peasants but the nobles and priests clamored for deliverance. King Charles may have been justly called the Simple, but he showed very good sense now. "We shall starve to death," the people were saying. "Nobody dares to work in the field or the vineyard; there is not an acre of corn from Blois to Senlis. Churches are burnt and people are murdered; the Northmen do as they please. See, it is all the fault of a weak king!"

King Charles roused himself to do a sensible thing; he may have planned it as a stroke of policy, and meant to avail himself of the Northmen's strength to keep himself on his throne. He consulted his barons and bishops, and they agreed with him that he must form a league with their enemies, and so make sure of peace. As we read the story of those days, we are hardly sure that Rolf was the subject after this rather than the king. He did homage to King Charles, and he received the sovereignty over most of what was to be called the dukedom of Normandy. The league was little more than an obligation of mutual defence, and King Charles was lucky to call Rolf his friend and ally. The vigorous Norwegian was likely to keep his word better than the French dukes and barons, who broke such promises with perfect ease. Rolf's duty and his interest led him nearly in the same path, but he was evidently disposed to do what was right according to his way of seeing right and wrong.

All this time he had been living with his wife Popa, the daughter of Count Berenger, who was slain at Bayeux. They had two children— William, and a daughter, Adela. According to the views of King Charles and the Christian church of that time, the marriage performed with Scandinavian rites was no marriage at all, though Rolf loved his wife devotedly and was training his son with great care, so that he might by and by take his place, and be no inferior, either, of the young French princes who were his contemporaries. As one historian says, the best had the best then, and this young William was being made a scholar as fast as possible.

For all this, when the king's messenger came to Rolf and made him an offer of Gisla, the king's daughter, for a wife, with the seigneury of all the lands between the river Epte and the border of Brittany, if he would only become a Christian and live in peace with the kingdom, Rolf listened with pleasure. He did not repeat now the words that Hasting heard on the bank of the Eure, "We will obey no one!" while with regard to the marriage he evidently felt free to contract a new one.

It was all a great step upward, and Rolf's clear eyes saw that. If he were not a Christian he could not be the equal of the lords of France. He was not a mere adventurer any longer, the leader of a band of pirates; other ambitions had come to him since he had been governor of his territory. The pagan fanaticism and superstition of his companions were more than half extinguished already; the old myths of the Northern gods had not flourished in this new soil. At last, after much discussion and bargaining about the land that should be given, Rolf gave his promise once for all, and now we may begin to call him fairly the Duke of Normandy and his people the Normans; the old days of the Northmen in France had come to an end. For a good many years the neighboring provinces called the new dukedom "the pirate's land" and "the Northman's land," but the great Norman race was in actual existence now, and from this beginning under Rolf, the tall Norwegian sea-king, has come one of the greatest forces and powers of the civilized world.

I must give you some account of the ceremonies at this establishment of the new duke, for it was a grand occasion, and the king's train of noblemen and gentlemen, and all the Norman officers and statesmen went out to do honor to that day. The place was in a village called St. Claire, on the river Epte, and the French pitched their tents on one bank of the river and the Normans on the other. Then, at the hour appointed, Rolf came over to meet the king, and did what would have astonished his father Rögnwald and his viking ancestors very much. He put his hand between the king's hands and said: "From this time forward I am your vassal and man, and I give my oath that I will faithfully protect your life, your limbs, and your royal honor."

After this the king and his nobles formally gave Rolf the title of duke or count, and swore that they would protect him and his honor too, and all the lands named in the treaty. But there is an old story that, when Rolf was directed to kneel before King Charles and kiss his foot in token of submission, he was a rebellious subject at once. Perhaps he thought that some of his French rivals had revived this old Prankish custom on purpose to humble his pride, but he said nothing, only beckoned quietly to one of his followers to come and take his place. Out steps the man. I do not doubt that his eyes were dancing, and that his yellow beard hid a laughing mouth; he did not bend his knee at all, but caught the king's foot, and lifted it so high that the poor monarch fell over backward, and all the pirates gave a shout of laughter. They did not think much of Charles the Simple, those followers of Rolf the Ganger.

Afterward the marriage took place at Rouen, and the high barons of France went there with the bride, though it was not a very happy day for Gisla, whom Rolf never lived with or loved. He was a great many years older than she, and when she died he took Popa, the first wife back again—if, indeed, he had not considered her the true wife all the time. Then on that wedding-day he became a Christian too, though there must have been more change of words and manner than of Rolf's own thoughts. He received the archbishop's lessons with great amiability, and gave part of his lands to the church before he divided the rest among his new-made nobles. They put a long white gown or habit on him, such as newly baptized persons wore, and he must have been an amusing sight to see, all those seven days that he kept it on, tall old seafarer that he was, but he preserved a famous dignity, and gave estates to seven churches in succession on each day of that solemn week. Then he put on his every-day clothes again, and gave his whole time to his political affairs and the dividing out of Normandy among the Norwegian chieftains who had come with him on that lucky last voyage.

It is said that Rolf himself was the founder of the system of landholding according to the custom of feudal times, and of a regular system of property rights, and customs of hiring and dividing the landed property, but there are no state papers or charters belonging to that early time, as there are in England, so nobody can be very sure. At any rate, he is said to have been the best ruler possible, and his province was a model for others, though it was the most modern in Gaul. He caused the dilapidated towns and cities to be rebuilt, and the churches were put into good repair and order. There are parts of some of the Rouen churches standing yet, that Rolf rebuilt.

There is a great temptation to linger and find out all we can of the times of this first Count of Normandy—so many later traits and customs date back to Rolfs reign; and all through this story of the Normans we shall find a likeness to the first leader, and trace his influence. His own descendants inherited many of his gifts of character—a readiness of thought and speech; clear, bright minds, and vigor of action. Even those who were given over to ways of vice and shame, had a cleverness and attractiveness that made their friends hold to them, in spite of their sins and treacheries. A great deal was thought of learning and scholarship among the nobles and gentle folk of that day, and Rolf had caught eagerly at all such advantages, even while he trusted most to his Northern traditions of strength and courage. If he had thought these were enough to win success, and had brought up his boy as a mere pirate and fighter, it would have made a great difference in the future of the Norman people and their rulers. The need of a good education was believed in, and held as a sort of family doctrine, as long as Rolf's race existed, but you will see in one after another of these Norman counts the nature of the sea-kings mixed with their later learning and accomplishments.

We cannot help being a little amused, however, when we find that young William, the grandson of old Rögnvald, loved his books so well that he begged his father to let him enter a monastery. The wise, good man Botho, who was his tutor, had taught him to be proud of his other grandfather, Count Berenger, who belonged to one of the most illustrious French families, and taught him also to follow the example of the good clergymen of Normandy, as well as the great conquerors and chieftains. By and by we shall see that he loved to do good, and to do works of mercy, though his people called him William Longsword, and followed him to the wars.

Normandy was wild enough when Rolf came to rule there, but before he died the country had changed very much for the better. He was very careful to protect the farmers, and such laws were made, and kept, too, that robbery was almost unknown throughout the little kingdom. The peasants could leave their oxen or their tools in the field now, and if by chance they were stolen, the duke himself was responsible for the loss. A pretty story is told of Rolf that has also been told of other wise rulers. He had gone out hunting one day, and after the sport, while he and his companions were resting and having a little feast as they sat on the grass, Rolf said he would prove the orderliness and trustiness of his people. So he took off the two gold bracelets which were a badge of his rank, and reached up and hung them on a tree close by, and there they were, safe and shining, a long time afterward, when he went to seek them. Perhaps this story is only a myth, though the tale is echoed in other countries—England, Ireland, and Lombardy, and others beside. At any rate, it gives an expression of the public safety and order, and the people's gratitude to their good kings. Rolf brought to his new home some fine old Scandinavian customs, for his own people were knit together with close bonds in Norway. If a farmer's own servants or helpers failed him for any reason, he could demand the help of his neighbors without paying them, and they all came and helped him gather his harvest. Besides, the law punished nothing so severely as the crime of damaging or stealing from a growing crop. The field was said to be under God's lock, with heaven for its roof, though there might be only a hedge for its wall. If a man stole from another man's field, and took the ripe corn into his own barn, he paid for it with his life. This does not match very well with the sea-kings' exploits abroad, but they were very strict rulers, and very honest among themselves at home. One familiar English word of ours—hurrah,—is said to date from Rolf's reign. *Rou* the Frenchmen called our Rolf; and there was a law that if a man was in danger himself, or caught his enemy doing any damage, he could raise the cry *Ha Rou!* and so invoke justice in Duke Rolf's name. At the sound of the cry, everybody was bound, on the instant, to give chase to the offender, and whoever failed to respond to the cry of *Ha Rou!* must pay a heavy fine to Rolf himself. This began the old English fashion of "hue and cry," as well as our custom of shouting Hurrah! when we are pleased and excited.

We cannot help being surprised to see how quickly the Normans became Frenchmen in their ways of living and even speaking. There is hardly a trace of their Northern language except a few names of localities left in Normandy. Once settled in their new possessions, Rolf and all his followers seem to have been as eager for the welfare of Normandy as they were ready to devastate it before. They were proud not of being Norsemen but of being Normans. Otherwise their country could not have done what it did in the very next reign to Rolf's, nor could Rouen have become so much like a French city even in his own lifetime. This was work worthy of his power, to rule a people well, and lift them up toward better living and better things. His vigor and quickness made him able to seize upon the best traits and capabilities of his new countrymen, and enforce them as patterns and examples, with no tolerance of their faults.

From the viking's ships which had brought Rolf and his confederates, all equal, from the Hebrides, it is a long step upward to the Norman landholders and quiet citizens with their powerful duke in his palace at Rouen. He had shared the lands of Normandy, as we have seen, with his companions, and there was a true aristocracy among them—a rule of the best, for that is what aristocracy really means. No doubt there was sin and harm enough under the new order of things, but we can see that there was a great advance in its first duke's reign, even if we cannot believe that all the fine stories are true that his chroniclers have told.

Rolf died in 927, and was a pious Christian according to his friends, and had a lingering respect for his heathen idols according to his enemies. He was an old man, and had been a brave man, and he is honored to this day for his justice and his courage in that stormy time when he lived. Some say that he was forty years a pirate before he came to Normandy, and looking back on these days of seafaring and robbery and violence must have made him all the more contented with his pleasant fields and their fruit-trees and waving grain; with his noble city of Rouen, and his gentle son William, who was the friend of the priests.

Rolf became very feeble in body and mind, and before his death he gave up the rule of the duchy to his son. He lingered for several years, but we hear nothing more of him except that when he lay dying he had terrible dreams of his old pirate days, and was troubled by visions of his slaughtered victims and the havoc made by the long-ships. We are glad to know that he waked from these sorrows long enough to give rich presents to the church and the poor, which comforted him greatly and eased his unhappy conscience. He was buried in his city of Rouen, in the cathedral, and there is his tomb still with a figure of him in stone—an old tired man with a furrowed brow; the strength of his fourscore years had become only labor and sorrow, but he looks like the Norseman that he was in spite of the ducal robes of French Normandy. There was need enough of bravery in the man who should fill his place. The wars still went on along the borders, and there must have been fear of new trouble in the duchy when this old chieftain Rolf had lain down to die, and his empty armor was hung high in the palace hall.

III. WILLIAM LONGSWORD.

"For old, unhappy, far-off things

And battles long ago."   —Wordsworth.

BEFORE we follow the fortunes of the new duke, young William Longsword, we must take a look at France and see what traditions and influences were going to affect our colony of Northmen from that side, and what relations they had with their neighbors. Perhaps the best way to make every thing clear is to go back to the reign of the Emperor Charlemagne, who inherited a great kingdom, and added to it by his wars and statesmanship until he was crowned at Rome, in the year 800, emperor not only of Germany and Gaul, but of the larger part of Italy and the northeastern part of Spain. Much of this territory had shared in the glories of the Roman Empire and had fallen with it. But Charlemagne was equal to restoring many lost advantages, being a man of great power and capacity, who found time, while his great campaigns were going on, to do a great deal for the schools of his country. He even founded a sort of normal school, where teachers were fitted for their work, and his daughters were busy in copying manuscripts; the emperor himself was fond of being read to when he was at his meals, and used to get up at midnight to watch the stars. Some of the interesting stories about him may not be true, but we can be sure that he was a great general and a masterly governor and lawgiver, and a good deal of a scholar. Like Rolf, he was one of the men who mark as well as make a great change in the world's affairs, and in whose time civilization takes a long step forward. When we know that it took him between thirty and forty years to completely conquer the Saxons, who lived in the northern part of his country, and we read the story of the great battle of Roncesvalles in which the Basque people won; when we follow Charlemagne (the great Charles, as his people love to call him) on these campaigns which take up almost all his history, we cannot help seeing that his enemies fought against the new order of things that he represented. It was not only that they did not want Charlemagne for their king, but they did not wish to be Christians either, or to forsake their own religion and their own ideas for his.

When he died he was master of a great association of countries which for years yet could not come together except in name, because of their real unlikeness and jealousy of each other. Charlemagne had managed to rule them all, for his sons and officers, whom he had put in command of the various provinces, were all dictated to by him, and were not in the least independent of his oversight. His fame was widespread. Embassies came to him from distant Eastern countries, and no doubt he felt that he was establishing a great empire for his successors. Thirty years after he died the empire was divided into three parts, and thirty-four years later it was all broken up in the foolish reign of his own great-grandson, who was called Charles also, but instead of Charles the Great became known as Charles the Fat. From the fragments of the old empire were formed the kingdoms of France, of Italy, and of Germany, with the less important states of Lorraine, Burgundy, and Navarre. But although the great empire had fallen to pieces, each fragment kept something of the new spirit that had been forced into it by the famous emperor. For this reason there was no corner of his wide domain that did not for many years after his death stand in better relation to progress, and to the influence of religion, the most potent civilizer of men.

All this time the power of the nobles had been increasing, for, whereas, at first they had been only the officers of the king, and were appointed to or removed from their posts at the royal pleasure, they contrived at length to make their positions hereditary and to establish certain rights and privileges. This was the foundation of the feudal system, and such a growth was sure to strike deep root. Every officer could hope to become a ruler in a small way, and to endow his family with whatever gains and holdings he had managed to make his own. And as these feudal chiefs soon came to value their power, they were ready to fight, not only all together for their king or over-lord, but for themselves; and one petty landholder with his dependents would go out to fight his next neighbor, each hoping to make the other his tributary. France proper begins to make itself heard about in these days.

If you have read "The Story of Rome" and "The Rise and Fall of the Roman Empire," you can trace the still earlier changes in the old province of Gaul. The Franks had come westward, a bold association of German tribes, and in that fifth century when the Roman rule was overthrown, they swarmed over the frontiers and settled by hundreds and thousands in the conquered provinces. But, strange to say, as years went on they disappeared; not because they or their children went away again and left Gaul to itself, but because they adopted the ways and fashions of the country. They were still called Franks and a part of the country was called France even, but the two races were completely mixed together and the conquerors were as Gallic as the conquered. They even spoke the new language; it appears like an increase or strengthening of the Gallic race rather than a subjugation of it, and the coming of these Franks founded, not a new province of Germany, but the French nation.

The language was changed a good deal, for of course many Frankish or German words were added, as Roman (or Romance) words had been added before, to the old Gallic, and other things were changed too. In fact we are not a bit surprised when we find that the German kings, Charlemagne's own descendants, were looked upon as foreigners, and some of the French leaders, the feudal lords and princes, opposed themselves to their monarchs. They were brave men and ready to fight for what they wanted. Charles the Fat could not keep himself on his unsteady throne, and in Rolf's day France was continually at war, sometimes at home, and almost always with the neighboring provinces and kingdoms. Rolf's contemporary, Charles the Simple, lost his kingship in 922, when his nobles revolted and put another leader in his place, who was called Hugh the Great, Count of Paris. Charles the Simple was kept a prisoner until he died, by a Count of Vermandois, of whom he had claimed protection, and whose daughter William Longsword had married.

There was a great deal of treachery among the French nobles. Each was trying to make himself rich and great, and serving whatever cause could promise most gain. There was diplomacy enough, and talking and fighting enough, but very little loyalty and care for public welfare. In Normandy, a movement toward better things showed itself more and more plainly; instead of wrangling over the fragments of an old dismembered kingdom, Rolf had been carefully building a strong new one, and had been making and keeping laws instead of breaking laws, and trying to make goodness and right prevail, and theft and treachery impossible. We must not judge those days by our own, for many things were considered right then that are wrong now; but Rolf knew that order and bravery were good, and that learning was good, and so he kept his dukedom quiet, though he was ready enough to fight his enemies, and he sent his son William Longsword to school, and made him a good scholar as well as soldier. This was as good training as a young man could have in those stormy times.

Under Rolf, Normandy had held faithfully to the king, but under his son's rule we find a long chapter of changes, for William was constantly transferring his allegiance from king to duke. When he succeeded his father, Normandy and France were at war—that is, Rolf would not acknowledge any king but Charles, who was in prison, while the usurper, Rudolph of Burgundy, was on the French throne. It is very hard to keep track of the different parties and their leaders. Everybody constantly changed sides, and it is not very clear what glory there was in being a king, when the vassals were so powerful that they could rebel against their sovereign and make war on him as often as they pleased. Yet they were very decided about having a king, if only to show how much greater they were by contrast. Duke Hugh of Paris takes the most prominent place just at this time, and with his widespread dominions and personal power and high rank, we cannot help wondering that he did not put himself at the head of the kingdom. Instead of that he chose to remain a subject, while he controlled the king's actions and robbed him of his territory and kept him in personal bondage. He had no objection to transferring his strange loyalty from one king to another, but he would always have a king over him, though at three different times there was nothing except his own plans to hinder him from putting the crown of France upon his own head. He had a stronger guiding principle than some of his associates, and seems to have been a better man.

From Charles the Simple had come the lands of Normandy, and to him the first vow of allegiance had been made, and so both Rolf and William took his part and were enemies to his usurper and his foes. When William came into possession of his dukedom, one of his first acts was to do homage to his father's over-lord, and he never did homage to Rudolph the usurper until Charles was dead, and even then waited three years; but Rudolph was evidently glad to be friends, and presented Longsword with a grant of the sea-coast in Brittany. The Norman duke was a formidable rival if any trouble should arise, and the Normans themselves were very independent in their opinions. One of Rolf's followers had long ago told a Frenchman that his chief, who had come to Neustria a king without a kingdom, now held his broad lands from the sun and from God. They kept strange faith with each other in those days. Each man had his own ambitious plans, and his leagues and friendships were only for the sake of bringing them about. This was not being very grateful, but Rolf's men knew that the Breton lands were the price of peace and alliance, and not a free gift for love's sake by any means.

As we try to puzzle out a distinct account of William's reign, we find him sometimes the enemy of Rudolph and in league with Hugh of Paris, sometimes he was in alliance with Rudolph, though he would not call him king, and oftener he would have nothing to do with either. It is very dull reading, except as we trace the characters of the men themselves.

Most of the Normans had accepted Christianity many years before, in the time of Rolf, and had been christened, but a certain number had refused it and clung to the customs of their ancestors. These people had formed a separate neighborhood or colony near Bayeux, and after several generations, while they had outwardly conformed to the prevailing observances, they still remained Northmen at heart. They were remarkable among the other Normans for their great turbulence and for an almost incessant opposition to the dukes, and some of them kept the old pagan devices on their shields, and went into battle shouting the Northern war-cry of *"Thor aide!"* instead of the pious *"Dieu aide!"* or *"Dex aide!"* of Normandy.

Whatever relic of paganism may have clung to Rolf himself, it is pretty certain that his son, half Frenchman by birth, was almost wholly a Frenchman in feeling. We must remember that he was not the son of Gisla the king's sister, however, but of Popa of Bayeux. There was a brother or half-brother of hers called Bernard de Senlis, who in spite of his father's murder and the unhappy beginning of their acquaintance with Rolf, seems to have become very friendly with the Norse chieftain.

The fortunes of war were so familiar in those days and kept so many men at fierce enmity with each other, that we are half surprised to come upon this sincere, kindly relationship in the story of the early Normans. Even Rolf's wife's foolish little nickname, "Popa," under cover of which her own name has been forgotten,—this name of puppet or little doll, gives a hint of affectionateness and a sign of homelikeness which we should be very sorry to miss. As for Bernard de Senlis, he protected not only the rights of Rolf's children and grandchildren, but their very lives, and if it had not been for his standing between them and their enemies Rolf's successors would never have been dukes of Normandy.

With all his inherited power and his own personal bravery, William found himself in a very hard place. He kept steadfastly to his ideas of right and might, and one thinks that with his half French and half Northman nature he might have understood both of the parties that quickly began to oppose each other in Normandy. He ruled as a French prince, and he and his followers were very eager to hold their place in the general confederacy of France, and eager too that Normandy should be French in religion, manners, and customs. Yet they did not wish Normandy to be absorbed into France in any political sense. Although there were several men of Danish birth, Rolf's old companions, who took this view of things, and threw in their lot with the French party, like Botho, William's old tutor, and Oslac, and Bernard the Dane, of whom we shall hear again, there was a great body of the Normans who rebelled and made much trouble.

William's French speech and French friends were all this time making him distrusted and even disliked by a large portion of his own subjects. There still remained a strong Northern and pagan influence in the older parts of the Norman duchy; while in the new lands of Brittany some of the independent Danish settlements, being composed chiefly of the descendants of men who had forced their way into that country before Rolf's time, were less ready for French rule than even the Normans. Between these new allies and the disaffected Normans themselves a grand revolt was organized under the leadership of an independent Danish chief from one of the Breton provinces. The rebels demanded one concession after another, and frightened Duke William dreadfully; he even proposed to give up his duchy and to beg the protection of his French uncle, Bernard de Senlis. We are afraid that he had left his famous longsword at home on that campaign, until it appears that his old counsellor, Bernard the Dane, urged him to go back and meet the insurgents, and that a great victory was won and the revolt ended for that time. The account of William's wonderful success is made to sound almost miraculous by the old chronicles.

The two Norman parties held separate territories and were divided geographically, and each party wished to keep to itself and not be linked with the other. The Christian duke who liked French speech and French government might keep Christian Rouen and Evreux where Frenchmen abounded, but the heathen Danes to the westward would rather be independent of a leader who had turned his face upon the traditions and beliefs of his ancestors. For the time being, these rebellious subjects must keep their grudges and bear their wrongs as best they might, for their opponents were the masters now, and William was free to aim at still greater influence in French affairs as his dominion increased.

Through his whole life he was swayed by religious impulses, and, as we have known, it was hard work at one time to keep him from being a monk. Yet he was not very lavish in his presents to the church, as a good monarch was expected to be in those days, and most of the abbeys and cathedrals which had suffered so cruelly in the days of the pirates were very poor still, and many were even left desolate. His government is described as just and vigorous, and as a general thing his subjects liked him and upheld his authority. He was very desirous all the time to bring his people within the bounds of Christian civilization and French law and order, yet he did not try to cast away entirely the inherited speech or ideas of his ancestors. Of course his treatment of the settlements to the westward and the Danish party in his dominion must have varied at different times in his reign. Yet, after he had made great efforts to identify himself with the French, he still found himself looked down upon by his contemporaries and called the Duke of the Pirates, and so in later years he concerned himself more with his father's people, and even, so the tradition goes, gave a new Danish colony direct from Denmark leave to settle in Brittany. His young son Richard was put under the care, not of French priests, but his own old tutor, Botho the Dane, and the boy and his master were sent purposely to Bayeux, the very city which young Richard's grandfather, Rolf, had helped to ravage. At Rouen the Northman's language was already almost forgotten, but the heir to the duchy was sent where he could hear it every day, though his good teacher had accepted French manners and the religion of Rome. William Longsword had become sure that there was no use in trying to be either wholly Danish or wholly French, the true plan for a Duke of Normandy was to be Dane and Frenchman at once. The balance seems to have swung toward the Danish party for a time after this, and after a troubled, bewildering reign to its very close, William died at the hands of his enemies, who had lured him away to hold a conference with Arnulf, of Flanders, at Picquigny, where he came to a mysterious and sudden death.

The next year, 943, was a marked one in France and began a new order of things. There was a birth and a death which changed the current of history. The Count of Vermandois, the same man who had kept the prison and helped in the murder of Charles the Simple, was murdered himself or at least died in an unexplained and horrible way, as men were apt to do who were called tyrants and were regicides beside. His dominion was divided among his sons, except some parts of it that Hugh of Paris seized. This was the death, and the birth was of a son and heir to Hugh of Paris himself. His first wife was an Englishwoman, Eadhild, but she had died childless, to his great sorrow. This baby was the son of his wife Hadwisa, the daughter of King Henry of Germany, and he was called Hugh for his father; Hugh Capet, the future king. After this Hugh of Paris changed his plans and his policy. True enough, he had never consented to being a king himself, but it was quite another thing to hinder his son from reigning over France by and by. Here the Frenchman begins to contrast himself more plainly against the Frank, just as we have seen the Norman begin to separate himself from the Northman. Under Rolf Normandy had been steadily loyal to King Charles the Simple; under William it had wavered between the king and the duke; under Richard we shall see Normandy growing more French again.

Under William Longsword, now Frenchman, now Northman was coming to the front, and everybody was ready to fight without caring so very much what it was all about. But everywhere we find the striking figure of the young duke carrying his great sword, that came to be the symbol of order and peace. The golden hilt and long shining blade are familiar enough in the story of William's life. Somehow we can hardly think of him without his great weapon. With it he could strike a mighty blow, and in spite of his uncommon strength, he is said to have been of a slender, graceful figure, with beautiful features and clear, bright color like a young girl's. His charming, cheerful, spirited manners won friendship and liking. "He had an eye for splendor," says one biographer; "well spoken to all, William Longsword could quote a text to the priest, listen respectfully to the wise sayings of the old, talk merrily with his young friends about chess and tables, discuss the flight of the falcon and the fleetness of the hound."

When he desired to be a monk, he was persuaded that his rank and duties would not permit such a sacrifice, and that he must act his part in the world rather than in the cloister, for Normandy's sake, but in spite of his gay life and apparent fondness for the world's delights and pleasures, when he died his followers found a sackcloth garment and scourge under his splendid clothes. And as he lay dead in Rouen the rough haircloth shirt was turned outward at the throat so that all the people could see. He had not the firmness and decision that a duke of Normandy needed; he was very affectionate and impulsive, but he was a miserly person, and had not the power of holding on and doing what ought to be done with all his might.

IV. RICHARD THE FEARLESS.

"By many a warlike feat

Lopped the French lilies."—Drayton.

AROUND the city of Bayeux, were the headquarters of the Northmen, and both Rolfs followers and the later colonists had kept that part of the duchy almost free from French influence. There Longsword's little son Richard (whose mother was Espriota, the duke's first wife, whom he had married in Danish fashion), was sent to learn the Northmen's language, and there he lived yet with his teachers and Count Bernard, when the news came of the murder of his father by Arnulf of Flanders, with whom William had gone to confer in good faith.

We can imagine for ourselves the looks of the little lad and his surroundings. He was fond even then of the chase, and it might be on some evening when he had come in with the huntsmen that he found a breathless messenger who had brought the news of Lonsgword's death. We can imagine the low roofed, stone-arched room with its thick pillars, and deep stone casings to the windows, where the wind came in and made the torches flare. At each end of the room would be a great fire, and the servants busy before one of them with the supper, and there on the flagstones, in a dark heap, is the stag, and perhaps some smaller game that the hunters have thrown down. There are no chimneys, and the fires leap up against the walls, and the smoke curls along the ceiling and finds its way out as best it can.

One end of the room is a step or two higher than the other, and here there is a long table spread with drinking-horns and bowls, and perhaps some beautiful silver cups, with figures of grapevines and fauns and satyrs carved on them, which the Norse pirates brought home long ago from Italy. The floor has been covered with rushes which the girls of the household scatter, and some of these girls wear old Norse ornaments of wrought silver, with bits of coral, that must have come from Italy too. The great stag-hounds are stretched out asleep after their day's work, and the little Richard is tired too, and has thrown himself into a tall carved chair by the fire.

Suddenly there comes the sound of a horn, and everybody starts and listens. Was the household to be attacked and besieged? for friends were less likely visitors than enemies in those rough times.

The dogs bark and cannot be quieted, and again the horn sounds outside the gate, and somebody has gone to answer it, and those who listen hear the great hinges creak presently as the gate is opened and the sound of horses' feet in the courtyard. The dogs have found that there is no danger and creep away lazily to go to sleep again, but when the men of the household come back to the great hall their faces are sadly changed. Something has happened.

Among them are two guests, two old counts whom everybody knows, and they walk gravely with bent heads toward the boy Richard, who stands by the smaller fire, in the place of honor, near his father's chair. Has his father come back sooner than he expected? The boy's heart must beat fast with hope for one minute, then he is frightened by the silence in the great hall. Nobody is singing or talking; there is a dreadful stillness; the very dogs are quiet and watching from their beds on the new-strewn rushes. The fires snap and crackle and throw long shadows about the room.

What are the two counts going to do—Bernard Harcourt and Rainulf Ferrières? They are kneeling before the little boy, who is ready to run away, he does not know why. Count Bernard has knelt before him, and says this, as he holds Richard's small hand: "Richard, Duke of Normandy, I am your liegeman and true vassal"; and then the other count does and says the same, while Bernard stands by and covers his face with his hands and weeps.

Richard stands, wondering, as all the rest of the noblemen promise him their service and the loyalty of their castles and lands, and suddenly the truth comes to him. His dear father is dead, and he must be the duke now; he, a little stupid boy, must take the place of the handsome, smiling man with his shining sword and black horse and purple robe and the feather with its shining clasp in the high ducal cap that is as splendid as any crown. Richard must take the old counts for his playfellows, and learn to rule his province of Normandy; and what a long, sad, frightened night that must have been to the fatherless boy who must win for himself the good name of Richard the Fearless!

Next day they rode to Rouen, and there, when the nobles had come, the dead duke was buried with great ceremony, and all the people mourned for him and were ready to swear vengeance on his treacherous murderer. After the service was over Richard was led back from the cathedral to his palace, and his heavy black robes were taken off and a scarlet tunic put on; his long brown hair was curled, and he was made as fine as a little duke could be, though his eyes were red with crying, and he hated all the pomp and splendor that only made him the surer that his father was gone.

They brought him down to the great hall of the palace, and there he found all the barons who had come to his father's burial, and the boy was told to pull off his cap to them and bow low in answer to their salutations. Then he slowly crossed the hall, and all the barons walked after him in a grand procession according to rank first the Duke of Brittany and last the poorest of the knights, all going to the Church of Notre Dame, the great cathedral of Rouen, where the solemn funeral chants had been sung so short a time before.

There were all the priests and the Norman bishops, and the choir sang as Richard walked to his place near the altar where he had seen his father sit so many times. All the long services of the mass were performed, and then the boy-duke gave his promise, in the name of God and the people of Normandy, that he would be a good and true ruler, guard them from their foes, maintain truth, punish sin, and protect the Church. Two of the bishops put on him the great mantle of the Norman dukes, crimson velvet and trimmed with ermine; but it was so long that it lay in great folds on the ground. Then the archbishop crowned the little lad with a crown so wide and heavy that one of the barons had to hold it in its place. Last of all, they gave him his father's sword, taller than he, but he reached for the hilt and held it fast as he was carried back to his throne, though Count Bernard offered to carry it. Then all the noblemen did homage, from Duke Alan of Brittany down, and Richard swore in God's name to be the good lord of every one and to protect him from his foes. Perhaps some of the elder men who had followed Rolf the Ganger felt very tenderly toward this grandchild of their brave old leader, and the friends of kind-hearted Longsword meant to be loyal and very fatherly to his defenceless boy, upon whom so much honor, and anxiety too, had early fallen.

See what a change there was in Normandy since Rolf came, and what a growth in wealth and orderliness the dukedom had made. All the feudal or clannish spirit had had time to grow, and Normandy ranked as the first of the French duchies. Still it would be some time yet before the Danes and Norwegians of the north could cease to think of the Normans as their brothers and cousins, and begin to call them Frenchmen or Welskes, or any of the other names they called the people in France or Britain. It was sure to be a hard dukedom enough for the boy-duke to rule, and all his youth was spent in stormy, dangerous times.

His father had stood godfather—a very close tie—to the heir of the new king of France, who was called Louis, and he was also at peace with Count Hugh of Paris. Soon after Longsword's death King Louis appeared in Rouen at the head of a body of troops, and demanded that he should be considered the guardian and keeper of young Richard during his minority. He surprised the counts who were in Rouen, and who were just then nearly defenceless. It would never do for them to resist Louis and his followers; they had no troops at hand; and they believed that the safest thing was to let Richard go, for a time at any rate. It was true that he was the king's vassal, and Normandy had always done homage to the kings of France. And with a trusty baron for protection the boy was sent away out of pleasant Normandy to the royal castle of Laon. The Rouen people were not very gracious to King Louis, and that made him angry. Indeed, the French king's dominion was none too large, and everybody knew that he would be glad to possess himself of the dukedom, or of part of it, and that he was not unfriendly to Arnulf, who had betrayed William Longsword. So the barons who were gathered at Rouen, and all the Rouen people, must have felt very anxious and very troubled about Richard's safety when the French horsemen galloped away with him. From time to time news came that the boy was not being treated very well. At any rate he was not having the attention and care that belonged to a duke of Normandy. The dukedom was tempestuous enough at any time, with its Northman party, and its French party, and their jealousies and rivalries. But they were all loyal to the boy-duke who belonged to both, and who could speak the pirate's language as well as that of the French court. If his life were brought to an untimely end what a falling apart there would be among those who were not unwilling now to be his subjects. No wonder that the old barons were so eager to get Richard home again, and so distrustful of the polite talk and professions of affection and interest on King Louis's part. Louis had two little sons of his own, and it would be very natural if he sometimes remembered that, if Richard were dead, one of his own boys might be Duke of Normandy instead that is, if old Count Hugh of Paris did not stand in the way.

So away went Richard from his pleasant country of Normandy, with its apple and cherry orchards and its comfortable farms, from his Danes and his Normans, and the perplexed and jealous barons. A young nobleman, named Osmond de Centeville, was his guardian, and promised to take the best of care of his young charge, but when they reached the grim castle of Laon they found that King Louis' promises were not likely to be kept. Gerberga, the French queen, was a brave woman, but eager to forward the fortunes of her own household, and nobody took much notice of the boy who was of so much consequence at home in his own castle of Rouen. We cannot help wondering why Richard's life did not come to a sudden end like his father's, but perhaps Osmond's good care and vigilance gave no chance for treachery to do its work.

After a while the boy-duke began to look very pale and ill, poor little fellow, and Osmond watched him tenderly, and soon the rest of the people in the castle had great hopes that he was going to die. The tradition says that he was not sick at all in reality, but made himself appear so by refusing to eat or sleep. At any rate he grew so pale and feeble that one night everybody was so sure that he could not live that they fell to rejoicing and had a great banquet. There was no need to stand guard any longer over the little chief of the pirates, and nobody takes much notice of Osmond even as he goes to and from the tower room with a long face.

Late in the evening he speaks of his war-horse which he has forgotten to feed and litter down, and goes to his stable in the courtyard with a huge bundle of straw. The castle servants see him, but let him pass as usual, and the banquet goes on, and the lights burn dim, and the night wanes before anybody finds out that there was a thin little lad, keeping very still, in the straw that Osmond carried, and that the two companions were riding for hours in the starlight toward the Norman borders. Hurrah! we can almost hear the black horse's feet clatter and ring along the roads, and take a long breath of relief when we know that the fugitives get safe to Crecy castle within the Norman lines next morning.

King Louis was very angry and sent a message that Richard must come back, but the barons refused, and before long there was a great battle. There could really be no such thing as peace between the Normans and the kingdom of France, and Louis had grown more and more anxious to rid the country of the hated pirates. Hugh the Great and he were enemies at heart and stood in each other's way, but Louis made believe that he was friendly, and granted his formidable rival some new territory, and displayed his royal condescension in various ways. Each of these rulers was more than willing to increase his domain by appropriating Normandy, and when we remember the two parties in Normandy itself we cannot help thinking that Richard's path was going to be a very rough one to follow. His father's enemy, Arnulf of Flanders, was the enemy of Normandy still, and always in secret or open league with Louis. The province of Brittany was hard to control, and while William Longsword had favored the French party in his dominions he had put Richard under the care of the Northmen. Yet this had not been done in a way to give complete satisfaction, for the elder Danes clung to their old religion and cared nothing for the solemn rites of the Church, by means of which Richard had been invested with the dukedom. They were half insulted by such silly pageantry, yet it was not to the leaders of the old pirate element in the dukedom, but to the Christianized Danes, whose head-quarters were at Rouen, that the guardianship of the heir of Normandy had been given. He did not belong to the Christians, but to the Norsemen, yet not to the old pagan vikings either. It was a curious and perhaps a very wise thing to do, but the Danes little thought when Longsword promised solemnly to put his son under their charge, that he meant the Christian Danes like Bernard and Botho. There was one thing that all the Normans agreed upon, that they would not be the vassals and lieges of the king of France. They had promised it in their haste when the king had come and taken young Richard away to Laon, but now that they had time to consider, they saw what a mistake it had been to make Louis the boy-duke's guardian. They meant to take fast hold of Richard now that he had come back, and so the barons were summoned, and when Louis appeared again in Normandy, with the spirit and gallantry of a great captain, to claim the guardianship and to establish Christianity, as well as to avenge the murder of Longsword, if you please!—he found a huge army ready to meet him.

Nobody can understand how King Louis managed to keep such a splendid army as his in good condition through so many reverses. He had lost heavily from his lands and his revenues, and there were no laws, so far as we know, that compelled military service, but the ranks were always full, and the golden eagle of Charlemagne was borne before the king on the march, and the banner of that great emperor, his ancestor, fluttered above his pavilion when the army halted. As for the

Danes (which means simply the Northern or Pirate party of Normandy), they were very unostentatious soldiers and fought on foot, going to meet the enemy with sword and shield. Some of them had different emblems on their shields now, instead of the old red and white stripes of the shields that used to be hung along the sides of the long-ships, and they carried curious weapons, even a sort of flail that did great execution.

We must pass quickly over the long account of a feigned alliance between Hugh of Paris and King Louis, their agreement to share Normandy between themselves, and then Hugh's withdrawal, and Bernard of Senlis's deep-laid plot against both the enemies of Normandy. It was just at this time that there was a great deal of enmity between Normandy and Brittany, and the Normans seem to be in a more rebellious and quarrelsome state than usual. If there was one thing that they clung to every one of them, and would not let go, it was this: that Normandy should not be divided, that it should be kept as Rolf had left it. Sooner than yield to the plots and attempted grasping and divisions of Hugh and Arnulf of Flanders, and Louis, they would send to the North for a fleet of dragon ships and conquer their country over again. They knew very well that however bland and persuasive their neighbors might become when they desired to have a truce, they always called them filthy Normans and pirates behind their backs, and were always hoping for a chance to push them off the soil of Normandy. There was no love lost between the dukedoms and the kingdom.

After sometime Louis was persuaded again that Normandy desired nothing so much as to call him her feudal lord and sovereign. Bernard de Senlis assured him, for the sake of peace, that they were no longer in doubt of their unhappiness in having a child for a ruler, that they were anxious to return to the old pledge of loyalty that Rolf gave to the successor of Charlemagne. He must be the over-lord again and must come and occupy his humble city of Rouen. They were tired of being harried, their land was desolated, and they would do any thing to be released from the sorrows and penalties of war. Much to our surprise, and very likely to his own astonishment too, we find King Louis presently going to Rouen, and being received there with all manner of civility and deference. Everybody hated him just as much as ever, and distrusted him, and no doubt Louis returned the compliment, but to outward view he was beloved and honored by his tributaries, and the Norman city seemed quiet and particularly servile to its new ruler and his bragging troops. Nobody understood exactly why they had won their ends with so little trouble, and everybody was on the watch for some amazing counterplot, and dared not trust either friend or foe. As for Louis, they had shamed and tormented him too much to make him a very affectionate sovereign now. To be sure he ruled over Normandy at last, but that brought him perplexity enough. In the city the most worthless of his followers was putting on the airs of a conqueror and aggravating the Norman subjects unbearably. The Frenchmen who had followed the golden eagle of Charlemagne so long without any reward but glory and a slender subsistence, began to clamor for their right to plunder the dukedom and to possess themselves of a reward which had been too long withheld already.

Hugh, of Paris, and King Louis had made a bold venture together for the conquest of Normandy, and apparently succeeded to their heart's content. Hugh had besieged Bayeux; and the country, between the two assailants, had suffered terribly. Bernard the Dane, or Bernard de Senlis either, knew no other way to reestablish themselves than by keeping Louis in Rouen and cheating him by a show of complete submission. The Normans must have had great faith in the Danish Bernard when they submitted to make unconditional surrender to Louis. Could it be that he had been faithless to the boy-duke's rights, and allowed him to be contemptuously disinherited?

Now that the king was safely bestowed in Rouen, his new liegemen began to say very disagreeable things. Louis had made a great fool of himself at a banquet soon after he reached Rolf's tower in the Norman city. Bernard the Dane, had spread a famous feast for him and brought his own good red wine. Louis became very talkative, and announced openly that he was going to be master of the Normans at last, and would make them feel his bonds, and shame them well. But Bernard the Dane left his own seat at the table and placed himself next the king. Presently he began, in most ingenious ways, to taunt him with having left himself such a small share of the lands and wealth of the ancient province of Neustria. He showed him that Hugh of Paris had made the best of the bargain, and that he had given up a great deal more than there was any need of doing. Bernard described in glowing colors the splendid dominions he had sacrificed by letting his rival step in and take first choice. Louis had not chosen to take a seventh part of the whole dukedom, and Hugh of Paris was master of all Normandy beyond the Seine, a beautiful country watered by fine streams whose ports were fit for commerce and ready for defence. More than this; he had let ten thousand fighting men slip through his hands and become the allies of his worst enemy. And so Bernard and his colleagues plainly told Louis that he had made a great mistake. They would consent to receive him as their sovereign and guardian of the young duke, but Normandy must not be divided; to that they would never give their consent.

Louis listened, half dazed to these suggestions, and when he was well sobered he understood that he was attacked on every side. Hugh of Paris had declared that if Louis broke faith with him now he would make an end to their league, and Louis knew that he would be making a fierce enemy if he listened to the Normans; yet if he refused, they would turn against him.

On the other hand, if he permitted Hugh to keep his new territory, he was only strengthening a man who was his enemy at heart, and who sooner or later would show his antagonism. Louis's own soldiers were becoming very rebellious. They claimed over and over again that Rolf had had no real right to the Norman lands, but since he had divided them among his followers, all the more reason now that the conquerors, the French owners of Normandy, should be put into possession of what they had won back again at last. They demanded that the victors should enforce their right, and not only expressed a wish for Bernard the Dane's broad lands, but for his handsome young wife. They would not allow that the Normans had any rights at all. When a rumor of such wicked plans began to be whispered through Rouen and the villages, it raised a great excitement. There would have been an insurrection at once, if shrewd old Bernard had not again insisted upon patience and submission. His wife even rebelled, and said that she would bury herself in a convent; and Espriota, young Richard's mother, thriftily resolved to provide herself with a protector, and married Sperling, a rich miller of Vaudreuil.

Hugh of Paris was Bernard's refuge in these troubles, and now we see what the old Dane had been planning all the time. Hugh had begun to believe that there was no use in trying to hold his new possessions of Normandy beyond the Seine, and that he had better return to his old cordial alliance with the Normans and uphold Rolf the Ganger's dukedom. So the Danish party, Christians and pagans, and the Normans of the French party, and Hugh of Paris, all entered into a magnificent plot against Louis. The Normans might have been contented with expelling the intruders, and a renunciation of the rights Louis had usurped, but Hugh the Great was very anxious to capture Louis himself.

Besides Hugh of Paris and the Norman barons who upheld the cause of young Richard, there was a third very important ally in the great rebellion against King Louis of France. When Gorm a famous old king of Denmark had died some years before, the successor to his throne was Harold Blaatand or Bluetooth, a man of uncommonly fine character for those times—a man who kept his promises and was noted for his simplicity and good faith and loyalty to his word. Whatever reason may have brought Harold to Normandy at this time, there he was, the firm friend of the citizens of the Bayeux country, and we find him with his army at Cherbourg.

All Normandy was armed and ready for a grand fight with the French, though it appears that at first there was an attempt at a peaceful conference. This went on very well at first, the opposing armies being drawn up on either side of the river Dive, when who should appear but Herluin of Montreuil, the insolent traitor who was more than suspected of having caused the murder of William Longsword. Since then he had ruled in Rouen as Louis's deputy and stirred up more hatred against himself, but now he took a prominent place in the French ranks, and neither Normans nor Danes could keep their tempers any longer. So the peaceful conference was abruptly ended, and the fight began.

Every thing went against the French: many counts were killed; the golden eagle of Charlemagne and the silk hangings and banners of the king's tent had only been brought for the good of these Normans, who captured them. As for the king himself, he was taken prisoner; some say that he was led away from the battle-field and secreted by a loyal gentleman of that neighborhood, who hid him in a secluded bowery island in the river near by, and that the poor gentleman's house and goods were burnt and his wife and children seized, before he would tell anything of the defeated monarch's hiding-place. There is another story that Harold Blaatand and Louis met in hand-to-hand combat, and the Dane led away the Frank as the prize of his own bravery. The king escaped and was again captured and imprisoned in Rouen. No bragging now of what he would do with the Normans, or who should take their lands and their wives. Poor Louis was completely beaten, but there was still a high spirit in the man and in his brave wife Gerberga, who seems to have been his equal in courage and resource. After a while Louis only regained his freedom by giving up his castle of Laon to Hugh of Paris, and the successor of Charlemagne was reduced to the pitiful poverty of being king only of Compiegne. Yet he was still king, and nobody was more ready to give him the title than Hugh of Paris himself, though the diplomatic treacheries went on as usual.

Harold had made a triumphant progress through Normandy after the great fight was over, and all the people were very grateful to him, and it is said that he reestablished the laws of Rolf, and confirmed the authority of the boy-duke. We cannot understand very well at this distance just why Harold should have been in Normandy at all with his army to make himself so useful, but there he was, and unless one story is only a repetition of the other, he came back again, twenty years after, in the same good-natured way, and fought for the Normans again.

Poor Louis certainly had a very hard time, and for a while his pride was utterly broken; but he was still young and hoped to retrieve his unlucky fortunes. Richard, the young duke, was only thirteen years old when Normandy broke faith with France. He had not yet earned his title of the Fearless, which has gone far toward making him one of the heroes of history, and was waiting to begin his real work and influence in the dukedom. Louis had sympathy enough of a profitless sort from his German and English neighbors. England sent an embassy to demand his release, and Hugh of Paris refused most ungraciously. Later, the king of the Germans or East Franks determined to invade Hugh's territory, and would not even send a message or have any dealings with him first; and when he found that the German army was really assembling, the Count of Paris yielded. But, as we have already seen, Louis had to give up a great piece of his kingdom. As far as words went, he was king again. He had lost his authority while he was in prison, but it was renewed with proper solemnity, and Hugh was again faithful liegeman and homager of his former prisoner. The other princes of Europe, at least those who were neighbors, followed Hugh's example—all except one, if we may believe the Norman historians. On the banks of the Epte, where Rolf had first done homage to the French king, the Norman duchy was now set free from any over-lordship, and made an independent country. The duke was still called duke, and not king, yet he was completely the monarch of Normandy, and need give no tribute nor obedience.

Before long, however, Richard, or his barons for him—wily Bernard the Dane, and Bernard de Senlis, and the rest—commended the lands and men of Normandy to the Count of Paris, benefactor and ally. The Norman historians do not say much about this, for they were not so proud of it as of their being made free from the rule of France. We are certain that the Norman soldiers followed Hugh in his campaigns, for long after this during the reign of Richard the Fearless there were some charters and state papers written which are still preserved, and which speak of Hugh of Paris as Richard's over-lord.

There are so few relics of that time that we must note the coinage of the first Norman money in Richard's reign. The chronicles follow the old fashion of the sagas in sounding the praises of one man—sometimes according to him all the deeds of his ancestors besides; but, unfortunately, they refer little to general history, and tell few things about the people. We find Normandy and England coming into closer relations in this reign, and the first mention of the English kings and of affairs across the Channel, lends a new interest to our story of the Normans. Indeed, to every Englishman and American the roots and beginnings of English history are less interesting in themselves than for their hints and explanations of later chapters and events.

Before we end this account of Duke Richard's boyhood, we must take a look at one appealing fragment of it which has been passed by in the story of the wars and tumults and strife of parties. Once King Louis was offered his liberty on the condition that he would allow the Normans to take his son and heir Lothair as pledge of his return and good behavior. No doubt the French king and Queen Gerberga had a consciousness that they had not been very kind to Richard, and so feared actual retaliation. But Gerberga offered, not the heir to the throne, but her younger child Carloman, a puny, weak little boy, and he was taken as hostage instead, and soon died in Rouen. Miss Yonge has written a charming story called "The Little Duke," in which she draws a touching picture of this sad little exile. It makes Queen Gerberga appear very hard and cruel, and it seems as if she must have been to let the poor child go among his enemies. We must remember, though, that these times were very hard, and one cannot help respecting the poor queen, who was very brave after all, and fought as gallantly as any one to keep her besieged and struggling kingdom out of the hands of its assailants.

We must pass over the long list of petty wars between Louis and Hugh. Richard's reign was stormy to begin with, but for some years before his death Normandy appears to have been tolerably quiet. Louis had seen his darkest times when Normandy shook herself free from French rule, and from that hour his fortunes bettered. There was one disagreement between Otto of Germany and Louis, aided by the king of Burgundy, against the two dukes, Hugh and Richard, and before Louis died he won back again the greater part of his possessions at Laon. Duke Hugh's glories were somewhat eclipsed for a time, and he was excommunicated by the Archbishop of Rheims and took no notice of that, but by and by when the Pope of Rome himself put him under a ban, he came to terms. The Normans were his constant allies, but there is not much to learn about their own military enterprises. The enthusiastic Norman writers give a glowing account of the failure of the confederate kings to capture Rouen, but say less about their marauding tour through the duchies of Normandy and Hugh's dominions. Rouen was a powerful city by this time, and a famous history belonged to her already. There are some fragments left still of the Rouen of that day, which is very surprising when we remember how battered and beleaguered the old town was through century after century.

Every thing was apparently prospering with the king of France when he suddenly died, only thirty-three years of age, in spite of his tempestuous reign and always changing career. He must have felt like a very old man, one would think, and somehow one imagines him and Gerberga, his wife, as old people in their Castle of Laon. Lothair was the next king, and Richard, who so lately was a child too, became the elder ruler of his time. Hugh of Paris died two years later, and the old enemy of Normandy, Arnulf of Flanders, soon followed him. The king of Germany, Otto, outlived all these, but Richard lived longer than he or his son.

The duchy of France, Hugh's dominion, passed to his young son, Hugh Capet, a boy of thirteen. When this Hugh grew up he did homage to Lothair, but Richard gave his loyalty to Hugh of Paris's son. The wars went on, and before many years went over Hugh Capet extinguished the succession of Charlemagne's heirs to the throne of

France, and was crowned king himself, so beginning the reign of France proper; as powerful and renowned a kingdom as Europe saw through many generations. By throwing off the rule of German princes, and achieving independence of the former French dynasty, an order of things began that was not overthrown until our own day. Little by little the French crown annexed the dominions of all its vassals, even the duchy of Normandy, but that was not to be for many years yet. I hope we have succeeded in getting at least a hint of the history of France from the time it was the Gaul of the Roman empire; and the empire of Charlemagne, and later, of the fragments of that empire, each a province or kingdom under a ruler of its own, which were reunited in one confederation under one king of France. All this time Europe is under the religious rule of Rome, and in Richard the Fearless's later years we find him the benefactor of the Church, living close by the Minster of Fécamp and buried in its shadow at last. There was a deep stone chest which was placed by Duke Richard's order near one of the minster doors, where the rain might fall upon it that dropped from the holy roof above. For many years, on Saturday evenings, the chest was filled to the brim with wheat, a luxury in those days, and the poor came and filled their measures and held out their hands afterward for five shining pennies, while the lame and sick people were visited in their homes by the almoner of the great church. There was much talk about this hollowed block of stone, but when Richard died in 996 at the end of his fifty-five years' reign, after a long, lingering illness, his last command was that he should be buried in the chest and lie "there where the foot should tread, and the dew and the waters of heaven should fall." Beside this church of the Holy Trinity at Fécamp he built the abbey of St. Wandville, the Rouen cathedral, and the great church of the Benedictines at St. Ouen. New structures have risen upon the old foundations, but Richard's name is still connected with the places of worship that he cared for.

"Richard Sans-peur has long been our favorite hero," says Sir Francis Palgrave, who has written perhaps the fullest account of the Third

Duke; "we have admired the fine boy, nursed on his father's knee whilst the three old Danish warriors knelt and rendered their fealty. During Richard's youth, adolescence, and age our interest in his varied, active, energetic character has never flagged, and we go with him in court and camp till the day of his death."

V. DUKE RICHARD THE GOOD.

"Then would he sing achievements high

And circumstance of chivalry."—Scott.

RICHARD THE FEARLESS had several sons, and when he lay dying his nobles asked him to say who should be his successor. "He who bears my name," whispered the old duke, and added a moment later: "Let the others take the oaths of fealty, acknowledge Richard as their superior; and put their hands in his, and receive from him those lands which I will name to you."

So Richard the Good came to his dukedom, with a rich inheritance in every way from the father who had reigned so successfully, and his brothers Geoffry, Mauger, William, and Robert, accepted their portions of the dukedom, to which Richard added more lands of his own accord.

During this reign there were many changes, some very gradual and natural ones, for Normandy was growing more French and less Scandinavian all the time, and the relationship grew stronger and stronger between vigorous young Normandy and troubled, failing England. Later we shall see how our Normans gave a new impulse to England, but already there are signs and forebodings of what must come to pass in the days of Richard the Good's grandson, William the Conqueror.

We first hear now of many names which are great names in Normandy and England to this day. "It seems as if there were never any region more peopled with men of known deeds, known names, known passions and known crimes," says Palgrave; and the Norman annals abound with historical titles "rendered illustrious by the illusions of time and blazonry which imagination imparts." It is very strange how few records there are, among the state papers in France, of all this period. Every important public matter in England was carefully recorded long before this, but with all the proverbial love of going to law, and all the well-ordered priesthood, and good education of the upper classes, there are only a few scattered charters until Normandy is really merged in France. This almost corresponds to the absence, in the literary world, of papers relating to Shakespeare, which is such a puzzle to antiquarians. Here was a man well-known and beloved both in his native village and the world of London, a man who must have covered thousands of pages with writing, and written letters and signed his name times without number, and yet not one of his manuscripts and very few signatures can be found. Only the references to him in contemporary literature remain to give us any facts at all about the greatest of English writers. Of far less noteworthy men, of his time and before that, we can make up reasonably full biographies. And Normandy is known only through the records of other nations, and the traditions and reports of romancing chroniclers. There are no long lists of men and money, and no treasurer or general of Rolf's, or Longsword's time has left us his accounts. Rolf's brother, who went to Iceland while Rolf came to Normandy, in the tyrannical reign of Harold Haarfager, established in that storm-bound little country a nation of scholars and record-makers. Perhaps it was easier to write there where the only enemies were ice and snow and darkness and the fury of the sea and wind.

Yet we can guess at a great deal about the condition of Normandy. There was so much going to and fro, such a lively commerce and transportation of goods, that we know the old Roman roads had been kept in good repair, and that many others must have been built as the population increased. The famous fairs which were held make us certain that there was a large business carried on, and besides the maintenance and constant use of a large army, in some years there was also a thrifty devotion to mercantile matters and agriculture. Foreign artisans and manufacturers were welcomed to the Norman provinces, and soon formed busy communities like the Flemish craftsmen, weavers and leather-makers, at Falaise. The Normans had an instinctive liking for pomp and splendor; so their tradesmen flourished, and their houses became more and more elegant, and must be carved and gilded like the dragon ships.

A merry, liberal duke was this Richard; fond of his court, and always ready to uphold Normandy's honor and his own when there was any righting to be done. He had a great regard for his nobles, and we begin to find a great deal said about gentlemen; the duke would have only gentlemen for his chosen followers, and the aristocrats make themselves felt more distinctly than before. The rule of the best is a hard thing to manage, it sinks already into a rule of the lucky, the pushing, or the favored in the Rouen court. The power and reign of chivalry begins to blossom now far and wide.

We begin to hear rumors too on the other side that there were wrong distinctions between man and man, and tyranny that grew hard to bear, and one Norman resents the truth that his neighbor is a better and richer man than he, and moreover has the right to make him a servant, and to make laws for him. The Norman citizens were equal in civil rights—that is to say, they were not taxed without their own consent, need pay no tolls, and might hunt and fish; all could do these things except the villeins and peasants, who really composed the mass of the native population, the descendants of those who lived in Normandy before Rolf came there. Even the higher clergy did not form part of the nobility and gentry at first, and in later years there was still a difference in rank and privileges between the priests of Norwegian and Danish race and the other ecclesiastics.

Before Richard the Good had been long on his throne there was a great revolt and uprising of the peasantry, who evidently did not think that their new duke deserved his surname at all. These people conceived the idea of destroying the inequality of races, so that Normandy should hold only one nation, as it already held one name. We cannot help being surprised at the careful political organization of the peasantry, and at finding that they established a regular parliament with two representatives from every district. In all the villages and hamlets, after the day's work was over, they came together to talk over their wrongs or to listen to some speaker more eloquent than his fellows. They "made a commune," which anticipates later events in the history of France in a surprising way. Freeman says that "such a constitution could hardly have been extemporized by mere peasants," and believes that the disturbance was founded in a loyalty to the local customs and rights which were fast being trampled under foot, and that the rebels were only trying to defend their time-honored inheritance. The liberty which they were eager to grasp might have been a great good, scattered as it would have been over a great extent of country, instead of being won by separate cities. The ancient Norman constitutions of the Channel Islands, Jersey and Guernsey and the rest, antiquated as they seem, breathe to-day a spirit of freedom worthy of the air of England or Switzerland or Norway.

The peasants clamored for their right to be equal with their neighbors, and no doubt many a small landholder joined them, who did not wish to swear fealty to his over-lord. In the *Roman de Rou*, an old chronicle which keeps together many traditions about early Normandy that else might have been forgotten, we find one of these piteous harangues. Perhaps it is not authentic, but it gives the spirit of the times so well that it ought to have a place here:

"The lords do nothing but evil; we cannot obtain either reason or justice from them; they have all, they take all, eat all, and make us live in poverty and suffering. Every day with us is a day of pain; we gain nought by our labors, there are so many dues and services. Why do we allow ourselves to be thus treated? Let us place ourselves beyond their power; we too are men, we have the same limbs, the same height, the same power of endurance, and we are a hundred to one. Let us swear to defend each other; let us be firmly knit together, and no man shall be lord over us; we shall be free from tolls and taxes, free to fell trees, to take game and fish, and do as we will in all things, in the wood, in the meadow, on the water!"

At this time the larger portion of Normandy was what used to" be called forest. That word meant something more than woodland; it belonged then to tracts of wild country, woodland and moorland and marshes, and these were the possession of the crown. The peasants had in the old days a right, or a custom at any rate, of behaving as if the forests were their own, but more and more they had been restricted, and the unaccustomed yoke galled them bitterly. Besides their being forbidden to hunt and fish in the forests, the water-ways were closed from them, taxes imposed, and their time and labor demanded on the duke's lands. There had been grants of these free tracts of country to the new nobility, and with the lands the new lords claimed also the service of the peasantry.

The people do not appear to have risen against the duke himself, so much as against their immediate oppressors, and it was one of these who was to be their punisher. You remember that Richard the Fearless' mother, Espriota, married, in the troublous times of his boyhood, a rich countryman called Sperling. They had a son called Raoul of Ivry, who seems to have been high in power and favor with the second Richard, his half-brother, and who now entered upon his cruel task with evident liking. He had been brought up among the country-folk, although he stood at this time next to the duke in office.

He was very crafty, and sent spies all through Normandy to find out when the Assembly or Parliament was to be held, and then dispersed his troops according to the spies' report, and seized upon all the deputies and these peasants who were giving oaths of allegiance to their new commanders. Whether from design or from anger and prejudice Raoul next treated his poor prisoners with terrible cruelty. He maimed them in every way, putting out their eyes, cutting off their hands or feet; he impaled them alive, and tortured them with melted lead. Those who lived through their sufferings were sent home to be paraded through the streets as a warning. So fear prevailed over even the love of liberty in their brave hearts, for the association of Norman peasants was broken up, and a sad resignation took the place, for hundreds of years, of the ardor and courage which had been lighted only to go out again so quickly.

There was another rebellion besides this, of which we have some account, and one man instead of a whole class was the offender. One of Richard's brothers, or half-brothers, the son of an unknown mother, had received as his inheritance the county of Exmes, which held three very rich and thriving towns. These were Exmes, Argentan, and Falaise in which we have already learned that there was a colony of Flemings settled, skilful, industrious weavers and leather-makers and workers in cloth and metals. Falaise itself was already very old indeed, and there remain yet the ruins of an old Roman camp, claimed to belong to the time of Julius Caesar, beside the earliest specimen of that square gray tower which is really of earlier date though always associated with Norman feudalism. The Falaise Fair, which was of such renown in the days of the first dukes, is supposed to be the survival of some pagan festival of vast antiquity. The name of Guibray, the suburb of Falaise which gave its name to the Fair, is said to be derived from the Gaulish word for mistletoe, and wherever we hear of mistletoe in ancient history it reminds us, not of merry-makings and Christmas holidays, but of the grim rites and customs of the Druids.

William, Duke Richard's brother, does not seem to have been grateful for these rich possessions, and before long there is a complaint that he fails to respond to the royal summons, and that he will not render service or do homage in return for his holding. Raoul of Ivry promptly counselled the Duke to take arms against the offender.

It was not long before William found himself a prisoner in the old tower of Rolf at Rouen. He was treated with great severity, and only avoided being hanged by making his escape in most romantic fashion. A compassionate lady contrived to supply him with a rope, and he came down from his high tower-window to the ground hand over hand. Luckily he found none of his keepers waiting for him, and succeeded in getting out of the country. Raoul had been hunting his partisans, and now he had the pleasure of hunting William himself, by keeping spies on his track and forcing him from one danger to another until he was tired of his life, and boldly determined to go to his brother the Duke and beg for mercy. He was very fortunate, for Richard not only listened to him, and was not angry at being stopped on a day when he had gone out to amuse himself with hunting, but he pardoned the suppliant and pitied his trials and sufferings, and more than all, though he did not give back the forfeited county of Exmes, he did give him the county of Eu. We hear nothing of what Raoul thought of such a pleasant ending to the troubles after he had shown such zeal himself in pursuing and harassing the Duke's enemy.

We must take a quick look at the relations between Richard the Good and Hugh Capet, Hugh of Paris's successor, and Robert of France, Hugh Capet's son, who was trying to uphold the fading dignities and power of the Carlovingian throne. Truly Charlemagne's glories were almost spent, and the new glories of the great house of the Capets were growing brighter and brighter. Our eyes already turn toward England and the part that the Norman dukes must soon play there, but there is something to say first about France.

Robert and Richard were great friends; they had many common interests, and were bound by solemn oaths and formal covenants of loyalty toward and protection of each other. Robert was a very honorable man; his relation to his father was a most curious one, for they seem to have been partners in royalty and to have reigned together over France. Richard the Fearless had done much to establish the throne of the Capets, and there was a firm bond between the second Richard and young Robert, to whom he did homage. There were several powerful chiefs and tributaries, but Richard the Good outranks them all, and takes his place without question as the first peer of France. The golden lilies of France are already in flower, and though history is almost silent through the later years of Hugh Capet's life, there are signs of great activity within the kingdom and of growing prosperity. There is an old proverb: "Happy is that nation which has no history!" and whenever we come to a time that the historians pass over or describe in a few sentences, we take a long breath and imagine the people busy in their homes and fields and shops, blest in the freedom from war and disorder.

Robert of France was a famous wit and liked to play tricks upon his associates. He was a poet too, and wrote some beautiful Latin rhymes which are still sung in the churches. There is a good story about his being at Rome once at a solemn church festival. When he approached the altar he held a chalice in his hands with great reverence, and everybody could see that it held a roll of parchment.

There could be no doubt that the king meant to bestow a splendid gift upon the church, perhaps, a duchy or even his whole kingdom; but after the service was over, and the pope and cardinals, full of expectation, hurried to see what prize was put into their keeping, behold! only a copy of Robert's famous chant "*Cornelius Centurio!*" It was a sad disappointment indeed when they looked at this unexpected offering!

But Robert was more than a good comrade, he was a remarkably good king, as kings went; he kept order and was brave, decided, and careful. It was true that he had fallen heir to a prosperous and well-governed kingdom, but it takes constant effort and watchfulness and ready strength to keep a kingdom or any lesser responsibilities up to the right level. He had one great trial, for his wife Bertha, being his first cousin, should not have been his wife according to the laws of the Roman Church. For the first time there was a pope of Rome who was from beyond the Alps, a German; and Robert and he were on bad terms, which resulted in the excommunication of the king of France and the queen, and at one time they were put so completely under the ban that even their servants forsook them and the whole kingdom was thrown into confusion. The misery became so great that the poor queen presently had to be separated from her husband, and this was the more grievous as she had no children, and so Robert was obliged to put her away from him and marry again for the sake of having an heir to the throne. Bertha's successor was very handsome, but very cross, and in later years King Robert used to say: "There are plenty of chickens in the nest, but my old hen pecks at me!"

In spite of the new queen's bad temper there are a good many things to be said in her praise.

She was much better educated than most women of her day, and she had a great admiration for Robert's poetry, and these things must have gone far to make up for her faults.

Duke Richard's marriage was a very fortunate one. His sister Hawisa, of whom he was guardian, was asked in marriage by Duke Godfrey of Brittany, and this was a very welcome alliance, since it bound the two countries closer together than ever before, and made them forget the rivalries which had sometimes caused serious trouble. Especially this was true when a little later Richard himself married Godfrey's sister Judith, who was distinguished for her wisdom. They had a most splendid wedding at the Abbey of St. Michael's Mount, and in course of time one of their daughters married the Count of Burgundy and one the Count of Flanders.

In spite of much immorality and irregularity in those days, there was enough that was proper and respectable in the alliances of the noble families, and we catch many a glimpse of faithful lovers and gallant love-making. It was often said that Normandy's daughters did as much for the well-being of the country as her sons, and when we read the lists of grand marriages we can understand that the dukes' daughters won as many provinces by their beauty as the sons did by their bravery in war.

It is hard to keep the fortunes of all these races and kingdoms clear in our minds. We cannot help thinking of England, and looking at all this early history of the Normans and their growth in relation to it. Then we must keep track of the Danes and Northmen, who have by no means outgrown their old traits and manners, though their cousins in Normandy have given up privateering and the long ships. The history of France makes a sort of background for Normandy and England both.

These marriages of which I have just told you greatly increased the magnificence and the power of the Norman duchy and widened the territory in every way. The Norman dukes could claim the right to interfere in the affairs of those states to which they were allied, and they improved their opportunities. But the most important of all the alliances has not been spoken of at all—the marriage of Richard the Fearless' daughter Emma to Æthelred the Unready of England.

Æthelred himself was the black sheep of his illustrious family—a long line of noble men they were for the most part. In that age much of the character of a nation's history depended upon its monarch, and it is almost impossible to tell the fortunes of a country except by giving the biographies of the reigning king. This Æthelred seems to have had energy enough, but he began many enterprises and never ended them, and wasted a great deal of strength on long, needless expeditions, and does not appear to have made effective resistance to the enemies who came knocking at the very gates of England. He had no tact and little bravery, and was given to putting his trust in unworthy and treacherous followers. Æthelred was the descendant of good King Ælfred and his noble successors, but his own kingdom was ready to fall to pieces before he reigned over it very long, and his reign of thirty-eight years came near to being the ruin of England. There were two or three men who helped him in the evil work, who were greater traitors at heart than Æthelred himself, and we can hardly understand why they were restored to favor after their treason and selfishness were discovered. As one historian says, if we could only have a few of the private letters, of which we have such abundance two or three centuries later, they would be the key to many difficulties.

The Danes were nibbling at the shores of England as rats would gnaw at a biscuit. They grew more and more troublesome. Over in Normandy, Richard the Good was treating these same Danes like friends, and allowing them to come into his harbors to trade with the Norman merchants. In the Côtentin country they found a people much like themselves, preserving many old traditions, and something of the northern speech. The Côtentin lands were poor and rocky, but the hills were crowded with castles, well armed and well fortified, and the men were brave soldiers and sailors, true descendants of the old vikings. They sought their fortunes on the sea too, and we can trace the names of these Côtentin barons and their followers through the army of William the Conqueror to other castles in the broad English lands that were won in less than a hundred years from Æthelred's time. Very likely some of these Côtentin Normans were in league with the northern Danes who made their head-quarters on the Norman shores, and went plundering across the Channel. Soon Æthelred grew very angry, which was to be expected, and he gathered his fleets at Portsmouth, and announced that he should bring Duke Richard back a captive in chains, and waste the whole offending country with fire, except the holy St. Michael's Mount.

The fleet obeyed Æthelred's foolish orders, and went ashore at the mouth of the river Barfleur, only to find the Normans assembled from the whole surrounding country—not a trained army by any means, but an enraged peasantry, men and women alike, armed with shepherds' crooks, and reaping-hooks and flails, and in that bloody battle of Sanglac, they completely routed the English. All the invaders who escaped crowded into six of their vessels and abandoned the rest, and hurried away as fast as they could go. This was a strong link in the chain that by and by would be long enough to hold England fast, and put her at the mercy of the Normans altogether. There was peace made before very long, though the Normans considered themselves to have been grievously insulted, and laughed at the English for being so well whipped. Perpetual peace, the contract unwisely promises, and the pope interfered between the combatants, to prevent the shedding of innocent blood. After the promises were formally made, Æthelred tried to make the alliance even closer. He had children already—one, the gallant Eadmund Ironside, who might have saved the tottering kingdom if he had only held the authority which was thrown away in his father's hands. The name of Æthelred's first queen has been lost, but she was "a noble lady, the daughter of Thored, an Ealdorman," and had been some time dead, so with great diplomacy King Æthelred the Unready, "by the grace of God Basileus of Albion, King and Monarch of all the British Nations, of the Orkneys and the surrounding Islands," as he liked to sign himself, came wooing to Normandy. Emma, the duke's sister, married him and went to England.

Æthelred gave her a splendid wedding-present of wide domains in the counties of Devon and Hants, part of which held the cathedral cities of Winchester and Exeter, the pride and defence of Southern Britain. Queen Emma gave the governorship of Exeter to her chief adviser and officer, Hugh the Norman, and her new subjects called her the Gem of Normandy, and treated her with great deference. She had the beauty of her race and of Rolf's descendants, and her name was changed to Ælfgifu, because this sounded more familiar to the English ears. At least that is the explanation which has come down to us.

Things were in a very bad way in England—the Anglo-Saxon rule of that time was founded upon fraud and violence, and the heavy misfortunes which assailed the English made them fear worse troubles later on. The wisest among them tried to warn their countrymen, but the warnings were apparently of little use. The make-believe rejoicings at Queen Emma's coming were quickly over with, and soon we hear of her flight to Normandy. Many reasons were given for this ominous act. Some say that Æthelred disgusted her by his drunkenness and lawlessness, and others that Hugh the Norman was treacherous, and betrayed his trust to the Danes, and that the queen was a partner in the business. There is still another story, that Æthelred was guilty of a shocking massacre, and that Emma fled in the horror and confusion that it made. Yet later she returned to England as the queen of Cnut the Dane.

Now we must change from England to France altogether for a few pages, and see how steadily the power of the Normans was growing, and how widely it made itself felt. We must see Richard the Good as the ally of France in the warfare waged by King Robert against Burgundy, which was the most important event of Robert's reign. Old Hugh of Paris had carefully avoided any confusion between the rights of Burgundy and the rights of France when he established the foundation of his kingdom. He was a wise politician, and understood that it would not do to conflict with such a power as Burgundy's, which held the Low Countries, Spain, and Portugal and Italy within its influence. Since his day Burgundy had been divided, but it was still distinguished for its great piety and the number of its religious institutions. Robert's uncle was Duke of Burgundy, and he was a very old man; so Robert himself had high hopes of becoming his successor. His chief rival was the representative of the Lombard kings in Italy—Otho William, who was son of Adalbert, a pirate who had wandered beyond the Alps, and Gerberga, the Count of Chalons' daughter. After Adalbert died Gerberga married old Duke Henry of Burgundy, and prevailed upon him to declare her son as his successor. This was illegal, but Otho William was much admired and beloved, and the great part of the Burgundians upheld his right.

Behold, then, Richard the Good and his Norman soldiery marching away to the wars! Duke Henry was dead, and King Robert made haste to summon his ally. Thirty thousand men were mustered under the Norman banner, and the black raven of war went slowly inland. What an enterprise it was to transport such a body of men and horses across country! Supplies could not be hurried from point to point as readily as in after-times, and the country itself must necessarily be almost devastated as if a swarm of locusts had crept through it. Normandy was overflowing with a military population anxious for something to do, with a lingering love for piracy and plundering. They made a swift journey, and Richard and his men were at the gates of the city of Auxerre almost as soon as the venerable duke was in his grave.

There was a tremendous siege; Robert's rival had won the people's hearts, and in the natural strongholds of the mountain slopes they defended themselves successfully. Besides this brave opposition of the Burgundians, the Normans were fought against in a more subtle way by strange phenomena in the heavens. A fiery dragon shot across the sky, and a thick fog and darkness overspread the face of the earth. Auxerre was shrouded in night, and the Norman archers could not see to shoot their arrows. Before long the leagued armies raised the siege of the border city and marched on farther into the country up among the bleak, rocky hills. Only one of the Burgundian nobles Hugh, Count of Chalons and Bishop of Auxerre—was loyal to the cause of King Robert of France. Presently we shall see him again under very surprising circumstances for a count, not to speak of a bishop! The country was thoroughly ravaged, but some time passed before it was finally conquered. At last there was a compromise, and Robert's son was elected duke. His descendants gave France a vast amount of trouble in later years, and so Burgundy revenged herself and Otho William's lost cause.

Richard of Normandy had kept his army well drilled in this long Burgundian campaign, but before his reign was over he had another war to fight with the Count of Dreux. The lands of Dreux were originally in the grant made to Rolf, but later they were held by a line of counts, whose last representative disappeared in Richard the Fearless reign. We find the country in Richard's possession without any record of war, so it had probably fallen to the crown by right. There was a great Roman road through the territory like the Watling Street that ran from Dover to Chester through England, and this was well defended as the old Roman roads always were. Chartres was joined to Dreux by this road, and Chartres was not at peace with Normandy. So a new fort and a town sprung up on the banks of the river to keep Chartres in check: Tillières, or the Tileries, which we might call the ancestor of the famous Tuileries of modern Paris.

There were several fierce battles, and sometimes gaining and sometimes losing, the Normans found themselves presently in a hard place. We are rather startled to hear of the appearance of king Olaf of Norway and the king of the Swedes as Richard's allies. The French people had not wholly outgrown their hatred—or fear and distrust either—of the pirates, and when the news came that bands of Northmen were landing in Brittany there was a wild excitement. Richard and the Chartres chieftain were making altogether too much of their quarrel, and King Robert, as preserver of the public peace, was obliged to interfere. After this episode everybody was more afraid of Normandy than ever, and Chartres was the gainer by the town of Dreux, with its forest and castle, that being the king's award. We cannot help wondering why Richard was persuaded to yield so easily, with all his Northmen eager enough to fight—but they disappear for the time being, and many stones were told of their treacherous warfare in Brittany; of the pitfalls covered with branches into which they tempted their mounted enemies on the battle-field of Dôl. All this seems to have been a little private diversion on their way to the Norman capital, where they were bidden for the business with Chartres.

Then there was a fight with the bishopric of Chalons, which interests us chiefly because Richard's son and namesake first makes his appearance. Renaud, the son of Otho William, who had lost the dukedom of Burgundy, had married a Norman damsel belonging to the royal family of Rolf. This Renaud was defeated and captured by the Count-Bishop of Chalons, of whom we know something already. He was loyal to King Robert of France, you remember, in the war with Burgundy, and now he treated Renaud with terrible severity, and had broken his vows, moreover, by getting married.

King Robert gave the Normans permission to march through his dominions, and seems to have turned his back upon the Count-Bishop. There was a succession of sieges, and the army burned and destroyed on every side as it went through Burgundy, and finally made great havoc in one of the chief towns, called Mirmande in the chronicles, though no Mirmande can be heard of now in that part of the world, and perhaps the angry Normans determined to leave no trace of it for antiquarians and geographers to discover. The Count-Bishop flees for his life to Chalons, and when he was assailed there, he was so frightened that he put an old saddle on his back and came out of the city gates in that fashion to beg for mercy. The merry historian who describes this scene adds that he offered Richard a ride and that he rolled on the ground at the young duke's feet in complete humiliation. One might reasonably say that the count made a donkey of himself in good earnest, and that his count's helmet and his priestly, shaven crown did not go very well together.

The third Richard covered himself with glory in this campaign, however, and went back to Normandy triumphant, to give his old father great pleasure by his valor. But Richard the Good was very feeble now, and knew that he was going to die; so, like Richard the Fearless, he went to Fécamp to spend his last days.

When he had confessed to the bishops, he called for his faithful barons, and made his will. Richard was to be his successor, and his courage and honesty deserved it; but the old father appears to have had a presentiment that all would not go well, for he begged the barons to be loyal to the good youth. Robert, the second son, fell heir to the county of Exmes, upon the condition that he should be faithful to his brother. There was another son, Mauger, a bad fellow, who had no friends or reputation, even at that early day. He was a monk, and a very low-minded one; but later he appears, to our astonishment, as Archbishop of Rouen. No mention is made of his receiving any gift from his father; and soon Richard the Good died and was buried in the Fécamp Abbey. In after years the bones of Richard the Fearless were taken from the sarcophagus outside the abbey door, and father and son were laid in a new tomb near the high altar.

All this early history of Normandy is told mainly by two men, the saga-writers of their time—William of Jumièges, who wrote in the lifetime of William the Conqueror, and Master Wace, of Caen, who was born on the island of Jersey, between thirty and forty years after the conquest of England. His "Roman de Rou" is most spirited and interesting, but, naturally, the earlier part of it is not always reliable. Both the chroniclers meant to tell the truth, but writing at a later date for the glory of Normandy, and in such a credulous age, we must forgive them their inaccuracies.

They have a great deal more to say about Richard the Good than about his two sons, Richard and Robert. Richard was acknowledged as duke by all the barons after his father's death, and then went in state to Paris to do homage to King Robert. This we learn from the records of his contract of marriage with the king's daughter, Lady Adela, who was a baby in her cradle, and the copy of the settlements is preserved, or, at least, the account of the dowry which Richard promised. This was the *seigneurie* of the whole Côtentin country, and several other baronies and communes; Cherbourg and Bruot and Caen, and many cities and lands besides. Poor little Lady Adela! and poor young husband, too, for that matter; for this was quite a heartless affair of state, and neither of them was to be any happier for all their great possessions.

In the meantime Robert, the Duke's brother, was not in the least satisfied, and made an outcry because, though he was lord of the beautiful county of Exmes, the city of Falaise was withheld from him.

There was a man from Brittany who urged him to resent his wrongs, and made trouble between the brothers; Ermenoldus he was called, *the theosophist*; and there is a great mystery about him which the old writers stop to wonder over. He was evidently a sort of magician, and those records that can be discovered give rise to a suspicion that he had strayed far eastward with some pirate fleet toward Asia, and had learned there to work wonders and to compass his ends by uncanny means.

There was a siege of Falaise, which Robert seized and tried to keep by main strength; but Richard's army was too much for him, and at last he sued for peace. The brothers went back to Rouen apparently the best of friends; but there was a grand banquet in Rolf's old castle, and Richard was suddenly death-struck as he sat at the head of the feast, and was carried to his bed, where he quickly breathed his last. The funeral bell began to toll while the banquet still went on, and the barons made themselves merry in the old hall.

There was great lamentation, for Richard was already much beloved, and nobody doubted that he had been poisoned. So Robert came to the throne of Normandy with a black stain upon his character, and during all the rest of his life that stain was not overlooked nor forgotten.

As for the baby-widow, she afterward became the wife of the Count of Flanders, Baldwin de Lisle, and she was the mother of Matilda, who was the wife of William the Conqueror.

VI. ROBERT THE MAGNIFICENT.

"What exile from himself can flee?"—Byron.

BEFORE we begin the story of the next Duke of Normandy whose two surnames, the Devil, and the Magnificent, give us a broad hint of his character, we must take a look at the progress of affairs in the dukedom. There is one thing to be remembered in reading this history, or any other, that history is not merely the story of this monarch or that, however well he may represent the age in which he lived and signify its limitations and development.

In Normandy one cannot help seeing that a power has been at work bringing a new Northern element into the country, and that there has been a great growth in every way since Rolf came with his vikings and besieged the city of Jumièges. Now the dukedom that he formed is one of the foremost of its day, able to stand on equal ground with the royal kingdom and duchy of France, for Robert's homage is only the homage of equals and allies. Normandy is the peer of Burgundy and of Flanders, and every day increases in strength, in ambition, in scholarship and wealth. The influence and *prestige* of the dukedom are recognized everywhere, and soon the soldiers of Normandy are going to take hold of English affairs and master them with unequalled strength. Chivalry is in the bloom of its youth, and the merchants of Falaise, and Rouen, and their sister cities, are rich and luxurious. The women are skilled in needlework and are famous for their beauty and intelligence. Everywhere there are new castles and churches, and the land swarms with inhabitants who hardly find room enough, while the great army hardly draws away the over-plus of men from the farms and workshops. There are whole districts like the Côtentin peninsula, that are nearly ready to pour out their population into some new country, like bees when they swarm in early summer, and neither the fashion of going on pilgrimage to the holy shrines, nor the spirit that leads to any warlike adventure, are equal to the need for a new conquest of territory, and a general emigration.

There are higher standards everywhere in law and morals and customs of home-life. The nobles are very proud and keep up a certain amount of state in their high stone castles. In the Côtentin alone the ruins of more than a hundred of these can yet be seen, and all over Normandy and Brittany are relics of that busy, prosperous time. The whole territory is like a young man who has reached his majority, and who feels a strength and health and ambition that make him restless, and make him believe himself capable of great things.

From followers of the black ravens and worshippers of the god Thor, the Normans have become Christians and devout followers of the Church of Rome. They go on pilgrimage to distant shrines and build churches that the world may well wonder at to-day and try to copy. They have great houses for monks and nuns, and crowds of priests and scholars, and it would not be easy to find worshippers of the old faith unless among old people and in secluded neighborhoods. There is little left of the old Northman's fashions of life but his spirit is as vigorous as ever, and his courage, and recklessness, his love of a fight and hatred of cowardice, his beauty and shapeliness, are sent down from generation to generation, a surer inheritance than lands or money. We grow eager, ourselves, to see what will come of this leaven of daring and pride of strength. There is no such thing for Normandy now, as tranquillity.

Duke Robert's story is chiefly interesting to us because he was the father of William the Conqueror, and in most of the accounts of that time it is hard to find any thing except various versions of his course toward his more famous son. But in reality he was a very gifted and powerful man, and strange to say, the conquest of England was only the carrying out of a plan that was made by Duke Robert himself.

The two young sons of Emma and Æthelred were still in Normandy, and the Duke thought it was a great pity that they were neglected and apparently forgotten by their countrymen. He undertook to be their champion, and boldly demanded that King Cnut of England should consider their rights. He sent an embassy to England and bade Cnut "give them their own," which probably meant the English crown. Cnut disdained the message, as might have been expected, and Duke Robert armed his men and fitted out a fleet, and all set sail for England to force the Dane to recognize the young princes. It sounds very well that the Normans should have been so eager to serve the Duke's cousins, but no doubt they were talking together already about the possibility of extending their dominions across the Channel. They were disappointed now, however, for they were beaten back and out of their course by very bad weather, and had to put in at the island of Jersey. From there they took a short excursion to Brittany, because Robert and his cousin Alan were not on good terms, Alan having refused to do homage to Normandy. There was a famous season of harrying and burning along the Breton coast, which may have reconciled the adventurers to their disappointment, but at any rate the conquest of England was put off for forty years. One wonders how Cnut's Queen Emma felt about the claims of her sons. It was a strange position for her to be put into. A Norman woman herself who had virtually forsaken her children, she could hardly blame her brother for his efforts to restore them to their English belongings, and yet she was bound to her new English interests, and must have different standards as Danish Cnut's wife from those of Saxon Æthelred's. There is an announcement in one of the Norman chronicles that Cnut sent a message to the effect that he would give the princes their rights at his death. This must have been for the sake of peace, but it is not very likely that any such thing ever happened.

A new acquaintance between the countries must have grown out of the banishment of some of the English nobles in the early part of Cnut's reign, and they no doubt strengthened the interest of the Normans, and made their desire to possess England greater than ever before. We shall be conscious of it more and more until the time of the Conquest comes. The Normans plotted and planned again and again, and their intrigues continually grew more dangerous to England. It is plain to see that they were always watching for a chance to try their strength, and were not unwilling to provoke a quarrel. Eadward, one of the English princes, was ready to claim his rights, but he had learned to be very fond of Normandy, and his half-heartedness served his adopted country well when he came at last to the English throne. For the present we lose sight of him, but not of Ælfred his brother, who ventured to England on an expedition which cost him his life, but that failure made the Norman desire for revenge burn hotter and deeper than before, though the ashes of disappointment covered it for a time.

Duke Robert's reign began with a grand flourish, as if he wished to bribe his subjects into forgetfulness of his brother Richard's death. There were splendid feasts and presents of armor and fine clothes for his retainers, and he won his name of the Magnificent in the very face of those who whispered that he was a murderer. He was very generous, and seems to have given presents for the pleasure it gave himself rather than from any underhand motives of gaining popularity. We are gravely told that some of his beneficiaries died of joy, which strikes one as being somewhat exaggerated.

The old castle of Rolf at Rouen was forsaken for the castle of Falaise. No doubt there were unpleasant associations with Rolfs hall, where poor Richard had been seized with his mysterious mortal illness. Falaise, with its hunting-grounds and pleasant woods and waters and its fine situation, was Robert's favorite home forever after. There he brought his wife Estrith, Cnut's sister, who first had been the wife of Ulf the Danish king, and there he lived in a free companionship with his nobles and with great condescension towards his inferiors, with whom he was often associated in most familiar terms.

There were chances enough to show his valor. Once Baldwin the elder, of Flanders, was attacked by his son Baldwin de Lisle, who had put himself at the head of an army, and the poor Count was forced to flee to Falaise for shelter and safety. Any excuse for going to war seems to have been accepted in Normandy; the country was brimming over with people. There was almost more population than the land could support, and Robert led his men to Flanders with great alacrity, and settled the mutiny so entirely that there was no more trouble. Flanders was brought to a proper state of submission, as if in revenge for old scores. At last the noblemen who had upheld the insurrection all deserted the leader of it, and both they and young Baldwin besought Robert to make the terms of peace. After this, Flanders and Normandy were very friendly together, and before long they formed a most significant alliance of the royal houses.

In Robert's strolls about Falaise, perhaps in disguise, like another Haroun al Raschid, his beauty-loving eyes caught sight one day of a young girl who was standing bare-footed in a shallow brook, washing linen, and making herself merry with a group of busy young companions. This was Arlette, or Herleva, according as one gives her the Saxon or the Norman name; her father was a brewer and tanner, who had been attracted to Falaise from Germany by the reputation of its leather manufactures and good markets. The pastures and hunting-grounds made skins very cheap and abundant, but the trade of skinning of beasts was considered a most degrading one, and those who pursued it in ancient times were thought less of than those who followed almost any other occupation. If we were not sure of this, we might suspect the Norman nobles of casting undue shame and reproach upon this man Fulbert.

Duke Robert seems to have quite forgotten his lawful wife in his new love-making with Herleva. Even the tanner himself objected to the duke's notice of his daughter, but who could withstand the wishes of so great a man? Not Fulbert, who accepted the inevitable with a good grace, for later in the story he shows himself a faithful retainer and household official of his lord and master. Robert never seems to have recovered from his first devotion to the pretty creature who stood with slender, white feet in the brook, and turned so laughing a face toward him. They showed not long ago the very castle-window in Falaise from which he caught his first sight of the woman who was to rule his life. He did not marry her, though Estrith was sent away; but they had a son, who was named William, who himself added the titles of the Great and

The Conqueror, but who never escaped hearing to his life's end the shame and ignominy of his birth. We cannot doubt that it was as mean an act then as now to taunt a man with the disgrace he could not help; but of all the great men who were of illegitimate birth whom we know in the pages of history, this famous William is oftenest openly shamed by his title of the Bastard. He won much applause; he was the great man of his time, but from pique, or jealousy, or prejudice, perhaps from some faults that he might have helped, he was forever accused of the shame that was not his. The Bastard,—the Tanner's Grandson; he was never allowed to forget, through any heroism or success in war, or furthering of Norman fortunes, that these titles belonged to him.

The pride of the Norman nobles was dreadfully assailed by Duke Robert's shameful alliance with Herleva. All his relations, who had more or less right to the ducal crown, were enraged beyond control. Estrith had no children, and this beggarly little fellow who was growing plump and rosy in the tanner's house, was arch-enemy of all the proud lords and gentlemen. There was plenty of scandal and mockery in Falaise, and the news of Robert's base behavior was flying from village to village through Normandy and France. The common people of Falaise laughed in the faces of the barons and courtiers as they passed in the street, and one day an old burgher and neighbor of the tanner asked William de Talvas, the head of one of the most famous Norman families, to go in with him to see the Duke's son. The Lord of Alençon was very angry when he looked at the innocent baby-face. He saw, by some strange foreboding and prevision, the troubles that would fall upon his own head because of this vigorous young life, and, as he cursed the unconscious child again and again, his words only echoed the fear that was creeping through Normandy.

Robert was very bold in his defiance of public opinion, and before long the old tanner sheds his blouse like the cocoon of a caterpillar, and blooms out resplendent in the gay trappings of court chamberlain. Herleva was given the place as duchess which did not legally belong to her, and this hurt the pride of the ladies and gentlemen of the court and the country in a way that all Robert's munificence and generosity could not repay or cure. The age was licentious enough, but public opinion demanded a proper conformity to law and etiquette. All the aristocratic house of Rolf's descendants, the valor and scholarship and churchmanship of Normandy, were insulted at once. The trouble fermented more and more, until the Duke's uncle, the Archbishop of Rouen, called his nephew to account for such open sin and disgrace of his kindred, and finally ex-communicated him and put all Normandy under a ban.

Somehow this outbreak was quieted down, and just then Robert was called upon, not only to settle the quarrel in Flanders above mentioned, but to uphold the rights of the French king. For his success in this enterprise he was granted the district of the Vexin, which lay between Normandy and France, and so the Norman duchy extended its borders to the very walls of Paris. Soon other questions of pressing importance rose up to divert public comment; it was no time to provoke the Duke's anger, and there was little notice taken of Herleva's aggravating presence in the ducal castle, or the untoward growth and flourishing of her son.

At length Duke Robert announced his intention of going on a pilgrimage to Jerusalem. He wished to show his piety and to gain as much credit as possible, so the long journey was to be made on foot. The Norman barons begged him not to think of such a thing, for in the excited condition of French and Norman affairs nothing could be more imprudent than to leave the dukedom masterless. "By my faith!" Robert answered stoutly, "I do not mean to leave you without a lord. Here is my young son, who will grow and be a gallant man, by God's help; I command you to take him for your lord, for I make him my heir and give him my whole duchy of Normandy."

There was a stormy scene in the council, and however we may scorn Robert's foolish, selfish present-giving and his vulgarity, we cannot help pitying him as he pleads with the knights and bishops for their recognition of his innocent boy. We pity the Duke's shame, while his natural feeling toward the child wars with his disgust. With all his eloquence, with all his authority, he entreats the scornful listeners until they yield. They have warned him against the danger of the time, and of what he must expect, not only if he goes on pilgrimage and leaves the dukedom to its undefended fate, but also if he further provokes those who are already his enemies, and who resent the presence of his illegitimate child. But he dares to put the base-born lad over the dukedom of Normandy as his own successor. He even goes to the king of France and persuades him to receive the unworthy namesake of Longsword as vassal and next duke, and to Alan of Brittany, who consents to be guardian. Then at last the unwilling barons do homage to the little lord—a bitter condescension and service it must have been!

After all the ceremonies were finished, Robert lost no time in starting on his pilgrimage. He sought the shrine of Jerusalem, many a weary mile away, over mountain and fen, past dangers of every sort. Nothing could be more characteristic than his performance of his penance or his pleasure journey—whichever he called it—for although he went on foot, he spent enormous sums in showering alms upon the people who came out to greet him. Heralds rode before him, and prepared his lodging and reception, and the great procession of horses and grooms and beasts of burden grew longer and longer as he went on his way. Once they blocked up the gateway of a town, and the keeper fell upon the pilgrim Duke, ignorantly, and gave him a good thrashing to make him hurry on with his idle crowd. Robert piously held back those of his followers who would have beaten the warder in return, and said that it was well for him to show himself a pattern of humility and patience, and such suffering was meant for the good of one's soul.

The Duke did a great many foolish things; for one, he had his horses shod with silver shoes, held on by only one nail, and gave orders that none of his servants should pick up the shoes when they were cast, but let them lie in the road.

At last the pilgrims reached Constantinople, and Robert made a great display of his wealth, not to speak of his insolent bad manners.

The emperor, Michael, treated his rude guests with true Eastern courtesy, and behaved himself much more honorably than those who despised him and called him names. He even paid all the expenses of the Norman procession, but, no doubt, he was anxious not to give any excuse for displeasure or disturbance between the Northerners and his own citizens. When the visit was over, and Robert moved on toward Jerusalem, his already feeble health, broken by his bad life, grew more and more alarming, and at last he could not take even a very short journey on foot, and was carried in a litter by negroes. The Crusades were filling the roads with pilgrims and soldiers, and travellers of every sort. One day they met a Côtentin man, an old acquaintance of Robert's. The Duke said with grim merriment that he was borne like a corpse on a bier. "My lord," asked the Crusader, who seems to have been sincerely shocked and doleful at the sight of the Duke's suffering; "my lord, what shall I say for you when I reach home?" "That you saw me carried toward Paradise by four devils," said the Duke, readier at any time to joke about life than to face it seriously and to do his duty. He kept up the pretence of travelling unknown and in disguise, like a humbler pilgrim, but his lavishness alone betrayed the secret he would really have been sorry to keep. Outside the gates of Jerusalem there was always a great crowd of people who were not able to pay the entrance-fee demanded of every pilgrim; but Robert paid for himself and all the rest before he went in at the gate. The long journey was almost ended, for on the way home, at the city of Nicaea, the Duke was poisoned, and died, and was buried there in the cathedral with great solemnity and lamentation. He had collected a heap of relics of the saints, and these were brought safely home to Normandy by Tostin, his chamberlain, who seems to have served him faithfully all the way.

VII. THE NORMANS IN ITALY.

"And therefore must make room

Where greater spirits come."—MARVELL.

THERE is a famous old story about Hasting, the viking captain. Once he went adventuring along the shores of the Mediterranean, and when he came in sight of one of the Tuscan cities, he mistook it for Rome. Evidently he had enough learning to furnish him with generous ideas about the wealth of the Roman churches, but he had brought only a handful of men, and the city looked large and strong from his narrow ship. There was no use to think of such a thing as laying siege to the town; such a measure would do hardly more than tease and provoke it: so he planned a sharp stroke at its very heart.

Presently word was carried from the harbor side, by a long-faced and tearful sailor, to the pious priests of the chief church, that Hasting, a Northman, lay sick unto death aboard his ship, and was desirous to repent him of his sins and be baptized. This was promising better things of the vikings, and the good bishop visited Hasting readily, and ministered eagerly to his soul's distress. Next day word came that the robber was dead, and his men brought him early to the church in his coffin, following him in a defenceless, miserable group. They gathered about the coffin, and the service began; the priests stood in order to chant and pray, their faces bowed low or lifted heavenward. Suddenly up goes the coffin-lid, out jumps Hasting, and his men clutch at the shining knives hidden under their cloaks. They strip the jewelled vestments from the priests' backs; they shut the church doors and murder the poor men like sheep; they climb the high altar, and rob it of its decorations and sacred cups and candlesticks, and load themselves with wealth. The city has hardly time to see them dash by to the harbor side, to hear the news and give them angry chase, before the evil ships are standing out to sea again, and the pirates laugh and shout as they tug at the flashing oars. No more such crafty converts! the people cry, and lift their dead and dying priests sorrowfully from the blood-stained floor. This was the fashion of Italy's early acquaintance with the Northmen, whose grandchildren were to conquer wide dominions in Apulia, in Sicily, and all that pleasant country between the inland seas of Italy and Greece.

It must have seemed almost as bad to the Romans to suffer invasion of this sort as it would to us to have a horde of furious Esquimaux come down to attack our coasts. We only need to remember the luxury of the Italian cities, to recall the great names of the day in literature and art, in order to contrast the civilization and appearance of the invader and the invaded. Yet war was a constant presence then, and every nation had its bitter enemies born of race prejudice and the resentment of conquest. To be a great soldier was to be great indeed, and by the time of the third of the Norman dukes the relation of the Northmen and Italians was much changed.

Yet there was not such a long time between the time of Hasting the pirate, and that of Tancred de Hauteville and Robert Guiscard. Normandy had taken her place as one of the formidable, respectable European powers. The most powerful of the fiefs of France, she was an enemy to be feared and honored, not despised. She was loyal to the See of Rome; very pious and charitable toward all religious establishments; no part of Southern Europe had been more diligent in building churches, in going on pilgrimage, in maintaining the honor of God and her own honor. Her knights prayed before they fought, and they were praised already in chronicle and song. The troubadours sung their noble deeds from hall to hall. The world looked on to see their bravery and valor, and when they grew restless and went a-roving and showed an increasing desire to extend their possessions and make themselves lords of new acres, the rest of the world looked on with envy and approval. Unless the Normans happened to come their way; that of course was quite a different thing.

We cannot help thinking that the readiness of the Englishman of to-day to form colonies and to adapt himself to every sort of climate and condition of foreign life, was anticipated and foreboded in those Norman settlements along the shores of the Mediterranean sea. Perhaps we should say again that the Northmen of a much earlier date were the true ancestors of all English colonists with their raving spirit and love of adventure, but the Normandy of the early part of the eleventh century was a type of the England of to-day. Its power was consolidated and the territory became too narrow for so much energy to be pent up in. The population increased enormously, and the familiar love of conquest and of seeking new fortunes was waked again. The bees send out new swarms when summer comes, and, like the bees, both Normans and Englishmen must have a leader and centralization of the general spirit, else there is scattering and waste of the common force.

We might go on with this homely illustration of the bees to explain the way in which smaller or larger groups of pilgrims, and adventurers of a less pious inclination, had wandered southward and eastward, toward the holy shrines of Jerusalem, or the rich harvest of Oriental wealth and luxury. Not much result came from these enterprises, though as early as 1026, we find the Duke of Naples allowing a company of Norman wanderers to settle at Aversa, and even helping them to build and fortify the town, and to hold it as a kind of out-post garrison against his enemies in Capua. They were understood to be ready for all sorts of enterprises, and the bitter flowers of strategy and revolt appeared to yield the sweetest honey that any country-side could offer. They loved a fight, and so they were often called in by the different Italian princes and proved themselves most formidable and trustworthy allies in case of sudden troubles. This is what an historian of that time says about them:

"The Normans are a cunning and revengeful people; eloquence and dissimulation appear to be their hereditary qualities. They can stoop to flatter; but unless they are curbed by the restraint of law they indulge the licentiousness of nature and passion, and in their eager search for wealth and dominion they despise whatever they possess and hope whatever they desire. Arms and horses, the luxury of dress, the exercises of hawking and hunting, are the delight of the Normans; but on pressing occasions they can endure with incredible patience the inclemency of every climate, and the toil and abstinence of a military life."

How we are reminded of the old vikings in this striking description! and how we see certain changes that have overlaid the original Norse and Danish nature. There are French traits now, like a not very thick veneering of more delicate and polished wood upon the sturdy oak.

Aversa was quickly made of great importance to that part of the world. The Norman colony did good missionary work, and Robert Guiscard, the chief Norman adventurer and founder of the kingdom of Naples, was leader and inspirer of great enterprises. In following the history of the time through many volumes, it is very disappointing to find such slight reference to this most interesting episode in the development of Norman civilization.

In one of the green valleys of the Côtentin, near a small stream that finds its way into the river Dove, there are still standing the crumbling walls of an ancient Norman castle. The neighboring fields still keep their old names of the Park, the Forest, and the Dove-Cot; and in this way, if in no other, the remembrance is preserved of an old feudal manor-house. Not long ago some huge oaks were clustered in groups about the estate, and there was a little church of very early date standing in the shade of a great cedar tree. Its roof had a warlike-looking rampart, and a shapely tower with double crosses lifted itself high against the sky.

In the early years of the eleventh century there lived in this quiet place an old Norman gentleman who was one of Duke Richard the Good's best soldiers. He had wandered far and wide in search of gain and glory. The Duke had given him command of ten armed men who formed his body-guard, and after a long service at court this elder Tancred returned to his tranquil ancestral home to spend the rest of his days. He was poor, and he had a very large family. His first wife, Muriel, had left several children, and their good step-mother treated them all with the same tenderness and wise helpfulness that she had shown to her own flock. The young de Hautevilles had received such education as gentlemen gave their children in those days, and, above every thing else, were expert in the use of arms and of horses and the pleasures of the chase. They trained their falcons, and grew up brave and strong. There were twelve sons, all trained to arms. Three of the elder family were named William, Drogo, and Humphrey, and the sixth, their half-brother, was Robert, who early won for himself the surname of Guiscard, or the Wise. Tall fellows they were, these sons of the Chevalier de Hauteville. One of the old French historians tells us that they had an air of dignity, and even in their youth great things were expected of them; it was easy to prophesy their brilliant future.

While they were still hardly more than boys, Serlon, their eldest brother, who had already gone to court, killed one of Duke Robert's gentlemen who had offered him some insult, and was banished to England where he spent some time in the dreariness of exile, longing more and more to get back to Normandy. This brought great sorrow to the household in the Côtentin valley; it was most likely that a great deal depended upon Serlon's success, and the eager boys at home were looking to him for their own advancement. However, the disappointment was not very long-lived, for at the time when Henry of France was likely to lose his throne through the intrigues of his brother and his mother, Constance of Provence, and came to the Duke of Normandy for aid, Serlon came home again without being asked, and fought like a tiger at the siege of Tillières. You remember that this siege lasted a long time, and it gives us a good idea of the warfare of that age to discover that every day there came out of the city gate an awesome knight who challenged the conqueror to single combat. The son of brave old Tancred was not frightened by even the sight of those unlucky warriors who lay dead under the challenger's blows, and one morning Serlon went to the gate at daybreak and called the knight out to fight with him.

The terrible enemy did not wait; he presently appeared in glistening armor and mounted upon a fiery steed. He asked Serlon who he was, and as if he knew by instinct that he had met his match at last, counselled the champion of Normandy to run away, and not try to fight with him.

Nobody had recognized the banished man, who carefully kept the visor of his helmet down over his face, and when the fight was over and the enemy's head was off and borne at the head of his victorious lance, he marched silently along the ranks of the Norman knights, who were filled with pride and glory, but for all their cheering he was still close-helmeted. Duke Robert heard the news of this famous deed, and determined that such a valiant knight must not hide himself or escape, so he sent a messenger to command the stranger to make himself known. When he found that Serlon himself had been the hero, he ran to meet him, and embraced him and held him to his heart, and still more, gave back to him all the lands and treasures which had come to him by his marriage and which had been confiscated when he was sent into exile. All these glories of their elder brother made the other sons more eager now than ever to show their prowess, but there was slight chance in Normandy, for the war lasted but little longer. But when Robert had put the French king on his throne again, he determined, as we have seen already, to go on a pilgrimage. There was not much prospect of winning great fame at home while young William the heir was so unpopular and Alan of Brittany was his careful guardian. The de Hautevilles were impatient at the prospect of years of petty squabbles and treacherous intrigues; they longed for a broader field for their energies. There was no such thing as staying at home and training the falcons; their hungry young brothers and sisters were pushing their way already, and the ancient patrimony was growing less and less. So William and Drogo and Humphrey went away to seek their fortunes like fairy-book princes, and hearing vague rumors of Rainulf's invitation to his countrymen, and of his being made count of the new possessions in Aversa, they turned their faces towards Italy. We cannot help lingering a moment to fancy them as they ride away from the door of their old home—the three brave young men together. The old father looks after them wistfully, but his eyes are afire, and he lives his own youth over again and wishes with all his heart that he were going too. The little sisters cry, and the younger brothers long for the day when their turn will come to go adventuring. The tame falcons flutter and peck at their hoods, there where they stand on their perches with fettered claws; the grass runs in long waves on the green hill-sides and dazzles the eyes that look after the sons as they ride towards the south; and the mother gives a little cry and goes back into the dark hall and weeps there until she climbs the turret stairs to see if she cannot catch one more look at the straight backs and proud heads of the young knights, or even one little glint of their horses' trappings as they ride away among the orchard leaves.

They would have to fight their way as best they could, and when they reached Apulia at last they still found work enough for their swords. South of Rome were the territories of the independent counts of Naples and the republic of Amalfi. South of these the Greek possessions of Lombardy, which had its own governor and was the last remnant of the Eastern empire.

The beautiful island of Sicily had been in the hands of the Moslems and belonged to the African kingdom of Tunis. In 1038 the governor of Lombardy believed he saw the chance that he had long been waiting for, to add Sicily to his own dominions. The Arabs were fighting among themselves and were split up already into several weak and irreconcilable factions, and he begged the Normans to go and help his own army to conquer them. After a while Sicily was conquered, but the Normans were not given their share of the glory of the victories; on the contrary, the Lombard governor was too avaricious and ungrateful for his own good, and there was a grand quarrel when the spoils were divided. Two years afterwards the indignant Normans came marching back to attack Apulia, and defeated the Greeks at Cannae so thoroughly that they were only left in possession of a few towns.

This was in 1043, and we cannot help feeling a great satisfaction at finding William de Hauteville president of the new republic of Apulia. Had not the three brothers shown their bravery and ability? Perhaps they had only remembered their old father's wise talk, and profited by his advice, and warning lest they should spend their strength by being great in little things instead of aiming at nobler pieces of work. All the high hopes which filled their hearts as they rode away from Normandy must have come true. They were already the leaders in Apulia, and had been foremost in the organization of an aristocratic republic. Twelve counts were elected by popular suffrage, and lived at their capital of Melfi, and settled their affairs in military council. And William, as I have said, was president.

Presently from East and West envious eyes began to look at this powerful young state. Europe knew well enough what had come from giving these Normans foothold in Gaul not so very long ago, and the Pope and the emperors of the West and East formed a league to chase the builders of this new Normandy out of their settlements. The two emperors, however, were obliged to hurry back to defend their own strongholds, and Leo the Tenth was left to fight his neighbors alone, with the aid of some German soldiers, a mere handful, whom Henry the Third had left. The Normans proposed fair terms to his Holiness, but he ventured to fight the battle of Civitella, and was overpowered and beaten, and taken prisoner himself. Then the shrewd Normans said how grieved they had been to fight against the Father of the Church, and implored him, captive as he was, to receive Apulia as a fief of the Holy See. This seems very puzzling, until we stop to think that the Normans would gain an established position among the Italian powers, and this amounted to an alliance with the power of the papal interests.

William de Hauteville died, and the office of president, or first count, passed to his next brother, Drogo, and after him to Humphrey. One day, while Drogo was count, a troop of pilgrims appeared in Amalfi, with their wallets and staves. This was no uncommon sight, but at the head of the dusty company marched a young man somewhere near twenty-five years of age, and of remarkable beauty. The high spirit, the proud nobility in his face, the tone of his voice even, showed him to be an uncommon man; his fresh color and the thickness of his blond hair gave nobody a chance to think that he had come from any of the Southern countries. Suddenly Drogo recognized one of his step-brothers, whom he had left at home a slender boy—this was Robert, already called Guiscard. He had gathered a respectable little troop of followers—five knights and thirty men-at-arms made his escort,—and they had been forced to put on some sort of disguise for their journey, because the court of Rome, jealous of the growing power of the Normans in Italy, did every thing to hinder their project, and refused permission to cross their territories to those who were coming from the North to join the new colony. Humbert de Hauteville was with Robert —indeed the whole family, except Serlon, went to Italy sooner or later after the old knight Tancred died; even the mother and sisters.

Robert arrived in time for the battle of Civitella, and distinguished himself amazingly. Indeed he was the inspirer and leader of the Norman successes in the South, and to him rather than to either of his elder brothers belongs the glory of the new Normandy.

His frank, pleasant manners won friends and followers without number, who loved him dearly, and rallied to his standard. He was well furnished with that wiliness and diplomacy which were needed to cope with Southern enemies, and his wild ambition led him on and on without much check from feelings of pity, or even justice. Like many other Normans, he was cruel, and his acts were those of a man who sees his goal ahead, and marches straight toward it. While William the Conqueror was getting ready to wear the crown of England, Robert Guiscard was laying his plans for the kingdom of the two Sicilies.

After a while Drogo was assassinated, and then Humphrey was put in his place, but he and Robert were always on bad terms with each other apparently. Robert's faults were the faults of his time, and yet his restlessness and ambition seem to have given his brother great disquietude; perhaps Humphrey feared him as a rival, but at any rate he seems to have kept him almost a prisoner of state. The Guiscard gained the votes of the people before long, when the count died and left only some young children, and in 1054 he was made Count of Apulia and general of the republic. We need not be surprised to find his title much lengthened a little later; he demanded the ducal title itself from Pope Nicholas, and styles himself "by the grace of God and St. Peter, Duke of Apulia, Calabria, and hereafter of Sicily." "The medical and philosophical schools of Salerno, long renowned in Italy, added lustre to his kingdom, and the trade of Amalfi, the earliest of the Italian commercial cities, extending to Africa, Arabia, India, with affiliated colonies in Constantinople, Antioch, Jerusalem, and Alexandria, enriched his ample domain. Excelling in the art of navigation, Amalfi is said to have discovered the compass. Under her Norman dukes, she held the position of the queen of Italian commerce, until the rise of the more famous cities of Pisa, Genoa, and Venice.

Roger de Hauteville, the youngest brother of all, who was much like Robert in every way, was the conqueror of Sicily, and the expedition was piously called a crusade against the unbelievers. It was thirty years before the rich island was added to the jurisdiction of Rome, from which the Mussulmans had taken it. Roger was given the title of count, but his dominion was on a feudal basis instead of being a republic. This success induced Robert to make a campaign against the Eastern empire, and the invasions continued as long as he lived. They were not very successful in themselves, but they were influential in bringing about great changes. The first crusade was an outcome of these plans of Robert's, and all the altered relations of the East and West for years afterward.

We must go far ahead of the slow pace of our story of the Normans in Normandy and England to give this brief sketch of the Southern dukedoms. The story of the de Hautevilles is only another example of Norman daring and enterprise. The spirit of adventure, of conquest, of government, of chivalry, and personal ambition shines in every page of it, and as time goes on we watch with joy a partial fading out of the worse characteristics of cruelty and avarice and trickery, of vanity and jealous revenge. "Progress in good government," says Mr. Green in his preface to A Short History of England, "is the result of social developments." The more we all think about that, the better for us and for our country. No doubt the traditions of Hasting the Northman and his barbarous piracies had hardly died out before the later Normans came, first in scattered groups, and then in legions, to settle in Italy. One cannot help feeling that they did much to make amends for the bad deeds of their ancestors. The south of Italy and the Sicilian kingdom of Roger were under a wiser and more tolerant rule than any government of their day, and Greeks, Normans, and Italians lived together in harmony and peace that was elsewhere unknown. The people were industrious, and all sorts of trades flourished, especially the silk manufacture. Perhaps the soft air and easy, luxurious fashion of life quieted the Norman restlessness a little. Who can tell?

Yet we get a hint of a better explanation of the prosperity of the two Sicilies in this passage from an old chronicle about King Roger: "He was a lover of justice and most severe avenger of crime. He abhorred lying; did every thing by rule, and never promised what he did not mean to perform. He never persecuted his private enemies, and in war endeavored on all occasions to gain his point without shedding of blood. Justice and peace were universally observed throughout his dominions."

A more detailed account of the reigns of the De Hautevilles will be found in the "Story of Sicily," but before this brief review of their conquests is ended, it is only fair to notice the existing monuments of Norman rule. The remains of Norman architecture, dating back to their time, may still be seen in Palermo and other cities, and give them a romantic interest. There are ruins of monasteries and convents almosts without number, and many churches still exist, though sometimes more or less defaced by modern additions and ignorant restoration. The Normans raised the standard of Western forms of architecture here as they did elsewhere, and their simpler buildings make an interesting contrast with Eastern types left by the Saracens. Outside the large cities almost every little town has at least some fragments of Norman masonry, and in Aderno—to note only one instance of the sort—there is a fine Norman castle in excellent preservation, which is used as a prison now. At Troina, a dreary mountain fortress, there is a belfry and part of the wall of a cathedral that Roger I. built in 1078. It was in Troina that he and his wife bravely established their court fifteen years earlier, and withstood a four months' siege from the Saracens. Galfridus, an old chronicler, tells sadly that the young rulers only had one cloak between them, and grew very hungry and miserable; but Eremburga, the wife, was uncomplaining and patient. At last the count was so distressed by the sight of her pallor and evident suffering, that he rallied his men and made a desperate charge upon his foes, and was happily victorious. Galfridus says of that day: "The single hand of Roger, with God's help, did such execution that the corpses of the enemy lay around him on every side like the branches of trees in a thick forest when strewn by a tempest." Once afterward, when Roger was away fighting in Calabria, Eremburga was formally left in command, and used to make the round with the sentinels on the walls every night.

We must look in Palermo for the noblest monuments of Norman days, and beside the churches and palaces, for the tombs of the kings and archbishops in San Rosario Cathedral. There lies Roger himself, "mighty Duke and first King of Sicily." Mr. Symonds says: "Very sombre and stately are these porphyry resting-places of princes born in the purple, assembled here from lands so distant, from the craggy heights of Hohenstauffen, from the green orchards of Côtentin, from the dry hills of Aragon. They sleep and the centuries pass by. Rude hands break open the granite lids of their sepulchres to find tresses of yellow hair, and fragments of imperial mantles embroidered with the hawks and stags the royal hunter loved. The church in which they lie changes with the change of taste in architecture and the manners of successive ages. But the huge stone arks remain unmoved, guarding their freight of mouldering dust beneath gloomy canopies of stone, that tempers the sunlight as it streams from the chapel windows."

And again at Venosa, the little town where the poet Horace was born, and where William de Hauteville with his brothers Drogo, Humphrey, and Robert Guiscard are buried, we cannot do better than quote the same charming writer:

"No chapter of history more resembles a romance than that which records the sudden rise and brief splendor of the house of Hauteville. In one generation the sons of Tancred de Hauteville passed from the condition of squires in the Norman vale of Côtentin to Kinghood in the richest island of the Southern Sea. The Norse adventurers became sultans of an Oriental capital. The sea-robbers assumed, together with the sceptre, the culture of an Arabian court . . . lived to mate their daughters with princes and to sway the politics of Europe with gold. . . . What they wrought, whether wisely or not, for the ultimate advantage of Italy, endures to this day, while the work of so many emperors, republics, and princes, has passed and shifted like the scenes in a pantomime. Through them the Greeks, the Lombards, and the Moors were extinguished in the South. The Papacy was checked in its attempt to found a province of St. Peter below the Tiber. The republics of Naples, Caëta, Amalfi, which might have rivalled perchance with Milan, Genoa, and Florence, were subdued to a master's hand. In short, to the Norman, Italy owed that kingdom of the two Sicilies, which formed one third of her political balance; and which proved the cause of all her most serious revolutions."

Much has been lost of the detailed history of the Norman-Italian states, and lost especially to English literature. If the development of Southern Italy had gone steadily forward to this time, with the eagerness and gathering force that might have been expected from that vigorous impulse of the eleventh century, no doubt there would have been a permanent factor in history rather than a limited episode. The danger of the climate, to those born and reared in Northern or Western Europe, was undoubtedly in the way of any long-continued progress. To-day the Norman buildings look strangely different from their surroundings, and are almost the only evidence of the once brilliant and prosperous government of the Normans in the South. One enthusiastic historian, who wrote before the glories of the de Hautevilles had faded, would have us believe that "there was more security in the thickets of Sicily than in the cities of other kingdoms."

VIII. THE YOUTH OF WILLIAM THE CONQUEROR.

"One equal temper of heroic hearts

Made weak by time and fate, but strong in will

To strive, to seek, to find, and not to yield."

—Tennyson.

THERE was one man, famous in history, who more than any other Norman seemed to personify his race, to be the type of the Norman progressiveness, firmness, and daring. He was not only remarkable among his countrymen, but we are forced to call him one of the great men and great rulers of the world. Nobody has been more masterful, to use a good old Saxon word, and therefore he came to be master of a powerful, venturesome race of people and gathered wealth and widespread territory. Every thing would have slipped through his fingers before he was grown to manhood if his grasp had not been like steel and his quickness and bravery equal to every test. "He was born to be resisted," says one writer; "to excite men's jealousy and to awaken their life-long animosity, only to rise triumphant above them all, and to show to mankind the work that one man can do—one man of fixed principles and resolute will, who marks out a certain goal for himself, and will not be deterred, but marches steadily towards it with firm and ruthless step. He was a man to be feared and respected, but never to be loved; chosen, it would seem, by Providence . . . to upset our foregone conclusions, and while opposing and crushing popular heroes and national sympathies, to teach us that in the progress of nations there is something required beyond popularity, something beyond mere purity and beauty of character—namely, the mind to conceive and the force of will to carry out great schemes and to reorganize the failing institutions and political life of states. Born a bastard, with no title to his dukedom but the will of his father; left a minor with few friends and many enemies, with rival competition at home and a jealous over-lord only too glad to see the power of his proud vassal humbled, he gradually fights his way, gains his dukedom, and overcomes competition at an age when most of us are still under tutors and governors; extends his dominions far beyond the limits transmitted to him by his forefathers, and then leaves his native soil to seek other conquests, to win another kingdom, over which again he has no claim but the stammering will of a weak king and his own irresistible energy, and what is still more strange, securing the moral support of the world in his aggression, and winning for himself the position of an aggrieved person recovering his just and undoubted rights. Truly the Normans could have no better representative of their extraordinary power."

William was only seven years old or a little more when his father left him to go on pilgrimage. No condition could have appeared more pitiable and desperate than his—even in his childhood we become conscious of the dislike his character inspired. Often just and true to his agreements, sometimes unexpectedly lenient, nothing in his nature made him a winner and holder of friendship, though he was a leader of men and a controller of them, and an inspirer of faithful loyalty besides the service rendered him for fear's sake. His was the rule of force indeed, but there is one thing to be particularly noted—that in a licentious, immoral age he grew up pure and self-controlled. That he did not do some bad things must not make us call him good, for a good man is one who does do good things. But his strict fashion of life kept his head clearer and his hands stronger, and made him wide-awake when other men were stupid, and so again and again he was able to seize an advantage and possess himself of the key to success.

While his father lived, the barons paid the young heir unwilling respect, and there was a grim acquiescence in what could not be helped. Alan of Brittany was faithful to his trust, and always able to check any dissensions and plots against his ward. The old animosity between him and Robert was quite forgotten, apparently; but at last Alan was poisoned. Robert's death was the signal for a general uprising of the nobles, and William's life was in peril for a dozen years. He never did homage to the king of France, but for a long time nobody did homage to him either; the barons disdained any such allegiance, and sometimes appear to have forgotten their young duke altogether in their bitter quarrels, and murders of men of their own rank. We trace William de Talvas, still the bastard's fierce enemy, through many plots and quarrels;—it appears as if he were determined that his curse should come true, and made it the purpose of his life. The houses of Montgomery and Beaumont were linked with him in anarchy and treachery; it was the Montgomeries' deadly mischief to which the faithful Alan fell victim. William himself escaped assassination by a chance, and several of his young followers were not so fortunate. They were all in the strong castle of Vaudreuil, a place familiar to the descendants of Longsword, since it was the home of Sperling, the rich miller, whom Espriota married. The history of the fortress had been a history of crime, but Duke Robert was ready to risk the bad name for which it was famous, and trust his boy to its shelter. There had never been a blacker deed done within those walls than when William was only twelve years old, and one of his playmates, who slept in his chamber, was stabbed as he lay asleep. No doubt the Montgomery who struck the cruel blow thought that he had killed the young duke, and went away well satisfied; but William was rescued, and carried away and hidden in a peasant's cottage, while the butchery of his friends and attendants still went on. The whole country swarmed with his enemies. The population of the Côtentin, always more Scandinavian than French, welcomed the possibility of independence, and the worst side of feudalism began to assert itself boldly. Man against man, high rank against low rank, farmer against soldier, the bloody quarrels increased more and more, and devastated like some horrible epidemic.

There were causes enough for trouble in the state of feudalism itself to account for most of the uproar and disorder, let alone the claim of the unwelcome young heir to the dukedom. It is very interesting to see how, in public sentiment, there was always an undertone of resentment to the feudal system, and of loyalty to the idea, at least, of hereditary monarchy. Even Hugh the Great, of France, was governed by it in his indifference to his good chances for seizing the crown years before this time; and though the great empire of Charlemagne had long since tottered to its fall and dismemberment, there was still much respect for the stability and order of an ideal monarchical government.

The French people had already endured some terrible trials, but it was not because of war and trouble alone that they hated their rulers, for these sometimes leave better things behind them; war and trouble are often the only way to peace and quietness. They feared the very nature of feudalism and its political power. It seemed to hold them fast, and make them slaves and prisoners with its tangled network and clogging weights. The feudal lords were petty sovereigns and minor despots, who had certain bonds and allegiances among themselves and with each other, but they were, at the same time, absolute masters of their own domain, and their subjects, whether few or many, were under direct control and surveillance. Under the great absolute monarchies, the very extent of the population and of the country would give a greater security and less disturbance of the middle and lower classes, for a large army could be drafted, and still there would be a certain lack of responsibility for a large percentage of the subjects. Under the feudal system there were no such chances; the lords were always at war, and kept a painfully strict account of their resources. Every field and every family must play a part in the enterprises of their master, and a continual racking and robbing went on. Even if the lord of a domain had no personal quarrel to settle, he was likely to be called upon by his upholder and ally to take part with him against another. In the government of a senate or an ecclesiastical council, the common people were governed less capriciously; their favor was often sought, even in those days, by the different factions who had ends to gain, and were willing to grant favors in return; but the feudal lords were quite independent, and could do as they pleased without asking anybody's advice or consent.

This concerns the relation of the serfs to their lords, but among the lords themselves affairs were quite different. From the intricate formalities of obligation and dependence, from the necessity for each feudal despot's vigilant watchfulness and careful preparation and self-control and quick-sighted decision, arose a most active, well-developed class of nobles. While the master of a feudal castle (or robber-stronghold, whichever we choose to call it) was absent on his forays, or more determined wars, his wife took his place, and ruled her dependents and her household with ability. The Norman women of the higher classes were already famous far and wide through Europe, and, since we are dealing with the fortunes of Normandy, we like to picture them in their castle-halls in all their dignity and authority, and to imagine their spirited faces, and the beauty which is always a power, and which some of them had learned already to make a power for good.

No matter how much we deplore the condition of Normandy and the lower classes of society, and sympathize with the wistfulness and enforced patience of the peasantry; no matter how perplexed we are at the slowness of development in certain directions, we are attracted and delighted by other aspects. We turn our heads quickly at the sound of martial music. The very blood thrills and leaps along our veins as we watch the Norman knights ride by along the dusty Roman roads. The spears shine in the sunlight, the horses prance, the robber-castles clench their teeth and look down from the hills as if they were grim stone monsters lying in wait for prey. The apple-trees are in blossom, and the children scramble out of the horses' way; the flower of chivalry is out parading, and in clanking armor, with flaunting banners and crosses on their shields, the knights ride by to the defence of Jerusalem. Knighthood was in its early prime, and in this gay, romantic fashion, with tender songs to the ladies they loved and gallantly defended, with a prayer to the Virgin Mary, their patroness, because they reverenced the honor and purity of womanhood, they fought through many a fierce fight, with the bitter, steadfast courage of brave men whose heart is in their cause. It was an easy step from their defiance of the foes of Normandy to the defence of the Church of God. Religion itself was the suggester and promoter of chivalry, and the Normans forgot their lesser quarrels and petty grievances when the mother church held up her wrongs and sufferings to their sympathy. It was to Christianity that the mediaeval times owed knighthood, and, while historians complain of the lawlessness of the age, the crimes and violence, the social confusion and vulgarity, still the poetry and austerity and real beauty of the knightly traditions shine out all the brighter. Men had got hold of some new suggestions; the best of them were examples of something better than the world had ever known. As we glance over the list of rules to which a knight was obliged to subscribe, we cannot help rejoicing at the new ideal of Christian manhood.

Rolf the Ganger had been proud rather than ashamed of his brutal ferocity and selfishness. This new standard demands as good soldiery as ever; in fact, a greater daring and utter absence of fear, but it recognizes the rights of other people, and the single-heartedness and tenderness of moral strength. It is a very high ideal.

A little later than the time of William the Conqueror's youth, there were formal ceremonies at the making of a knight, and these united so surprisingly the poet's imaginary knighthood and the customs of military life and obligations of religious life, that we cannot wonder at their influence.

The young man was first stripped of his clothes and put into a bath, to wash all former contaminations from body and soul—a typical second baptism, done by his own free will and desire. Afterward, he was clothed first in a white tunic, to symbolize his purity; next in a red robe, a sign of the blood he must be ready to shed in defending the cause of Christ; and over these garments was put a tight black gown, to represent the mystery of death which must be solved at last by him, and every man.

Then the black-robed candidate was left alone to fast and pray for twenty-four hours, and when evening came, they led him to the church to pray all night long, either by himself, or with a priest and his own knightly sponsors for companions. Next day he made confession; then the priest gave him the sacrament, and afterward he went to hear mass and a sermon about his new life and a knight's duties. When this was over, a sword was hung around his neck and he went to the altar, where the priest took off the sword, blessed it, and put it on again. Then the candidate went to kneel before the lord who was to arm him, and was questioned strictly about his reasons for becoming a knight, and was warned that he must not desire to be rich or to take his ease, or to gain honor from knighthood without doing it honor; at last the young man solemnly promised to do his duty, and his over-lord to whom he did homage granted his request to be made a knight.

After this the knights and ladies dressed him in his new garments, and the spurs came first of all the armor, then the haubert or coat of mail; next the cuirass, the armlets, and gauntlets, and, last of all, the sword. Now he was ready for the *accolade*; the over-lord rose and went to him and gave him three blows with the flat of the sword on his shoulder or neck, and sometimes a blow with the hand on his breast, and said: "In the name of God, of St. Michael and St. George, I make thee knight. Be valiant and fearless and loyal."

Then his horse was led in, and a helmet was put on the new knight's head, and he mounted quickly and flourished his lance and sword, and went out of the church to show himself to the people gathered outside, and there was a great cheering, and prancing of horses, and so the outward ceremony was over, and he was a dubbed knight, as the old phrase has it—adopted knight would mean the same thing to-day; he belonged to the great Christian brotherhood of chivalry. We have seen how large a part religion played in the rites and ceremonies, but we can get even a closer look at the spirit of knighthood if we read some of the oaths that were taken by these young men, who were the guardians and scholars of whatever makes for peace, even while they chose the ways of war and did such eager, devoted work with their swords. M. Guizot, from whose "History of France" I have taken the greater part of this description, goes on to give twenty-six articles to which the knights swore, not that these made a single ritual, but were gathered from the accounts of different epochs. They are so interesting, as showing the steady growth and development of better ideas and purposes, that I copy them here. Indeed we can hardly understand the later Norman history, and the crusades particularly, unless we make the knights as clear to ourselves as we tried to make the vikings.

We must thank the clergymen of the tenth and eleventh centuries for this new thought about the duties and relationships of humanity,—men like Abelard and St. Anselm, and the best of their contemporaries. It is most interesting to see how the church availed herself of the feudal bonds and sympathies of men, and their warlike sentiment and organization, to develop a better and more peaceful service of God. Truthfulness and justice and purity were taught by the church's influence, and licentiousness and brutality faded out as the new order of things gained strength and brightness. Later the pendulum swung backward, and the church used all the terrors of tyranny, fire, and sword, to further her ends and emphasize her authority, instead of the authority of God's truth and the peace of heavenly living. The church became a name and cover for the ambitions of men.

Whatever the pretences and mockeries and rivalries and thefts of authority may be on the part of unworthy churchmen, we hardly need to remind ourselves that in every age the true church exists, and that true saints are living their holy, helpful lives, however shadowed and concealed. Even if the harvest of grain in any year is called a total loss, and the country never suffered so much before from dearth, there is always enough wheat or corn to plant the next spring, and the fewer handfuls the more precious it is sure to seem. In this eleventh century, a century which in many ways was so disorderly and cruel, we are always conscious of the presence of the "blameless knights" who went boldly to the fight; the priests and monks of God who hid themselves and prayed in cell and cloister. "It was feudal knighthood and Christianity together," says Guizot, "which produced the two great and glorious events of that time—the Norman conquest of England, and the Crusades."

These were the knight's promises and oaths as Guizot repeats them, and we shall get no harm from reading them carefully and trying to keep them ourselves, even though all our battles are of another sort and much duller fights against temptations. It must be said that our enemies often come riding down upon us in as fine away and break a lance with us in as magnificent a fashion as in the days of the old tournaments. But our contests are apt to be more like the ancient encounters with cruel treachery of wild beasts in desert places, than like those at the gay jousts, with all the shining knights and ladies looking on to admire and praise.

The candidates swore: First, to fear, reverence, and serve God religiously, to fight for the faith with all their might, and to die a thousand deaths rather than renounce Christianity;

To serve their sovereign prince faithfully, and to fight for him and fatherland right valiantly;

To uphold the rights of the weaker, such as widows, orphans, and damsels, in fair quarrel, exposing themselves on that account according as need might be, provided it were not against their own honor or against their king or lawful princes.

That they would not injure any one maliciously, or take what was another's, but would rather do battle with those who did so.

That greed, pay, gain, or profit should never constrain them to do any deed, but only glory and virtue.

That they would fight for the good and advantage of the common weal.

That they would be bound by and obey the orders of their generals and captains, who had a right to command them.

That they would guard the honor, rank, and order of their comrades, and that they would, neither by arrogance nor by force, commit any trespass against any one of them.

That they would never fight in companies against one, and that they would eschew all tricks and artifices.

That they would wear but one sword, unless they had to fight against two or more enemies.

That in tourney or other sportive contests, they would never use the point of their swords.

That being taken prisoner in a tourney, they would be bound on their faith and honor to perform in every point the conditions of capture, besides being bound to give up to the victors their arms and horses, if it seemed good to take them, being also disabled from fighting in war or elsewhere without their victor's leave.

That they would keep faith inviolably with all the world, and especially with their comrades, upholding their honor and advantage wholly in their absence.

That they would love and honor one another, and aid and succor one another whenever occasion offered.

That having made vow or promise to go on any quest or adventure, they would never put off their arms save for the night's rest.

That in pursuit of their quest or adventure, they would not shun bad and perilous passes, nor turn aside from the straight road for fear of encountering powerful knights, or monsters, or wild beasts, or other hindrance, such as the body and courage of a single man might tackle.

That they would never take wage or pay from any foreign prince.

That in command of troops or men-at-arms, they would live in the utmost possible order and discipline, and especially in their own country, where they would never suffer any harm or violence to be done.

That if they were bound to escort dame or damsel, they would serve, protect, and save her from all danger and insult, or die in the attempt.

That they would never offer violence to any dame or damsel, though they had won her by deeds of arms.

That being challenged to equal combat, they would not refuse without wound, sickness, or other reasonable hindrance.

That, having undertaken to carry out any enterprise, they would devote to it night and day, unless they were called away for the service of their king and country.

That, if they made a vow to acquire any honor, they would not draw back without having attained it or its equivalent.

That they would be faithful keepers of their word and pledged faith, and that, having become prisoners in fair warfare, they would pay to the uttermost the promised ransom, or return to prison at the day and hour agreed upon, on pain of being proclaimed infamous and perjured.

That, on returning to the court of their sovereign, they would render a true account of their adventures, even though they had sometimes been worsted, to the king and the registrar of the order, on pain of being deprived of the order of knighthood.

That, above all things, they would be faithful, courteous, and humble, and would never be wanting to their word for any harm or loss that might accrue to them."

It would not do to take these holy principles, or the pageant of knight-errantry, for a picture of Normandy in general. We can only remind ourselves with satisfaction that this leaven was working in the mass of turbulent, vindictive society. The priests worked very hard to keep their hold upon their people, and the authority of the church proved equal to many a subtle weakness of faith and quick strain of disloyalty. We should find it difficult to match the amazing control of the state by the church in any other country,—even in the most superstitiously devout epochs. When the priesthood could not make the Normans promise to keep the peace altogether, they still obtained an astonishing concession and truce. There was no fighting from Wednesday evening at sunset until Monday morning at sunrise. During these five nights and four days no fighting, burning, robbing, or plundering could go on, though for the three days and two nights left of the week any violence and crime were not only pardonable, but allowed. In this Truce of God, not only the days of Christ's Last Supper, Passion, and Resurrection were to remain undesecrated, but longer periods of time, such as from the first day of Advent until the Epiphany, and other holy seasons. If the laws of the Truce were broken, there were heavy penalties: thirty years' hard penance in exile for the contrite offender, and he must make reparation for all the evil he had committed, and repay his debt for all the spoil. If he died unrepentant, he was denied Christian burial and all the offices of the church, and his body was given to wild beasts and the fowls of the air.

To be sure, the more ungodly portion of the citizens fought against such strict regulations, and called those knights whom the priests armed, "cits without spirit," and even harder names, but for twelve years the Truce was kept. The free days for murder and theft were evidently made the most of, and from what we can discover, it appears as if the Normans used the Truce days for plotting rather than for praying. Yet it was plain that the world was getting ready for great things, and that great emergencies were beginning to make themselves evident. New ideas were on the wing, and in spite of the despotism of the church, sometimes by very reason of it, we can see that men were breaking their intellectual fetters and becoming freer and wiser. A new order of things was coming in; there was that certain development of Christian ideas, which reconciles the student of history in every age to the constant pain and perplexity of watching misdirected energies and hindering blunders and follies.

"It often happens that popular emotions, however deep and general, remain barren, just as in the vegetable world many sprouts come to the surface of the ground, and then die without growing any more or bearing any fruit. It is not sufficient for the bringing about of great events and practical results, that popular aspirations should be merely manifested; it is necessary further that some great soul, some powerful will, should make itself the organ and agent of the public sentiment, and bring it to fecundity, by becoming its type—its personification."

In the middle of this eleventh century, the time of William the Conqueror's youth, the opposing elements of Christian knighthood, and the fighting spirit of the viking blood, were each to find a champion in the same leader. The young duke's early years were a hard training, and from his loveless babyhood to his unwept death, he had the bitter sorrows that belong to the life of a cruel man and much-feared tyrant. It may seem to be a strange claim to make for William the Conqueror—that he represented Christian knighthood—but we must remember that fighting was almost the first duty of man in those days, and that this greatest of the Norman dukes, with all his brutality and apparent heartlessness and selfishness, believed in his church, and kept many of her laws which most of his comrades broke as a matter of course. We cannot remind ourselves too often that he was a man of pure life in a most unbridled and immoral age, if we judge by our present standards of either purity or immorality. There is always a temptation in reading or writing about people who lived in earlier times, to rank them according to our own laws of morality and etiquette, but the first thing to be done is to get a clear idea of the time in question. The hero of Charlemagne's time or the Conqueror's may prove any thing but a hero in our eyes, but we must take him in relation to his own surroundings. The great laws of truth and justice and kindness remain, while the years come and go; the promises of God endure, but while there is, as one may say, a common law of heavenly ordering, there are also the various statute laws that vary with time and place, and these forever change as men change, and the light of civilization burns brighter and clearer.

In William the Conqueror's lifetime, every landed gentleman fortified his house against his neighbors, and even made a secure and loathsome prison in his cellar for their frequent accommodation. This seems inhospitable, to say the least, and gives a tinge of falseness to such tender admonitions as prevailed in regard to charity and treatment of wayfarers. Yet every rich man was ambitious to go down to fame as a benefactor of the church; all over Normandy and Brittany there was a new growth of religious houses, and those of an earlier date, which had lain in ruins since the Northmen's time, were rebuilt with pious care. There appears to have been a new awakening of religious interest in the year 1000, which lasted late into the century. There was a surprising fear and anticipation of the end of the world, which led to a vast number of penitential deeds of devotion, and it was the same during the two or three years after 1030, at the close of the life of King Robert of France.

Normandy and all the neighboring countries were scourged by even worse plagues than the feudal wars. The drought was terrible, and the famine which followed desolated the land everywhere. The trees and fields were scorched and shrivelled, and the poor peasants fought with the wild beasts for dead bodies that had fallen by the roadside and in the forests. Sometimes men killed their comrades for very hunger, like wolves. There was no commerce which could supply the failure of one country's crops with the overflow of another's at the other side of the world, but at last the rain fell in France, and the misery was ended. A thousand votive offerings were made for very thankfulness, for again the people had expected the end of the world, and it had seemed most probable that such an arid earth should be near its final burning and desolation.

In the towns, under ordinary circumstances, there was a style of living that was almost luxurious. The Normans were skilful architects, and not only their minsters and monasteries, but their houses too, were fit for such proud inhabitants, and rich with hangings and comfortable furnishings. The women were more famous than ever for needlework, some of it most skilful in design, and the great tapestries are yet in existence that were hung, partly for warmth's sake, about the stone walls of the castles. Sometimes the noble ladies who sat at home while their lords went out to the wars, worked great pictures on these tapestries of various events of family history, and these family records of battles and gallant bravery by land and sea are most interesting now for their costume and color, beside their corroboration of historical traditions.

We have drifted away, in this chapter, from William the Conqueror himself, but I believe that we know more about the Normandy which he was to govern, and can better understand his ambitions, his difficulties, and his successes. A country of priests and soldiers, of beautiful women and gallant men; a social atmosphere already alive with light, gayety, and brightness, but swayed with pride and superstition, with worldliness and austerity; loyal to Rome, greedy for new territory, the feudal lords imperious masters of complaining yet valiant serfs; racked everywhere by civil feuds and petty wars and instinctive jealousies of French and foreign blood this was Normandy. The Englishmen come and go and learn good manners and the customs of chivalry, England herself is growing rich and stupid, for Harthacnut had introduced a damaging custom of eating four great meals a day, and his subjects had followed the fashion, though that king himself had died of it and of his other habit of drinking all night long with merry companions.

IX. ACROSS THE CHANNEL.

"———One decree

Spake laws to them, and said that, by the soul

Only, the nations should be great and free."

—Wordsworth.

It is time to take a closer look at England and at the shameful degradations of Æthelred's time. The inroads of the Danes read like the early history of Normandy, and we must take a step backward in the condition of civilization when we cross to the other side of the Channel. There had been great changes since Ælfred's wise and prosperous reign, or even since the time of Æthelred's predecessor, Eadgar, who was rowed in his royal-barge at Chester by eight of his vassal kings— Kenneth of Scots, Malcolm of Cumberland, Maccus of the Isles, and five Welsh monarchs. The lord of Britain was gracious enough to do the steering for so noble a company of oarsmen, and it was considered the proudest day that ever had shone upon an English king.

We must remind ourselves of the successive waves of humanity which had overspread England in past ages, leaving traces of each like less evident geologic strata. From the stone and bronze age people, through the Celts with their Pictish and Scottish remnant, through the Roman invasion, and the Saxon, more powerful and enduring than any from our point of view, we may trace a kinship to our Normans across the water. But the English descendants of Celts, Danes, Angles, Saxons, and Jutes needed to feel a new influence and refreshing of their better instincts by way of Normandy.

Perhaps each one of the later rulers of Britain thought he had fallen upon as hard and stormy times and had as much responsibility as anybody who ever wielded a sceptre, but in the reign of the second Æthelred, there are much greater dramas being played, and we feel, directly we get a hint of it, as children do who have been loitering among petty side-shows on their way to a great play. Here come the

Danes again, the kings of Denmark and the whole population of Norway one would think, to read the records, and this time they attack England with such force and determination that within less than forty years a Danish king is master of Britain.

If Æthelred had been a better man this might never have happened, but among all the Saxon kings he seems to have been the worst—thoroughly bad, weak, cowardly, and cruel. He was sure to do things he had better have left alone, and to neglect his plain duty. Other kings had fallen on as hard, perplexing times as he, but they had been strong enough to keep some sort of control of themselves at any rate. Dunstan the archbishop warned the people, when Æthelred was crowned, that they had no idea of the trouble that was coming, and through the whole reign things went from bad to worse. Dreadful things happened which we can hardly blame the silly king for—like a plague among cattle, and the burning of London in 982; and a few years afterward there was a terrible invasion of the Norwegians, and we have seen that aid and comfort were ready for them over in Bayeux and the pirate cities of Normandy.

Now we first hear of the Danegelt, great sums of money, always doubling and increasing, that were paid the Northmen as bribes to go away and leave England in peace. The paying of this Danegelt became a greater load than the nation could carry, for the pirates liked nothing better than to gather a great fleet of ships every few months and come to anchor off the coast, sending a messenger to make the highwayman's favorite request, your money or your life! One of the first sums boldly demanded of Æthelred's aldermen was ten thousand pounds. We can see how rapidly the wealth of England had increased, for in Ælfred's time the fine for killing a king was a hundred and twenty shillings, and this was considered a great sum of money; the penalty for taking a peasant's life was only five shillings, which makes us understand, without any doubt, the scarceness and value of money. Here are some extracts from the English chronicle, which had been kept since Bede's time and for many years after this, which will show how miserably every thing was going on:

1001. "The army [the Danes of course] went over the land and did as was their wont. Slew and burned . . . it was sad in every way for they never ceased from their evil."

1002. "In this year the king and his witan resolved, that tribute would be paid and peace made with them, on condition that they should cease from their evil. This they accepted and were paid £24,000.

1006. "At midwinter the Winchester folk might see an insolent and fearless army as they went by their gate to the sea, and fetched them food and treasure over fifty miles from the sea. Then was there so great awe of the army that no one could think or devise how they should be driven from the country. Every shire in Wessex had they cruelly marked with burning and with harrying. The king began then with his witan earnestly to consider what might seem most advisable to them all, so that the country might be protected ere it were at last undone." This time the tribute was £36,000, and another time the ships put to sea with a Danegelt of £48,000.

England grew more and more miserable and shamefully unable to defend herself, the captains of her fleet were incapable or treacherous, and at last, when some of the ships had been wrecked and there had been some sad disasters at sea, the chronicle has a more despairing tone than ever. "It was as if all counsel had come to an end," the writer says, "and the king and aldermen and all the high witan went home, and let the toil of all the nation lightly perish."

Æthelred the Unready won for himself, in his reign of thirty-eight years, the hearty contempt and distrust of all his people. There is a temptation to blame him for the misery of England, and to attribute it all to his faults and to the low aims and standards of his character, to his worthless ambitions. But, in a general way, the great men, or notorious men of history, who stand out before a dim and half-forgotten background, are only typical of their time and representative of it. One very good man, or bad man, cannot be absolutely a single specimen of his kind; there must be others who rank with him, and who have been his upholders and influencers. So while the story of any nation is in its early chapters, and seems to be merely an account of one ruler or statesman after another, we must not forget that each symbolized his day and generation, a brave leader of a brave race, or a dull or placid or serene representative of a secure, inactive age.

Although there was blundering enough and treachery in Æthelred's reign, there was a splendid exception in the victories and steadfastness of the city of London, which was unsuccessfully attacked again and again by the Danes. The heathen, as the English called their enemies, were lucky in their two leaders, the king of Norway, and the king of Denmark. Olaf, the first-named, was converted after a while, and going from the islands of Orkney to England, he was baptized there, and the English bishops were very kind to him, and Æthelred gave him some presents, and made him promise that he would not come plundering to England any more. We are quite surprised to hear that the promise was kept. Swegen the Dane promised too, but he appeared again after a while, and Æthelred thought he would improve upon the fashion of paying Danegelt by ordering a general massacre of all the Danes instead. Afterward somebody tried to excuse such a piece of barbarianism by saying that the Danes had plotted against the king, but even if they had, Æthelred showed a wretched spirit. It was a time of peace, but he sent secret messengers all through the country, and as the English were only too glad to carry out such orders, there was a terrible slaughter of men, women, and children.

Next year Swegen came back to avenge the wrong, all the more readily because his own sister and her husband and son were among the murdered, and the poor woman had made a prophecy, as she fell, dying, that misery and vengeance should fall upon the English for their sins. For a long time afterward the Danes were very fierce and kept England in fear and disorder. Once they laid siege to Canterbury, and when it had fallen into their hands they demanded Danegelt from the Archbishop, a very good old man. He had a heart full of pity for his poor people already so abominably taxed and oppressed in every way, and was brave enough to squarely refuse, so the Danes slew him with horrible torture; one might tell many such stories of the cruelty and boldness of the invaders. Æthelred was perfectly helpless or else cowardly and indifferent, and presently Swegen, who had gone back to the North returned with a great fleet and a swarm of followers, and not long afterward he conquered every sort of opposition, even that of the brave Londoners, and was proclaimed king of England. Here was a change indeed! the silly Saxon king and his wife and children fled across the sea to Normandy, and Swegen sat upon the throne. He began to reign in splendid state; he had the handsomest ships afloat, all decked out with figures of men and birds and beasts wrought in silver and amber and gold, and fine decorations of every sort. No doubt he had made fine plans and meant to do great deeds, but he died suddenly within a very short time, and the people believed he was frightened to death by a vision.

Æthelred was in Normandy at the court of Richard the Fearless. You remember that Richard's sister Emma went over to England to marry the unready king, Æthelred had one older son, Eadmund Ironside, beside the two boys who were Emma's children, and the hearts of the English turned to their old king, and at last they sent for him to come back, in spite of his faults. He made many fine promises, and seems to have done a great deal better most of the time during the last two years that he lived. Perhaps he had taken some good lessons from the Norman court. But Cnut, Swegen's son, came back to England, just before he died, as fearless as a hawk, and led his men from one victory to another, and Æthelred faded out of life to everybody's relief. When he was dead at last, the witan chose Cnut for king in his stead, but the Londoners, who were rich and strong, and who hated the Danes bitterly—the Londoners would have none of the pirates to reign over them, and elected young Eadmund Ironside, a valiant soldier and loyal-hearted fellow who feared nothing and was ready to dare every thing. The two young kings were well matched and fought six great battles, in most of which Ironside gained the advantage, but at last the Danes beat him back and though everybody was ready for a seventh battle, the witan showed their wisdom for once and forbade any more fighting, and somehow managed to proclaim peace. The young kings treated each other most generously, and called each other brother, and were very cordial and good-natured. They agreed to divide the kingdom, so that Eadmund Ironside had all England south of the Thames—East Anglia and Essex and London. Cnut took all the northern country and owned Eadmund for his over-lord, but within the year Cnut reigned alone. Eadmund died suddenly—some say that he was murdered, and some that he had worn himself out with his tremendous activity and anxiety. It is a great temptation to follow out the story of such a man, and especially because he lived in such an important time, but we must hurry now to the point where Norman and English history can be told together, and only stop to explain such things as will make us able to understand and take sides in the alliance of the two vigorous, growing nations.

Cnut's life, too, is endlessly interesting. He began by behaving like a pirate, and the latter part of his reign was a great reform and a very comfortable time for England, so scarred and spoiled by war. In the beginning there was a great question about the kingship. In those days it was a matter of great importance that the king should be able to rule and able to fight, and the best and most powerful member of the royal family was the proper one to choose. The English for a long time had elected their kings, and Cnut, though he held half the country, was very careful not to seize the rest by force. We watch with great interest his wielding of rude politics before the witan; he called them into council and laid his claim before them.

Eadmund Ironside had left two little sons, but nobody thought of their being his successors. Indeed Cnut showed a great fear of the royal family, and took care that his rivals should be disposed of; he knew that the witan and everybody else were tired of the everlasting war and bloodshed. He was fierce and downright in his demands, and in the end the heirs of Ironside were all passed over—the Athelings or princes were all set aside, and Cnut the Dane was king of England.

Ironside's brother, Eadwy, of whom the best things are said, was outlawed, and died within a few months under very suspicious circumstances. The two little boys, Ironside's sons, were sent out of the country to Cnut's half-brother, the king of Sweden, with orders that they should be put out of the way. The king felt such pity for the innocent children, that he sent them away to Hungary instead of having them murdered. The Hungarian king, Stephen, was a saint and a hero, and he was very kind to the poor exiles, and brought them up carefully. One died young, but we shall hear again about the other.

Cnut did a very surprising thing next. He sent for Queen Emma to come back again from the Norman court to marry him. She must have been a good deal older than he, but she was still a beautiful woman, and marked with the famous Norman dignity and grace. Cnut promised that if they should ever have a son born, he should be the next king of England. Emma's two elder sons, Ælfred and Eadward, were left in Normandy, and there they grew up quite apart from their mother, and thinking much more of their Norman descent and belonging than of their English heritage.

Cnut now appears in the light of a model sovereign for those days. He had renounced all his pagan ideas, and been christened and received into the Church. We might expect that he would have pushed his own countrymen forward and all the Danish interests, but it was quite the other way. At the beginning of his reign he had executed several powerful English nobles whose influence and antagonism he had reason to fear; but now he favored the English in a marked way, and even ordered his ships and all the pirates and fighting men back to the North. It seems very strange, now, that a king of England ever reigned over Sweden and Denmark, and Norway beside, but it seems as if Cnut were prouder of being king of England than of all his other powers and dignities. He was not only very gracious and friendly with his English subjects at home, but he sent them abroad to be bishops, and displeased the Danish parishes by such arrangements.

We all know the story of the rising tide, and Cnut's reproof to his courtiers on the sea-shore. As we read about him we are reminded a little of Rolf the Ganger, and his growth from pirate fashions to a more gentle and decent humanity. The two men were not so very unlike after all, but I must confess that I think with a good deal of sympathy of Cnut's decision to go on a pilgrimage to Rome. It was expecting a good deal of the young sea-rover that he should stay quietly at home to rule his kingdom. The spirit of adventure stirred in his veins, and we may be sure that he enjoyed his long and perilous overland journey to Italy. He made the road safer for his countrymen who might also have a pious desire to worship at the famous foreign shrines. He complained to the emperor and the priests at Rome about the robber-chiefs who pounced down upon travellers from their castles in the Alps, and they promised to keep better order. The merchants and pilgrims were often laden with rich offerings for the churches, besides goods which they wished to sell, and the robbers kept watch for them. Their ruined fortresses are still perched along the Alpine passes, and one cannot help hoping that Cnut had some exciting disputes with his enemies, and a taste of useful fighting and proper discipline among the bold marauders.

He wrote a famous letter about his pilgrimage, directed to the archbishops, and bishops, the great men, and all the people. He tells whom he saw in Rome—the Pope, and the German Emperor, and other great lords of the earth; and says, with pride, that every one has treated him handsomely, and what fine presents he has had given him to carry home. He had come to Rome for the good of his people, and for the salvation of his own soul, he tells them seriously; and one thing he did for England was to complain of the heavy taxes the church had put upon it, and the Pope promised that such injustice should not happen any more. There is something very touching in the way that he says he had made a great many good resolves about his future life, and that he is not ashamed to own that he has done wrong over and over again, but he means, by God's help, to amend entirely. He vows to Heaven that he will govern his life rightly, and rule his kingdom honestly and piously, and that neither rich nor poor shall be oppressed or hardshipped. There never was a better letter, altogether, and Cnut kept his promises so well that the old Anglo-Saxon chronicle, which aches with stories of war and trouble, grows quite dull now in the later years of his reign. There was nothing to tell any more, the monks thought who kept the record; but we know, for that very reason, that the English farms flourished, and the wheat fields waved in the summer wind, the towns grew rich, and the merchants prosperous; and when the English-Northman king died, it was a sad day for England. Cnut was only forty years old, but that was a long time for a king to live. His son, Harold Harefoot, reigned in his stead, and many of the old troubles of the country sprang up at once, as if they had only been asleep for a little while, and were by no means out-grown or ended.

Harold Harefoot was not in the least pious, and behaved himself with most unreasonable folly, and fortunately died at the close of four years of insult and unworthiness. Then Harthacnut, the younger brother, was made king, and he promptly demanded a Danegelt, the most hateful of taxes, and did a great many things which only reopened the breach between Dane and Englishman, though it had seemed to be smoothed over somewhat in his father's time. Harold had done one brutal thing that towered above all the rest. The two princes who had been living in Normandy thought there might be some chance of their gaining a right to the throne, and the younger one, Ælfred, had come over to England with his knights and gentlemen. Harold seized them and was most cruel; he first blinded his half-brother and then had him put to death. This made a great noise in Normandy, and there is one good thing to be said about Harthacnut, that he was bitterly angry with his brother, and also with Earl Godwine, a famous nobleman, who was the most powerful man in England next the king. He was Cnut's favorite and chief adviser, but Harthacnut suspected that he had a hand in Ælfred's murder. Nobody has ever been quite clear about the matter. Godwine and all his lords swore that he was innocent, and gave the king a magnificent ship with all sorts of splendors belonging to it, besides nearly a hundred men in full armor, and gold bracelets to make them as grand as could be. So the king accepted Godwine's oath in view of such a polite attention, but he asked Eadward to leave the Norman court and come over to live with him. Eadward came, and in two years he was king of England, Harthacnut having died a wretched drunken death.

So again there was a descendant of Ælfred the Great and the house of Cerdic on the throne. Eadward was the last of the line, and in his day began the most exciting and important chapter of English history—the Norman Conquest.

We have come quickly along the line of Danish kings, and now it is time to stop and take a more careful look at the state of manners and customs in England, and make ourselves sure what the English people of that time were like, how they lived in their houses, and what changes had come to the country in general. There were certain hindrances to civilization, and lacks of a fitting progress and true growth. Let, us see what these things were, and how the greater refinement of the Normans, their superior gifts and graces, must come into play a little later. There was some deep meaning in the fusion of the two peoples, and more than one reason why they could form a greater nation together than either Normans or Englishmen could alone.

First, the dwellers on English soil had shown a tendency, not yet entirely outgrown, to fall back into a too great indulgence in luxurious living. When the storm and strain of conquest, of colonization, had spent itself, the Englishmen of Eadward's and Cnut's time betook themselves to feasting and lawlessness, of the sort that must undermine the vigor of any people. The fat of the land tempted them in many ways, and they sank under such habits as quickly as they had risen under the necessities that war makes for sacrifices and temperance. They were suffering, too, from their insularity; they were taken up with their own affairs, and had kept apart from the progress of the rest of Europe. There was a new wave and impulse of scholarship, which had not yet reached them. It was ebb-tide in England in more ways than one; and time for those Normans to appear who, to use the words of one of their historians, "borrow every thing and make it their own, and their presence is chiefly felt in increased activity and more rapid development of institutions, literature, and art. Thus . . . they perfect, they organize every thing, and everywhere appear to be the master spirits of their age."

The English people had become so impatient of the misrule of Cnut's sons, that the remembrance of Cnut's glories was set aside for the time being, and no more Danish kings were desired. "All folk chose Eadward to king," says the chronicle, and evidently the hearts of the people were turned, full of hope and affection, to the exiled son of Æthelred and Emma, who had been since his childhood at the Norman court. His murdered brother Ælfred had been canonized by the romantic sympathy of his English friends; he was remembered now as a saintly young martyr to English patriotism, and the disreputable reign of Cnut's sons had made the virtues of the ancient race of English kings very bright by comparison. The new king must be of English blood and a link with past prosperity. The son of Eadmund Ironside was an exile also in the distant court of Hungary, but Eadward, a gentle, pious man, was near at hand, and there were a thousand voices ready to shout for him even while Harthacnut lay unburied in the royal robes and trappings.

There was an opposition on the part of the Danes, who were naturally disinclined to any such change, and when the formal election and consecration of the new king took place, some months after this popular vote, all Earl Godwine's power and influence were brought to bear before certain important votes could be won. Indeed, at first Eadward himself was apparently hard to persuade to accept his high office. He seems to have been much more inclined to a religious life than to statesmanship, but between much pushing from behind in Normandy and the eager entreaties of his English friends, he was forced to make his way again across the Channel. There are interesting accounts, which may or may not be true, of his conversations with Godwine; but the stronger man prevailed. The very promise he made to uphold the new king's rights might make Eadward feel assured and hopeful of some stability and quietness in his reign. England was far behind Normandy in social or scholarly progress; to reign over Englishmen did not appear the most rewarding or alluring career to the fastidious, delicate, cloister-man. The rough-heartiness and red-cheeked faces of his subjects must have contrasted poorly with his Norman belongings, so much more refined and thoughtful, not to say adroit and dissembling. England was still divided into four parts, as Cnut had left it. His scheme of the four great earldoms had proved a bad one enough, for it had only made the nation weaker, and kept up continual rivalries and jealousies between the lords of Northumbria, Mercia, East Anglia, and Wessex. The northern territory was chiefly Danish in its traditions, and though there was a nominal subjection to the king, Northumbria was almost wholly independent of any over-rule. In Mercia, Lady Godiva and Earl Leofric were spending their lives and their great wealth, chiefly in furthering all sorts of religious houses and good works of the churches.

The greatest earl of all was Godwine of Wessex, the true leader of the English and a most brave and loyal man. Cnut had trusted him, and while there were enough jealous eyes to look at his kingly prosperity, and malicious tongues ready to whisper about his knowledge of young Ælfred's murder, or his favor and unrighteous advancement of his own family to places of power, Godwine still held the confidence of a great faction among the English people. His son Harold was earl of East Anglia, and they were lawful governors, between them, of the whole southern part of the kingdom. It was mainly through Godwine's influence that Eadward was crowned king, and we may look to the same cause for his marriage with the earl's daughter Edith, but the line of English princes, of whom Godwine hoped to be ancestor, never appeared, for the king was childless, and soon made an enemy of his father-in-law. Some people say that Godwine did not treat his royal son with much respect having once put him on the throne. Eadward too never was able to forget the suspicion about Ælfred's murder, so the breach between him and the great earl was widened year by year. Eadward was not the sturdy English monarch for whom his people had hoped; he was Norman at heart, as a man might well be who had learned to speak in the foreign tongue, and had made the friendships of his boyhood and manhood in the duke's court and cloisters. Priestcraft was dearer to him than statecraft, and his name of The Confessor showed what almost saintly renown he had won from those who were his friends and upholders.

It did not suit very well that one Norman gentleman after another came to London to fill some high official position. Eadward appeared to wish to surround himself wholly with Normans, and the whole aspect of the English court was changed little by little. The king proved his own weakness in every way—he was as like Æthelred the Unready as a good man could be like a bad one.

Godwine grew more and more angry, and his determination to show that England could do without the crowds of interlopers who were having every thing their own way worked him disaster for a time. There was a party of the king's friends journeying homeward to Normandy, who stopped overnight in the city of Dover and demanded its hospitality in insolent fashion. The Dover men would not be treated like slaves, and a fight followed in which the Frenchmen were either killed or driven out of the town. Eadward of course sided with his friends, and was very indignant; he sent orders to Earl Godwine, who was governor of the region, to punish the offenders, but Godwine refused squarely unless the men should have been fairly tried and given a chance to speak for themselves. This ended in a serious quarrel, and the king gained a victory without any battle either, for there was a sudden shifting of public feeling in Eadward's favor—God wine's own men forsook him and were loyal to the crown, and the great earl was banished for conscience sake, he and all his family, for the king even sent away his own wife, though he kept all her lands and treasures, which was not so saint-like and unworldly as one might have expected.

One of Godwine's sons had proved himself a very base and treacherous man, and the earl had shielded him; this was one reason why his defence of English liberty was so overlooked by his countrymen, but the Normans had a great triumph over this defeat, and praised the pious king and told long stories of his austere life, his prayers, and holy life. After he was canonized these stories were lengthened still more, but while he was yet without a halo some of his contemporaries charge him with laziness and incapacity. He certainly was lacking in kingly qualities, but he gained the respect and love of many of his subjects, and was no doubt as good as so weak a man could be. After his death Englishmen praised him the more because they liked William the Conqueror the less, and as for the Normans they liked anybody better than Harold, who had been a much more formidable opponent in his claim to the English crown. Mr. Freeman says: "——The duties of secular government . . . were . . . always something which went against the grain. His natural place was not on the throne of England, but at the head of a Norman abbey. . . . For his virtues were those of a monk; all the real man came out in his zeal for collecting relics, in his visions, in his religious exercises, in his gifts to churches and monasteries, in his desire to mark his reign as its chief result, by the foundation of his great abbey of Saint Peter at Westminster. In a prince of the manly piety of Alfred things of this sort form only a part, a pleasing and harmonious part, of the general character. In Eadward they formed the whole man."

The chronicler who writes most flatteringly of him acknowledges that he sometimes had shocking fits of bad temper, but that he was never betrayed into unbecoming language. On some occasions he was hardly held back by Godwine or Harold from civil war and massacre; though he was conscientious within the limit of his intelligence, and had the art of giving a gracious refusal and the habit of affability and good manners. William of Malmesbury, the chronicler, tells us that he kept his royal dignity, but that he took no pleasure in wearing his robes of state, even though they were worked for him by his affectionate queen. Like his father, he was ever under the dominion of favorites, and this was quickly enough discovered and played upon by Norman ecclesiastics and Norman and Breton gentlemen in search of adventure and aggrandizement. It makes a great difference whether we read the story of this time in English or in French records. Often the stories are directly opposite to each other, and only the most careful steps along the path keep one from wandering off one way or the other into unjust partisanship. Especially is this true of Godwine, the confessor's great contemporary. He seems, at any rate, to have been a man much ahead of his time in knowledge of affairs and foresight of the probable effects from the causes of his own day. His brother earls were jealous of him; the Church complained of his lack of generosity; even his acknowledged eloquence was listened to incredulously; and his good government of his own provinces, praised though it was, did not gain him steady power. His good government made him, perhaps more than any thing else, the foremost Englishman of his time, and presently we shall see how deep a feeling there was for him in England, and how much confidence and affection were shown in his welcome back from exile, though he had been allowed to go away with, such sullen disapproval. Godwine's wife, Gytha, was a Danish woman, which was probably a closer link with that faction in the northern earldom than can be clearly understood at this late day. Lord Lytton's novel, called "Harold," makes this famous household seem to live before our eyes, and the brief recital of its fortunes and conditions here cannot be more than a hint of the real romance and picturesqueness of the story.

The absence of Godwine in Flanders—a whole year's absence—had taught his countrymen what it was to be without him. They were sadly annoyed and troubled by the king's continued appointment of Normans to every place of high honor that fell vacant. Bishoprics and waste lands alike were pounced upon by the hangers-on at court, and castles were lifting their ugly walls within sight of each other almost, here and there in the quiet English fields. Even in London itself the great White Tower was already setting its strong foundations; a citadel for the town, a fort to keep the borderers and Danes at bay were necessary enough to a country, but England was being turned into another Normandy and Brittany, with these new houses that were built for war, as if every man's neighbor were his enemy. The square high towers were no fit places for men to live in who tilled the soil and tended their flocks and herds. There were too many dark dungeons provided among the foundation stones beside, and the English farmers whispered together about their new townsfolk and petty lords, and feared the evil days that were to come.

The ruined Roman houses and strange tall stones of the Druid temples were alike thrown down and used to build these new castles. Men who had strayed as far as the Norman coasts had stories enough to tell; what landmarks of oppression these same castles were in their own country, and how the young Duke William had levelled many of them to the ground in quarrelsome Normandy. There was no English word for this awesome new word—*castles!* The free and open halls of the English thanes were a strange contrast to the new order of dwelling-places. Robert of Jumièges had been made Archbishop of Canterbury, and a host of his countrymen surrounded the king more and more closely and threatened to deprive the English of their just rights. It was this monk Robert who had "beat into the king's head" that his brother Ælfred had come to his death through Earl Godwine.

It is very easy to tell the story of the Normans from the English side. Let us cross the Channel again to Rouen and see what effect the condition of English affairs was having upon the young duke. It would not be strange if his imagination were busy with some idea of enlarging his horizon by a look at his neighbors. Eadward had no heir, they had talked together oftentimes, perhaps, about the possibility of making one noble great kingdom by the joining of England and Normandy. Every day more stories reached his ears of the wealth and fruitfulness of the Confessor's kingdom.

X. THE BATTLE OF VAL-ÈS-DUNES.

"Who stood with head erect and shining eyes,

As if the beacon of some promised land

Caught his strong vision, and entranced it there."

—A. F.

THE Viking's grandchildren had by no means lost their love for journeying by land or sea. As in old Norway one may still find bits of coral and rudely shaped precious stones set in the quaintly wrought silver ornaments made by the peasants, so in Normandy there are pieces of Spanish leather and treasures from the east and from the south, relics of the plundering of a later generation. Roger de Toesny, one of William's fiercest enemies, does not become well-known to us until we trace out something of his history as a wanderer before he came to join Talvas in a well-planned rebellion.

In Duke Richard the Good's time there was a restless spirit of adventure stirring in Norman hearts, and the foundations were laid of the Southern kingdoms which made such a change in Europe. A Norman invasion of Spain came to nothing in comparison with those more important settlements, but in 1018 Roger de Toesny carried the Norman arms into the Spanish peninsula. A long time before this Richard the Fearless had persuaded a large company of his Scandinavian subjects to wander that way, being pagan to the heart's-core and hopelessly inharmonious. Roger followed them on a grand crusade against the infidel Saracen, and also hoped to gain a kingdom for himself. He was of the noblest blood in Normandy, of Rolf the Ganger's own family, and well upheld the warlike honor of his house in his daring rights with the infidel. Almost unbelievable stories are told of his cannibal-like savagery with his captives, but the very same stories are told of another man, so we will not stop to moralize upon Roger's wickedness. He married the Spanish countess of Barcelona, who did homage to the king of France, and every thing looked prosperous at one time for his dominion, but it never really took root after all, and de Toesny went back again to Normandy, and blazed out instantly with tremendous wrath at the pretentions of William the Bastard. He could not believe that the proud Norman barons and knights would ever submit to such a degradation. De Talvas was only too glad to greet so sympathetic an ally, and the opposition to the young duke took a more formidable shape than ever before.

All through William's earliest years the feudal lords spent most of their strength in quarrelling with each other, but de Toesny's appearance gave the signal for a league against the ruler whom they despised. William was no longer a child, and rumors of his premature sagacity, and his uncommon strength and quickness in war, were flying about from town to town and warned his enemies that they had no time to lose if they meant to crush him down. He was a noble-looking lad and had shown a natural preference for a soldier's life; at fifteen he had demanded to be made a knight of the old Norman tradition in which lurked a memory of Scandinavian ceremonies. None save Duke William could bend Duke William's bow, and while these glowing accounts of him were written from a later standpoint, and his story might easily be read backward, as a fulfilment of prophecy, we can be sure, at least, that his power asserted itself in a marked way, and that he soon gained importance and mustered a respectable company of followers as the beginning of a brilliant and almost irresistible court and army. Even King Henry of France was jealous of his vassal's rising fame and popularity, and felt obliged to pay William a deference that his years did not merit. All through the first twelve years men felt that the boy William's life was in danger, and that, whatever respect Henry paid him, was likely to be changed to open animosity and disdain the moment that there was a good excuse. We have a glimpse now and then of the lonely lad at his sport in the forest about Falaise and Valognes, where he set apart preserves for hunting. We follow him from Alan of Brittany's wardship, to the guardian he chose himself, who held the place of tutor with that of captain-general of the Norman army, but, guardian or no guardian, he pushed forward single-handed, and mastered others, beside himself, in a way that the world never will cease to wonder at.

Roger de Toesny refused allegiance to begin with, and with loud expressions of his scorn of the Bastard, began to lay waste his neighbors' lands as if they, too, had been Saracens and merited any sort of punishment. We first hear the name of De Beaumont, famous enough ever since, in an account of a battle which some of Roger's outraged victims waged against him. Grantmesnil, too, is a name that we shall know very well by and by, when William has gone over to England with his Norman lords. Normandy never got over its excitement and apparent astonishment at William's presence and claims; but even in his boyhood he was the leader of a party. "So lively and spirited was he, that it seemed to all a marvel," says one of the old chroniclers, with enthusiasm. When he began to take deep interest in his affairs, the news of revolts and disorderliness in the country moved him to violent fits of irritation, but he soon learned to hide these instinctively, and the chronicle goes on to say that he "had welling up in his child's heart all the vigor of a man to teach the Normans to forbear from all acts of irregularity." In this outbreak against de Toesny he found an irresistible temptation to assert his mastery, and boy as he was, he really made himself felt; De Toesny was killed in the fierce little battle, and his death gave a temporary relief from such uprisings; but William comes more and more to the front, and all Normandy takes sides either for or against him. This was no insignificant pretender, but one to be feared; his guardians and faithful men who had held to him for good or bad reasons, were mostly put out of the way by their enemies, and there was nobody at last who could lead the Bastard's men to battle better than he could himself.

Henry of France had been biding his time, and now Guy of Burgundy, the son of William's cousin whom he had welcomed kindly at his feudal court, puts in a claim to the dukedom of Normandy. He helped forward a conspiracy, and one night, while William was living in his favorite castle at Valognes, the jester came knocking with his bauble, and crying at the chamber door, begging him to fly for his life: "They are already armed; they are getting ready; to delay is death!" cried poor Golet the fool; and his master leaped out of bed, seized his clothes, and ran to the stables for his horse. Presently he was galloping away toward Falaise for dear life, and to this day the road he took is called the Duke's road. This was in 1044, and William was nineteen years old. He was not slow to understand that the rebels had again risen, and that the conspiracy was more than a conspiracy; it was a determined insurrection. All the night long, as he rode across the country in the bright moonlight, he was thinking about his plans, no doubt, and great energies and determinations were suddenly waked in his heart. This was more than a dislike of himself and the tan-yard inheritance; it was the old rivalry of the Frenchmen and Northmen. The old question of supremacy and race prejudice was to be fought over once more and for the last time with any sort of distinctness. This was not the petty animosity of one baron or another; it was almost the whole nobility of Normandy against their duke.

There was one episode of the duke's journey which is worth telling: He had ridden for dear life, and had forded many a stream, and one, more dangerous, tide inlet where the rivers Oune and Vire flowed out to sea; and when he got safe across, he went into the Church of St. Clement, in the Bayeux district, to kneel down and say his prayers.

As the sun rose, he came close to the church and castle of Rye, and the Lord of Rye was standing at the castle gate in the clear morning air. William spurred his horse, and was for hurrying by, but this faithful vassal, whose name was Hubert, knew him, and stopped him, and begged to be told the reason of such a headlong journey. The Lord of Rye was very hospitable, and the tired duke dismounted, and was made welcome in the house; and presently a fresh horse was brought out for him, and the three brave sons of the loyal house were mounted also to ride by his side to Falaise. This hospitality was not forgotten. Later, in

England, their grateful guest set them in high places, and favored them in princely fashion. Guy, of Burgundy had been brought up with William as a friend and kinsman, and had been treated with great generosity. He was master of some great estates, and one of these was a powerful border fortress between Normandy and France. His friends were many, and he found listeners enough to his propositions. Born of the princely houses of Burgundy and Normandy, he claimed the duchy as his inherited right; and while so many in court and camp were ashamed of their lawful leader, and ready to deny his authority, came Guy's opportunity.

William was cautious, and not without experience. When he was only a baby he had caught at the straw on which he lay, and would not let go his hold, and this sign of his future power and persistence had been proved a true one. The quarrelsome, lawless lords felt that their days of liberty for themselves, and oppression of everybody else, would soon be over if they did not strike quickly. They dreaded so strong and stern a master, and rallied to the standard of the Bastard's rival, Guy of Burgundy.

There were some of the first nobles of the Côtentin who forsook their young duke for this rival who was hardly Norman at all, as they usually decided such points. His Norman descent was on the spindle side rather than the sword, to use the old distinction, and his mother's ancestors would not have prevented him in other days from being called almost a Frenchman. There is a tradition that Guy promised to divide the lands of Normandy with his allies, keeping only the old French grant to Rolf for himself, and this must have been the cause of the treason of the descendants of Rolf's and William Longsword's loyal colonists. It would amaze us to see the change in the life and surroundings of the feudal lords even in the years of William's minority. The leader of the barons in the revolt was the Viscount of Coutances, the son of that chief who had defeated Æthelred of England and his host nearly half a century before. He lived in a castle on the river Oune, near which he afterward built his great St. Saviour's Abbey. This was the central point of the insurrection, and from his tower Neal of St. Saviour could take a wide survey of his beautiful Côtentin country with its plough-land and pastures and forests, the great minster of Lessay, and the cliffs and marshes; the sturdy castles of his feudal lords scattered far and wide. There came to Saint Saviour's also Randolf of Bayeux, and Hamon of Thorigny and of Creuilly, and Grimbald of Plessis, and each of them made his fortress ready for a siege, and swore to defend Guy of Burgundy and to use every art of war and even treachery to subdue and disgrace William. I say "even treachery," but that was the first resort of these insurgents rather than the last. They had laid the deep plot to seize and murder him at Valognes, and Grimbald was to have struck the blow.

King Henry of France was another enemy at heart. It is difficult at first to understand his course toward his young neighbor. He never had fairly acknowledged him, and William on his part had never put his hands into the king's and announced with the loyal homage of his ancestors that he was Henry's man. While Normandy was masterless in William's youth, there was a good chance, never likely to come again in one man's lifetime, for the king to assert his authority and to seize at least part of the Norman territory. The discontent with the base-born heir to the dukedom might not have been enough by itself to warrant such usurpation, but then, while the feudal lords were in such turmoil and so taken up with, for the most part, merely neighborhood quarrels; while they had so little national and such fierce sectional feeling, would have been the time for an outsider to enrich himself at their expense. It was not yet time for Normandy to be provoked into a closer unification by any outside danger. The French and Scandinavian factions were still distinct and suspicious of each other, but it was already too late when King Henry at last, without note or warning, poured his soldiers across the Norman boundary and invaded the Evreçin; too late indeed in view of what followed, and in spite of the temporary blazing up of new jealousies and the revival of old grievances and hatreds. Henry won a victory and triumph for the time being; he demanded the famous border castle of Tillières and insisted that it should be destroyed, and though the brave commander held out for some time even against William's orders, he finally surrendered. Henry placed a strong garrison there at once, and after getting an apparently strong hold on Normandy there followed a time of peace. The king seemed to be satisfied, but no doubt the young duke's mind was busy enough with a forced survey of his enemies, already declared or still masked by hypocrisy, and of his own possible and probable resources. A readiness to do the things that must be done was making a true man of Duke William even in his boyhood. For many years he had seen revolt and violence grow more easy and more frequent in his dukedom; the noise of quarrels and fighting grew louder and louder. In his first great battle at Val-ès-dunes the rule of the Côtentin lords and Guy of Burgundy, or the rule of William the Bastard, struggled for the mastery.

It was a great battle in importance rather than in numbers. William called to his loyal provinces for help, and the knights came riding to court from the romance-side of Normandy, while from the Bessin and the Côtentin the rebels came down to meet them. It seems strange that, when William represents to us the ideal descendant of the Northmen, the Scandinavian element in his dukedom was the first to oppose him. For once King Henry stood by his vassal, and when William asked for help in that most critical time, it was not withheld. Henry had not been ashamed to take part with the Norman traitors in past times, and now that there was a chance of breaking the ducal government in pieces and adding a great district to France, we are more than ever puzzled to know why he did not make the most, of the occasion. Perhaps he felt that the rule of the dukes was better than the rule of the mutinous barons of the Côtentin, and likely, on the whole, to prove less dangerous. So when William claimed protection, it was readily granted, and the king came to his aid at the head of a body of troops, and helped to win the victory.

We hear nothing of the Norman archers yet in the chronicler's story of the fight. They were famous enough afterward, but this battle was between mounted knights, a true battle of chivalry. The place was near the river Orne, and the long slopes of the low hills stretched far and wide, covered with soft turf, like the English downs across the Channel, lying pleasantly toward the sun. Master Wace writes the story of the day in the "Roman de Rou," and sketches the battle-field with vivid touches of his pen. Mr. Freeman says, in a note beneath his own description, that he went over the ground with Mr. Green, his fellow-historian, for company, and Master Wace's book in hand for guide. In the "Roman de Rou" there is a hint that not only the peasantry, but the poorer gentlemen as well, were secretly on William's side, that the prejudice and distrust toward the feudal lords was very great, and that there was more confidence in a sovereign than in the irksome tyranny of less powerful lords.

The barons of Saxon Bayeux and Danish Coutances were matched against the loyal burghers of Falaise, Romanized Rouen, and the men of the bishop's cities of Liseux and Evreux. King Henry stopped at the little village of Valmeray to hear mass, as he came up from the south with his followers, and presently the duke joined them in the great plain beyond. The rebels are there too; the horses will not stand in place together, they have caught the spirit of the encounter, and the bright bosses of the shields; the lances, tied with gay ribbons, glitter and shine, as the long line of knights bends and lifts and wavers like some fluttering gay decoration,—some many-colored huge silken splendor all along the green grass. The birds fly over swiftly, and return as quickly, puzzled by the strange appearance of their country-side. Their nests in the grass are trampled under foot—the world is alive with men in armor, who laugh loudly and swear roundly, and are there for something strange, to kill each other if they can, rather than live, for the sake of Normandy. Far away the green fields stretch into the haze, the cottages look like toys, and the sheep and cattle feed without fear in the pastures. Church towers rise gray and straight-walled into the blue sky. It is a great day for Normandy, and her best knights and gentlemen finger their sword-hilts, or buckle their saddle-girths, and wait impatiently for the battle to begin on that day of Val-ès-dunes.

Among the Côtentin lords was Ralph of Tesson, lord of the forest of Cinquelais and the castle of Harcourt-Thury. Behind him rode a hundred and twenty knights, well armed and gallant, who would follow him to the death. He had sworn on the holy relics of the saints at Bayeux to smite William wherever he met him, yet he had no ground for complaint against him. His heart fell when he saw his rightful lord face to face. A tanner's grandson, indeed, and a man whose father and mother had done him wrong; all that was true, yet this young Duke William was good to look upon, and as brave a gentleman as any son of Rolf's, or the fearless Richard's. Ralph Tesson (the Badger they called him), a man both shrewd and powerful, stood apart, and would not rank himself and his men with either faction, and his knights crowded round him, to remind him that he had done homage once to William, and would fight against his natural lord. The Côtentin lords were dismayed and angry, they promised him great rewards, but nothing touched him, and he stood silent, a little way from the armies. The young duke and the king noticed him, and the six-score-and-six brave knights in his troop, all with their lances raised and trimmed with their ladies' silk tokens. William said that they would come to his aid; neither Tesson nor his men had any grudge against him.

Suddenly Tesson put spurs to his horse, and came dashing across the open field, and all the lords and gentlemen held their breath as they watched him. "Thury! Thury!" he shouted as he came, and "Thury! Thury!" the cry echoed back again from the distance. He rode straight to the duke; there was a murmur from the Côtentin men; he struck the duke gently with his glove. It was but a playful mockery of his vow to the saints at Bayeux; he had struck William, but he and his knights were William's men again; the young duke said, "Thanks to thee!" and the fight began, all the hotter for the anger of the deserted barons and their desire for revenge. The day had begun with a bad omen for their success. "*Dexaide!*" the old Norman war-cry, rang out, and those who had followed the lilies of France cried *"Montjoie Saint Denis!"* as they fought.

Nowadays, a soldier is a soldier, and men who choose other professions can keep to them, unless in their country's extremity of danger, but in that day every man must go to the wars, if there were need of him, and be surgeon or lawyer, and soldier too; yes, even the priests and bishops put on their swords and went out to fight. It would be interesting to know more names on the roll-call that day at Val-ès-dunes, but we can almost hear the shouts to the patron saints, and the clash of the armor. King Henry fought like a brave man, and the storm of the battle raged fiercest round him. The knights broke their lances, and fought sword to sword. There was no play of army tactics and manœuvring, but a hand-to-hand fight, with the sheer strength of horse and man. Once King Henry was overthrown by the thrust of a Côtentin lance, and sprang up quickly to show himself to his men. Again he was in the thickest of the encounter, and was met by one of the three great rebel chiefs and thrown upon the ground, but this Lord of Thorigny was struck, in his turn, by a loyal French knight, and presently his lamenting followers carried him away dead on his shield like any Spartan of old. And the king honored his valor and commanded that he should be buried with splendid ceremonies in a church not far from the battlefield. Long afterward the Norman men and women loved to sing and to tell stones about the young Duke William's bravery and noble deeds of arms in that first great fight that made him duke from one end of Normandy to the other. He slew with his own hand the noblest and most daring warrior of Bayeux. Master Wace, the chronicler, tells us how William drove the sharp steel straight through his hardy foe, and how the body fell beneath his stroke and its soul departed. Wace was a Bayeux man himself, and though he was a loyal songster and true to his great duke, he cannot help a sigh of pride and sorrow over Hardrez' fate.

Neal of St. Saviour fought steadily and cheered his men eagerly as the hour went on, but Randolf of Bayeux felt his courage begin to fail him. Hamon was dead. Their great ally, Hardrez, had been the flower of his own knights, and he was lying dead of a cruel sword-thrust there in plain sight. He lost sight of Neal, perhaps, for he was suddenly afraid of betrayal, and grieved that he had ever put his helmet on. There is a touching bit of description in the "Roman de Rou" just now. The battle pleased him no more, is told in the quaint short lines. He thought how sad it was to be a captive, and sadder still to be slain. He gave way feebly at every charge; he wandered to and fro aimlessly, a thing to be stumbled over, we fancy him, now in the front of the fight, now in the rear; at last he dropped his lance and shield. "He stretched forth his neck and rode for his life," says Master Wace, quite ashamed of his countryman. But we can see the poor knight's head drooping low, and his good, tired horse—the better man of the two—mustering all his broken strength to carry his master beyond the reach of danger. All the cowards rode after him pell-mell, but brave Saint Saviour fought to the last and held the field until his right arm failed and he could not strike again. The French pressed him hard, the Norman men looked few and spent, and the mighty lord of the Côtentin knew that all hope was lost. There on the rising ground of Saint Lawrence the last blow was struck.

Away went the rebels in groups of three or four—away for dear life every one of them, riding this way and that, trying to get out of reach of their enemies and into some sort of shelter. The duke chased them like a hound on the track of hares on, on toward Bayeux, past the great Abbey of Fontenay and the Allemagne quarries, until they reached the river Orne with its deep current. Men and horses floundered in the water there, and many hot wounds tinged it with a crimson stain. They were drowned, poor knights, and poor, brave horses too. They went struggling and drifting down stream; the banks were strewn with the dead; and the mill-wheels of Borbillon, a little farther down, were stopped in their slow turning by the strange wreck and floating worthless fragments of those lords and gentlemen who had lost the battle of the Val-ès-dunes.

And William was the conqueror of Normandy. Guy of Burgundy was a traitor to his friends, and won a heritage of shame for his flight from the field. We hear nothing of him while the fight went on, only that he ran away. It appears that he must have been one of the first to start for a place of safety, because they blame him so much; there is nothing said about all the rebels running away together a little later. That was the fortune of war and inevitable; not personal cowardice, they might tell us. Guy of Burgundy was the man who had led the three Côtentin lords out by fair promises and taunts about their bastard duke, and he should have been brave and full of prowess, since he undertook to be the rival of so brave a man. He did not go toward the banks of the fateful river, but in quite another direction to his own castle of Brionne, and a troop of his vassals escaped with him and defended themselves there for a long time, until William fairly starved them out like rats in a hole. They held their own bravely, too, and no man was put to death when they surrendered, while Guy was even allowed to come back to court. Master Wace stoutly maintains that they should have been hung, and says long afterward that some of those high in favor at court were the traitors of the great rebellion.

Strange to say, nobody was put to death. Mr. Freeman says of this something that gives us such a clear look at William's character that I must copy it entire. "In those days, both in Normandy and elsewhere, the legal execution of a state criminal was an event that seldom happened. Men's lives were recklessly wasted in the endless warfare of the times, and there were men, as we have seen, who did not shrink from private murder, even in its basest forms. But the formal hanging or beheading of a noble prisoner, so common in later times, was, in the eleventh century, a most unusual sight. And, strange as it may sound, there was a sense in which William the Conqueror was not a man of blood. He would sacrifice any number of lives to his boundless ambition; he did not scruple to condemn his enemies to cruel personal mutilations; he would keep men for years as a mere measure of security, in the horrible prison-houses of those days; but the extinction of human life in cold blood was something from which he shrank."

At the time of the first great victory, the historian goes on to say, William was of an age when men are commonly disposed to be generous, and the worst points of his character had not begun to show themselves. Later in life, when he had broken the rule, or perhaps we must call it only his prejudice and superstition, we find that the star of his glory is already going down, pale and spent, into the mists of shame and disappointment.

None of the traitors of the Val-ès-dunes were treated harshly, according to the standard of the times. The barons paid fines and gave mortgages, and a great many of them were obliged to tear down their robber castles, which they had built without permission from the duke. This is the reason that there are so few ruins in Normandy of the towers of that date. The Master of St. Saviour's was obliged to take himself off to Brittany, but there was evidently no confiscation of his great estates, for we find him back again at court the very next year, high in the duke's favor and holding an honorable position. He lived forty-four years after this, an uncommon lifetime for a Norman knight, and followed the Conqueror to England, but he got no reward in lands and honor, as so many of his comrades did. Guy of Burgundy stayed at court a little while, and then went back to his native province and devoted himself to making plots against his brother, Count William. Grimbald de Plessis-fared the worst of all the conspirators; he was taken to Rouen and put into prison weighted down with chains, and given the poorest of lodgings. He confessed that he had tried to murder William that night at Valognes, when the court jester gave warning, and said that a knight called Salle had been his confederate. Salle denied the charge stoutly and challenged De Plessis to fight a judicial combat, but before the day came the scheming, unlucky baron from the Saxon lands was found dead in his dungeon. The fetters had ground their way into his very bones, and he was buried in his chains, for a warning, while his estates were seized and part of them given to the church of Bayeux.

Now, at last, the Norman priests and knights knew that they had a master. For some time it was surprisingly quiet in Normandy, and the country was unexpectedly prosperous. The great duchy stood in a higher rank among her sister kingdoms than ever before, and though there was another revolt and serious attacks from envious neighbors, yet the Saxons of the Bessin and the Danes of the Côtentin were overthrown, and Normandy was more unitedly Norman-French than ever. There had been a long struggle that had lasted from Richard the Fearless' boyhood until now, but it was ended at last, to all intents and purposes. Even now there is a difference between the two parts of Normandy, though so many years have passed; but the day was not far off after this battle of Val-ès-dunes when the young conqueror could muster a great army and cross the channel into England. "The Count of Rouen," says Freeman, "had overcome Saxons and Danes within his own dominions, and he was about to weld them into his most trusty weapons, wherewith to overcome Saxons and Danes beyond the sea."

Perhaps nothing will show the barbarous cruelty of these times or William's fierce temper better than the story of Alençon and its punishment. William Talvas, the young duke's old enemy, formed a rebellious league with Geoffry of Anjou, and they undertook to hold Alençon against the Normans. When William came within sight of the city, he discovered that they had sufficient self-confidence to mock at him and insult him. They even spread raw skins over the edge of the city walls, and beat them vigorously, yelling that there was plenty of work for the tanner, and giving even plainer hints at what they thought of his mother's ancestry.

William was naturally put into a great rage, and set himself and his army down before the walls his enemies thought so invincible. He swore "by the splendor of God" that he would treat them as a man lops a tree with an axe, and, sure enough, when the siege was over, and Alençon was at the Conqueror's mercy, he demanded thirty-two captives of war, and nose, hands, and feet were chopped off, and presently thrown back over the walls into the town.

XI. THE ABBEY OF BEC.

"He heard across the howling seas,

Chime convent bells on wintry nights."

—Matthew Arnold.

THE only way of escaping from the obligations of feudalism and constant warfare was by forsaking the follies of the world altogether for the shelter of a convent, and there devoting one's time and thought to holy things. A monastic life often came to be only an excuse for devotion to art or to letters, or served merely to cover the distaste for military pursuits. It was not alone ecclesiasticism and a love for holy living and thoughts of heaven that inspired rigid seclusion and monkish scorn of worldliness. Not only popular superstition or recognition of true spiritual life and growth of the Church made up the Church's power, but the presence of so much secular thought and wisdom in the fold. Men of letters, of science, and philosophy made it often more than a match for the militant element of society, the soldiery of Normandy, and the great captains, who could only prove their valor by the strength of their strategy and their swords. William was quick to recognize the vast strength of the clergy and the well-protected force of cloistered public opinion. A soldier and worldly man himself, he arrayed himself on the side of severe self-repression and knightly chastity and purity of life, and kept the laws of the convent in high honor; while he mixed boldly with the rude warfare of his age. He did not think himself less saintly because he was guilty of secret crimes against his rivals. A skilful use of what an old writer calls "the powder of succession" belonged as much to his military glory as any piece of field-tactics and strategy. He was anxious to stand well in the Pope's estimation, and the ban and malediction of the Church was something by all means to be avoided. The story of his marriage shows his bold, adventurous character and determination in a marked way, and his persistence in gaining his ends and winning the approval of his superior, in spite of obstacles that would have daunted a weaker man. To gain a point to which the Church objected he must show himself stronger than the Church.

So there were two great forces at work in Normandy: this military spirit, the love of excitement, of activity, and adventure; and this strong religious feeling, which often made the other its willing servant, and was sometimes by far the most powerful of the two. Whether superstition or true, devout acceptance and unfolding of the ideas of the Christian religion moved the Normans and their contemporaries to most active service of the Church, we will not stop to discuss. The presence of the best scholars and saints in any age is a leaven and inspiration of that age, and men cannot help being more or less influenced by the dwelling among them of Christ's true disciples and ministers. That there was a large amount of credulity, of superstitious rites and observances, we cannot doubt, neither can we question that these exercised an amazing control over ignorant minds. Standing so near to a pagan ancestry, the people of large, and, relatively speaking, remote districts of Normandy, were no doubt confused by lingering vestiges of the older forms of belief. As yet, religion, in spite of the creeds of knighthood, showed itself more plainly in stone and mortar, in vestments, and fasts, and penances, and munificent endowments, than in simple truth and godliness of life. A Norman nobleman, in the time of the Conqueror, or earlier, thought that his estate would lack its chief ornament if he did not plant a company of monks in some corner of it. It was the proper thing for a rich man to found a monastery or religious house of some sort or other, and this was a most blessed thing for the scholars of their time. The profession of letters was already becoming dignified and respectable, and the students of the Venerable Bede, and other noble teachers from both north and south, had already scattered good seeds through the states of Europe. It was in this time that many great schools were founded, and in the more peaceful years of the early reign of the Conqueror, religion and learning found time to strike a deeper root in Normandy than ever before. There was more wealth for them to be nourished with, the farms were productive, and the great centres of industry and manufacture, like Falaise, were thriving famously. It was almost as respectable to be a monk as to be a soldier. There is something very beautiful in these earlier brotherhoods—a purer fashion of thought and of life, a simplicity of devotion to the higher duties of existence. But we can watch here, as in the later movements in England and Italy, a gradual change from poverty and holiness of life, to a love of riches and a satisfaction with corrupt ceremonies and petty authority. The snare of worldliness finds its victims always, and the temptation was easy then, as it is easy now, to forget the things that belong to the spirit. We have seen so much of the sword and shield in this short history that we turn gladly away for a little space to understand what influences were coming from the great abbeys of Bec and Saint Evreuil, and to make what acquaintance we can with the men who dwelt there, and held for their weapons only their mass-books and their principles of education and of holy living. Lanfranc we must surely know, for he was called the right-hand man of the Conqueror; and now let us go back a little way and take a quick survey of the founding of the Abbey of Bec, and trace its history, for that will help us to understand the monastic life, and the wave of monasticism that left so plain a mark upon the headlands and valleys of Normandy. Both in England and Norman France, you can find the same redroofed villages clustered about high square church towers, with windows in the gray stone walls that look like dim fret-work or lacework. The oldest houses are low and small, but the oldest minsters and parish churches are very noble buildings.

The first entrance into one of the old cathedrals is an event in one's life never to be forgotten. It grows more beautiful the longer one thinks of it; that first impression of height and space, of silence and meditation; the walls are stored with echoes of prayers and chanting voices; the windows are like faded gardens, with their sober tints and gleams of brighter color. The saints are pictured on them awkwardly enough, but the glory of heaven beams through the old glass upon the worn tombstones in the floor; the very dust in the rays of sunlight that strike across the wide, solemn spaces, seems sacred dust, and of long continuance. We shut out this busy world when we go into the cathedral door, and look about us as if this were a waiting-room from whence one might easily find conveyance to the next world. There is a feeling of nearness to heaven as we walk up the great aisle of what our ancestors called, reverently enough, God's house. One is suddenly reminded of many unseen things that the world outside gives but little chance to think about. We are on the journey heavenward indeed. There where many centuries have worn away the trace of worldliness and the touch of builders' tools, so that the building itself seems almost to have grown by its own life and strength, you think about the builders and planners of such dignity and splendor more than any thing, after all. Who were the men that dared to lift the roof and plant the tall pillars, and why did they, in those poor, primitive times, give all they had to make this one place so rich and high. The bells ring a lazy, sweet chime for answer, and if you catch a glimpse of some brown old books in the sacristy, and even spell out the quaint records, you are hardly satisfied. We can only call them splendid monuments of the spirit of the time (almost uncivilized, according to our standard) when nevertheless there was a profound sentiment of worship and reverence.

Besides this, we are reminded that the lords of church and state were able, if it pleased them, to command the entire service of their vassals. All the liberties and aids and perquisites that belonged to rank ceased where the lowest rank ended, at the peasant. He was at anybody's command and mercy who chanced to be his master; he had but precious few rights and claims of his own. When Christ taught his disciples that whosoever would be chief among them must become as a servant, he suggested a truth and order of relationship most astonishing and contrary to all precedent. He that would be chief among Hebrews or Normans, chief, alas, even in our own day, is still misled by the old idea that the greatest is the master of many men. Wordly power and heavenly service are always apt to be mistaken for each other.

In an age when every man claimed the right of private war against every other man, unless he were lord or vassal, we naturally look for ferocity, and understand that the line between private war and simple robbery and murder was not very clearly kept. Those who were comparatively unable to defend themselves were the chief sufferers, and of course many peace-loving men were obliged to take on the appearance of fighters, and be ready for constant warfare in all its shapes. There was only the one alternative—first to the universal dissension of a nationality of armed men, and later to the more orderly and purposeful system of knighthood,—simply to retreat from the world altogether and lead a strictly religious life. The famous order of the Benedictine monks was built up in Normandy with surprising devotion. A natural love and respect for learning, which had long been smouldering half-neglected, now burst into a quick blaze in the hearts of many of the descendants of the old Norse skalds and Sagamen. While the Augustinian order of monks is chiefly famous for building great cathedrals, and the mendicant friars have left many a noble hospital as their monuments, so the Benedictines turned their energies toward the forming of great schools. The time has passed when the Protestant world belittled itself by contemptuously calling the monks lazy, sensual, and idle, and by seeing no good in these ancient communities. Learning of every sort, and the arts, as well, would have been long delayed in their development, if it had not been for such quiet retreats, where those men and women who chose could turn their thoughts toward better employments than the secular world encouraged or even allowed. The Benedictines were the most careful fosterers of scholarship; their brethren of monastic fame owed them a great deal in every way.

There was a noble knight named Herluin, who lived in the time of Duke Robert the Devil, and who was for thirty-seven years a knight-at-arms. He was a descendant of one of Rolf's companions, his lineage was of the very best, and his estates made part of the original grant of Charles the Simple. Herluin was vassal to Count Gilbert of Brionne, and had proved himself a brave and loyal knight, both to his overlord and the duke. He was high in favor, and unusually tender-hearted and just to those in trouble. We cannot help wishing that it had seemed possible to such a man that he should stay in the world and leaven society by his example, but to a thoughtful and gentle soul like Herluin the cloister offered great temptations. There was still great turbulence even among ecclesiastics—the worst of them "bore arms and lived the life of heathen Danes. . . . The faith of Herluin nearly failed him when he saw the disorder of one famous monastery, but he was comforted by accidentally beholding the devotions of one godly brother, who spent the whole night in secret prayer. He was thus convinced that the salt of the earth had not as yet wholly lost its savor."

Our pious knight forsook the world, and with a few companions devoted himself to building a small monastery on his own estate at Burneville, near Brionne. The church was consecrated, and its founder received benediction from his bishop, who ordained him a priest and made him abbot of the little community. Herluin was very diligent in learning to read, and achieved this mighty task without neglecting . any of the work which he imposed upon himself day by day. Soon he grew famous in all that part of Normandy for his sanctity and great wisdom in explaining the Bible. But it was discovered that the site of his flourishing young establishment was not well chosen; an abbey must possess supplies of wood and water, and so the colony was removed to the valley of a small stream that flows into the Lisle, near the town of Brionne. In the old speech of the Normans this brook was called a beck; we have the word yet in verse and provincial speech; and it gave a name to the most famous and longest remembered perhaps of all the Norman monasteries. Mr. Freeman says: "The hills are still thickly wooded; the beck still flows through rich meadows and under trees planted by the waterside, by the walls of what was once the renowned monastery to which it gave its name. But of the days of Herluin no trace remains besides these imperishable works of nature. A tall tower, of rich and fanciful design, one of the latest works of mediaeval skill, still attracts the traveller from a distance; but of the mighty minster itself, all traces, save a few small fragments, have perished. . . The truest memorial of that illustrious abbey is now to be found in the parish church of the neighboring village. In that lowly shelter is still preserved the effigy with which after-times had marked the resting-place of the founder. Such are all the relics which now remain of the house which once owned Lanfranc and Anselm as its inmates.

"In this valley it was that Herluin finally fixed his infant settlement, devoting to it his own small possession."

"By loving this world," he said, when he pleaded for his poor peasants in Gilbert of Brionne's court—"By loving this world and by obeying man I have hitherto much neglected God and myself. I have been altogether intent on training my body, and I have gained no education for my soul. If I have ever deserved well of thee, let me pass what remains of life in a monastery. Let me keep thy affection and with me give to God what I had of thee."

Herluin was not left alone in his enterprise; one companion after another joined him, and presently there was a busy company of monks at Bec. They subjected themselves to all sorts of self-denials and privations, working hard at building their new home, at ditching, gardening, or wood-cutting, and chanting their prayers with entire devotion. Herluin allowed himself one scanty meal a day, and went about his work poorly dressed, but serving God in most humble fashion. This was the story of many small religious houses and their founders, but we cannot help tracing the beginning of the abbey of Bec with particular interest for the sake of Lanfranc, who has kept its memory alive and made it famous in Norman and English history.

The story of this friar of Bec, who came to be archbishop of Canterbury, and whose influence and power were only second, a few years later, to William the Conqueror's own, reads like a romance, as indeed does many another story of that romantic age. He was born at Pavia, the City of the Hundred Towers, in Lombardy, and belonged to an illustrious family. He was discovered in early boyhood to be an uncommon scholar, and even in his university course he became well known by his brilliant talents and fine gift of oratory. He was looked upon as almost invincible in debate while he was still a school-boy, and when he left college it was supposed that he would give the benefit of his attainments and growth to his native city. For a little while he did stay there, and began his career, but he appears to have been made restless by a love of change and adventure, and a desire to see the world, and next we find him going northward with a company of admiring scholars, as if on pilgrimage, but in the wrong direction! The enthusiastic little procession crossed the St. Bernard pass into France and for some reason went to Avranches, where Lanfranc taught a school and quickly became celebrated. In spite of the more common profession or trade of fighting, there was never a time when learning or the profession of letters was more honored, and the Normans yielded to none of their contemporaries in the respect they had for scholars.

Lanfranc became dissatisfied with the honor and glory of his success at Avranches; and presently, in quest of something more deep and satisfying more in accordance with the craving of his spiritual nature, left his flourishing school and again started northward. The country was very wild and unsafe for a solitary wayfarer; and presently, so the tradition runs, he was attacked by a band of robbers, beaten, and left tied to a tree without food or money or any prospect of immediate release. The long hours of the night wore away and he grew more and more desperate; at last he bethought himself of spiritual aid as a last resort, and tried to repeat the service of the church. Alas! he could not remember the prayers and hymns, and in his despair he vowed a pious vow to God that he would devote himself to a holy life if his present sufferings might be ended. In good season some charcoal burners played the welcome part of deliverers and Lanfranc, yet aching with the pinch of his fetters and their galling knots, begged to know of some holy house near by, and was directed to Herluin's hermitage and the humble brotherhood of Bec.

The little colony of holy men was all astir that day. Soldiers and sober gentlemen were tilling the soil and patiently furthering their rural tasks. Herluin himself, the former knight-at-arms, was clad in simple monkish garb, and playing the part of master-mason in the building of a new oven. Out from the neighboring thicket comes a strange figure, pale yet from his uncomforted vigil, and prays to be numbered with those who give their lives to the service of God. "This is surely a Lombard!" says Herluin, wonderstruck and filled with sympathy; and when he discovers the new brother's name and eager devotion, he kneels before him in love and reverence. It was a great day for the abbey of Bec.

Such learning and ability to teach as Lanfranc's could not be hidden; indeed the church believed in using a man's great gifts, and each member was bound to give of his bounty in her service. The brothers who could till the ground and hew timber and build ovens kept at their tasks, and all the while Lanfranc, the theologian and teacher, the man of letters, gathered a company of scholars from far and wide. Bec became a famous centre of learning, and even from Italy and Greece young men journeyed to his school, and, as years went by, he was venerated more and more. His quick understanding and cleverness saved him many a disaster, and we recognize in him a charming inheritance of wit and good humor. He had the individuality and characteristics of his Italian ancestry, while he was that rare man in any social circle of his age, or even a later age,—a true man of the world. A Norman of the Normans in his adopted home, he was yet able to see Normandy, not as the world itself, but only a factor in it, and to put it and its ambitions and possessions in their true relation to wider issues. There was no such churchman-statesman as Lanfranc in the young duchy, and his fame and glory were felt more and more. William the duke himself might well set his wits at work to conquer this formidable opponent of his marriage, and win him over to his following, and the first attack was not by conciliatory measures. Lanfranc received a formidable order to quit the country and leave his abbey of Bec on penalty of worse punishment.

The future archbishop of English Canterbury meekly obeyed his temporal lord, and set out through the forest with a pitiful straggling escort affectingly futile in its appearance. He himself was mounted on the worst old stumbling horse in the despoiled abbey stables, and presently they meet the duke out hunting in most gallant array with a lordly following of knights and gentlemen. It looks surprisingly as if shrewd Lanfranc had arranged the scene beforehand. Along he comes on his feeble steed, limping slowly on the forest path; he, the greatest prior and book-man of Normandy, turned out of the house and home that his own learning had made famous through Christendom. "Under Lanfranc," says the chronicler, "the Normans first fathomed the art of letters, for under the six dukes of Normandy scarce any one among the Normans applied himself to liberal studies, nor was there any learning found till God, the provider of all things, brought Lanfranc to Normandy." All this, no doubt, flashed through William's mind, and the prior of Bec's Italian good-humor proved itself the best of weapons. "Give me a better horse," he cried, "and you shall see me go away faster." The duke laughed in spite of himself, and Lanfranc won a chance of pleading his cause. Before they parted they were sworn friends, and the prior's knowledge of civil law and of theology and of human nature (not least by any means of his famous gifts) were for once and all at the duke's service. He supported the cause of the unlawful marriage, and even won a dispensation from the Pope, long desired and almost hopeless, in William's favor.

But the abbey of Bec was a great power for good in its time, and carried a wonderful influence for many years. In the general scarcity of books in those days before printing, the best way of learning was to listen to what each great scholar had to say, and the students went about from school to school, and lingered longest at places like Bec, where the best was to be found. The men here were not only the patrons of learning and the guarders of their own copies of the ancient classics, but they taught the children of the neighborhood, and sheltered the rich and poor, the old people and the travellers, who wandered to their gates. They copied missals, they cast bells for churches, they were the best of farmers, of musicians, of artists. While Lanfranc waged his great battle with Berengarius about the doctrine of the Eucharist, and came out a victorious champion for the church, and won William's cause with the Pope with most skilful pleading of the value of Norman loyalty to the See of Rome, his humbler brethren tended their bees and ploughed straight furrows and taught the country children their letters. Such a centre of learning and of useful industry as Bec was the best flower of civilization. Lanfranc himself was true to his vow of humility. We catch some delightful glimpses of his simple life, and one in particular of his being met on a journey by some reverential pilgrims to his school. He was carefully carrying a cat behind him on the saddle, comfortably restrained from using her claws, and Lanfranc explained that he had sometimes been grievously annoyed by mice at his destination, and had provided this practical ally. One can almost see the twinkle in the good man's eyes, and the faces of the surprised scholars who had been looking forward with awe and dread to their first encounter with so renowned a man.

XII. MATILDA OF FLANDERS.

"It had been easy fighting in some plain,

Where victory might hang in equal choice;

But all resistance against her is vain."

—Marvell.

WE have occasionally had a glimpse of Flanders and its leading men in the course of our Norman story; but now the two dukedoms were to be linked together by a closer tie than either neighborhood, or a brotherhood, or antagonism in military affairs. While Normandy had been gaining new territory and making itself more and more feared by the power of its armies, and had been growing richer and richer with its farms and the various industries of the towns, Flanders was always keeping pace, if not leading, in worldly prosperity.

Flanders had gained the dignity and opulence of a kingdom. Her people were busy, strong, intelligent craftsmen and artists, and while her bell-towers lifted themselves high in the air, and made their chimes heard far and wide across the level country, the weavers' looms and the women's clever fingers were sending tapestries to the walls of the Vatican, and frost-like laces to the ladies of Spain.

The heavy ships of Flanders went and came with the richest of freights from her crowded ports; her picture-painters were at work, her gardens were green, and her noblemen's houses were filled with whatever a luxurious life could demand or invent. As the country became overcrowded, many of the inhabitants crossed over to Scotland, and gained a foothold, sometimes by the sword, and oftener by the plough and spade and weaver's shuttle. The Douglases and the Leslies, Robert Bruce and all the families of Flemings, took root then, and, whether by art or trade, established a right to be called Scotsmen, and to march in the front rank when the story is told of many a brave day in Scottish history.

The Count of Flanders was nominally vassal of both Rome and France, but he was practically his own man. Baldwin de Lisle, of the Conqueror's time, was too great a man to need anybody's help, or to be bought or sold at will by an over-lord. He stood well as the representative of his country's wealth and dignity. A firm alliance with such a neighbor was naturally coveted by such a far-seeing man as the young duke; and besides any political reasons, there was a closer reason still, in the love that had sprung up in his heart for Matilda, the count's daughter. In 1049, he had been already making suit for her hand, for it was in that year when the Council of Rheims forbade the banns, on some plea of relationship that was within the limit set by the Church. William's whole existence was a fight for his life, for his dukedom, for his kingdom of England, and he was not wanting in courage in this long siege of church and state, when the woman he truly loved was the desired prize. If history can be trusted, she was a prize worth winning; if William had not loved her, he would not have schemed and persisted for years in trying to win her in spite of countless hindrances which might well have ended his quest if he had been guided only by political reasons for the alliance.

His nobles had eagerly urged him to marry. Perhaps they would have turned their eyes toward England first if there had been a royal princess of Eadward's house, but failing this, Flanders was the best prize. The Norman dukedom must not be left without an heir, and this time there must be no question of the honesty of the heir's claim and right to succession. Normandy had seen enough division and dissension, and angry partisanship during the duke's own youth, and now that he had reached the age of twenty-four, and had made himself master of his possessions, and could take his stand among his royal neighbors, everybody clamored for his marriage, and for a Lady of Normandy. He was a pure man in that time of folly and licentiousness. He was already recognized as a great man, and even the daughter of Baldwin of Flanders might be proud to marry him.

Matilda was near the duke's own age, but she had already been married to a Flemish official, and had two children. She was a beautiful, graceful woman, and it is impossible to believe some well-known old stories of William's rude courtship of her, since her father evidently was ready to favor the marriage, and she seems to have been a most loyal and devoted wife to her husband, and to have been ready enough to marry him hastily at the end of a most troublesome courtship. The great Council of Rheims had forbidden their marriage, as we have already seen, and the pious Pope Leo had struck blows right and left among high offenders of the Church's laws; a whole troop of princes were excommunicated or put under heavy penances, and the Church's own officials were dealt justly with according to their sins. When most of these lesser contemporaries were properly sentenced, a decree followed, which touched two more illustrious men: the Count of Flanders was forbidden to give his daughter to the Norman duke for a wife, and William, in his turn, was forbidden to take her. For four long years the lovers—if we may believe them to be lovers—were kept apart on the Pope's plea of consanguinity. There is no evidence remaining that this was just, yet there truly may have been some relationship. It is much easier to believe it, at any rate, than that the count's wife Adela's former child-marriage to William's uncle could have been put forward as any sort of objection.

We must leave for another chapter the affairs of Normandy and William's own deeds during the four years, and go forward with this story of his marriage to a later time, when in the course of Italian affairs, a chance was given to bring the long courtship to a happy end. Strangely enough this came by means of the De Hautevilles and that Norman colony whose fortunes we have already briefly traced. In the conflict with Pope Leo, when he was forced to yield to the Normans' power and to recognize them as a loyal state, William either won a consent to his wedding or else dared to brave the Pope's disapproval. While Leo was still in subjection the eager duke hurried to his city of Eu, near the Flemish border, and met there Count Baldwin and his daughter. There was no time spent in splendid processions and triumphal pageants of the Flemish craftsmen; some minor priest gave the blessing, and as the duke and his hardly-won wife came back to the Norman capital there was a great cheering and rejoicing all the way; and the journey was made as stately and pompous as heart could wish. There was a magnificent welcome at Rolf's old city of Rouen; it was many years since there had been a noble lady, a true duchess, on the ducal throne of Normandy.

But the spirit of ecclesiasticism held its head too high in the pirates' land to brook such disregard of its canons, even on the part of its chief ruler. There was an uncle of William's, named Mauger, who was primate of the Norman church. He is called on every hand a very bad man—at any rate, his faults were just the opposite of William's, and of a sensual and worldly stamp. He was not a fit man for the leader of the clergy, in William's opinion. Yet Mauger was zealous in doing at least some of the duties of his office—he did not flinch from rebuking his nephew! All the stories of his life are of the worst sort, unless we give him the credit of trying to do right in this case, but we can too easily remember the hatred that he and all his family bore toward the bastard duke in his boyhood, and suspect at least that jealousy may have taken the place of scorn and despising. One learns to fear making point-blank decisions about the character of a man so long dead, even of one whom everybody blamed like Mauger. His biographers may have been his personal enemies, and later writers have ignorantly perpetuated an unjust hue and cry.

Perhaps Lanfranc may be trusted better, for he too blamed the duke for breaking a holy law, Lanfranc the merry, wise Italian, who loved his fellow-men, and who was a teacher by choice and by gift of God. All Normandy was laid under a ban at this time for the wrong its master had done. Lanfranc rebuked the assumed sinner bravely, and William's fierce stern temper blazed out against him, and ordered a vicious revenge of the insult to him and to his wife. The just William, who kept Normandy in such good order, who stood like a bulwark of hewn stone between his country and her enemies, was the same William who could toss severed hands and feet over the Alençon wall, and give orders to burn the grain stacks and household goods of the abbey of Bec. We have seen how the duke and the abbot met, and how they became friends again, and Lanfranc made peace with Pope Leo and won him the loyalty of Normandy in return. Very likely Lanfranc was glad to explain the truth and to be relieved from upholding such a flimsy structure as the church's honor demanded. At any rate, William gladly paid his Peter's pence and set about building his great abbey of St. Etienne, in Caen, for a penance, and made Lanfranc its prelate, and Matilda built her abbey of the Holy Trinity, while in four of the chief towns of Normandy hospitals were built for the old and sick people of the duchy. We shall see more of these churches presently, but there they still stand, facing each other across the high-peaked roofs of Caen; high and stately churches, the woman's tower and the man's showing characteristics of boldness and of ornament that mark the builders' fancy and carry us in imagination quickly back across the eight hundred years since they were planned and founded. Anselm, Maurilius, and Lanfranc, these were the teachers and householders of the great churches, and one must have a new respect for the young duke and duchess who could gather and hold three such scholars and saintly men to be leaders of the church in Normandy.

There were four sons and three daughters born to William and Matilda, and there is no hint of any difference or trouble between the duke and his wife until they were unable to agree about the misconduct of their eldest son. Matilda's influence for good may often be traced or guessed at in her husband's history, and there are pathetic certainties of her resignation and gentleness when she was often cruelly hurt and tried by the course of events.

Later research has done away with the old idea of her working the famous Bayeux tapestry with the ladies of her court to celebrate the Conqueror's great deeds; but he needed no tribute of needle-work, nor she either, to make them remembered. They have both left pictures of themselves done in fadeless colors and living text of lettering that will stand while English words are spoken, and Norman trees bloom in the spring, and Norman rivers run to the sea, and the towers of Caen spring boldly toward the sky.

We cannot be too thankful that so much of these historic churches has been left untouched. When it is considered that at five separate times the very fiends of destruction and iconoclasm seem to have been let loose in Normandy, it is a great surprise that there should be so many old buildings still in existence. From the early depredations of the Northmen themselves, down to the religious wars of the sixteenth century and the French revolution of the eighteenth, there have been other and almost worse destroying agencies than even the wars themselves. Besides the natural decay of masonry and timber, there was the very pride and growing wealth of the rich monastic orders and the large towns, who liked nothing better than to pull down their barns to build greater and often less interesting ones. The most prosperous cities naturally build the best churches, as they themselves increase, and naturally replace them oftenest, and so retain fewest that are of much historical interest in the end. The most popular weapon in the tenth and eleventh centuries was fire; and the first thing that Norman assailants were likely to do, was to throw burning torches over the walls into the besieged towns. Again and again they were burnt—houses, churches, and all.

The Normans were constantly improving, however, in their fashions of building, and had made a great advance upon the Roman architecture which they had found when they came to Neustria. Their work has a distinct character of its own, and perhaps their very ignorance of the more ornate and less effective work which had begun to prevail in Italy, gave them freedom to work out their own simple ideas. Instead of busying themselves with petty ornamentation and tawdry imagery, they trusted for effect to the principles of height and size. Their churches are more beautiful than any in the world; their very plainness and severity gives them a beautiful dignity, and their slender pillars and high arches make one think of nothing so much as the tall pine forests of the North. What the Normans did with the idea of the Roman arch, they did too in many other ways. They had a gift of good taste that was most exceptional in that time, and especially in that part of Europe; and whatever had been the power and efficiency of the last impulse of civilization from the South, this impulse from the North did a noble work in its turn. Normandy herself, in the days of William and Matilda, was fully alive and pervaded with dreams of growth and expansion.

Nobody can tell how early the idea of the conquest of England began to be a favorite Norman dream. In those days there was always a possibility of some day owning one's neighbor's land, and with weak Eadward on the throne of England, only too ready to listen to the suggestions and demands of his Norman barons and favorite counsellors, it must have seemed always an easier, not to say more possible, thing to take one step farther. There was an excellent antechamber across the Channel for the crowded court and fields of Normandy, and William and Eadward were old friends and companions. In 1051, when Normandy was at peace, and England was at any rate quiet and sullen, submissive to rule, but lying fast, bound like a rebellious slave that has been sold to a new master, William and a fine company of lords and gentlemen went a visiting.

All those lords and gentlemen kept their eyes very wide open, and took good notice of what they saw.

It was not a common thing by any means, for a great duke to go pleasuring. He was apt to be too busy at home; but William's affairs were in good order, and his cousin of England was a feeble man and more than half a Norman; besides, he had no heir, and in course of time the English throne would lack a proper king. The idea of such a holiday might have pleased the anxious suitor of Matilda of Flanders, too, and have beguiled the hard time of waiting. Nobody stopped to remember that English law gave no right of succession to mere inheritance or descent. Ralph the Timid was Æthelred's grandson; but who would think of making him king instead of such a man as William? The poor banished prince at the Hungarian court, half a world away, was not so much as missed or wished for. Godwine was banished, Harold was in Ireland; besides, it must be urged that there was something fine in the notion of adding such a state as Normandy to England. England was not robbed, but magnificently endowed by such a proposal.

Eadward was amiably glad to see this brave Duke of the Normans. There was much to talk over together of the past; the present had its questions, too, and it was good to have such a strong arm to lean upon; what could have been more natural than that the future also should have its veil drawn aside, not too rashly or irreverently? When Eadward had been gathered to his fellow saints, pioneered by visions that did not fade, and panoplied by authentic relics—nay, when the man of prayers and cloistered quietness was kindly taken away from the discordant painfulness of an earthly kingdom, what more easy than to dream of this warlike William in his place; William, a man of war and soldiery, for whom the government of two great kingdoms in one, would only harden and employ the tense muscles and heavy brain; would only provide his own rightful business? And, while Eadward thought of this plan, William was Norman, too, and with the careful diplomacy of his race, he joined the daring and outspokenness of old Rolf the Ganger; he came back with his lords and gentlemen to Normandy, weighed down with presents—every man of them who had not stayed behind for better gain's sake. He came back to Normandy the acknowledged successor to the English crown. Heaven send dampness now and bleak winds, and let poor Eadward's sufferings be short! There was work for a man to do in ruling England, and Eadward could not do it. The Englishmen were stupid and dull; they ate too much and drank too much; they clung with both hands to their old notions of state-craft and government. It was the old story of the hare and the tortoise, but the hare was fleet of foot and would win.

Win? Yes, this race and that race; and yet the tortoise was going to be somehow made over new, and keep a steady course in the right path, and learn speed, and get to be better than the old tortoise as the years went on and on.

Eadward had no right to will away the kingship of England; but this must have been the time of the promise that the Normans claimed, and that their chroniclers have recorded. All Normandy believed in this promise, and were ready to fight for it in after years. It is most likely that Eadward was only too glad, at this date, to make a private arrangement with the duke. He was on the worst of terms just then with Godwine and his family, and consequently with the displeased English party, who were their ardent upholders. Indeed, a great many of these men were in Ireland with Harold, having turned their backs upon a king and court that were growing more friendly to Normandy and disloyal to England day by day.

The very next year after William's triumphal visit the Confessor was obliged to change his course in the still stormier sea of English politics. The Normans had shown their policy too soon, and there was a widespread disapproval, and an outcry for Godwine's return from exile. Baldwin of Flanders, and King Henry of France, had already been petitioning for his pardon, and suddenly Godwine himself came sailing up the Thames, and London eagerly put itself under his control. Then Eadward the Confessor consented to a reconciliation, there being no apparent alternative, and a troop of disappointed and displaced foreigners went back to Normandy. Robert of Jumièges, was among them. The Anglo-Saxon chronicle tells us gravely, that at Walton-on-the-Naze, "they were lighted on a crazy ship, and the archbishop betook himself at once over the sea, leaving behind him his pall and all his Christendom here in the land even as God willed it, because he had taken upon him that worship as God willed it not." The plea for taking away his place was "because he had done more than any to cause strife between Godwine and the king"; and Godwine's power was again the strongest in England.

The great earl lived only a few months longer, and when he died his son Harold took his place. Already the eyes of many Englishmen were ready to see in him their future king. Already he stands out a bold figure, with a heart that was true to England, and though the hopes that centred in him were broken centuries ago, we cannot help catching something of the hope and spirit of the time. We are almost ready to forget that this brave leader, the champion of that elder English people, was doomed to fall before the on-rushing of a new element of manhood, a tributary stream that came to swell the mighty channel of the English race and history. William the Norman was busy at home, meanwhile. The old hostility between Normandy and Flanders, which dated from the time of William Longsword's murder, was now at a certain end, by reason of the duke's marriage. Matilda, the noble Flemish lady, the descendant of good King Alfred of England, had brought peace and friendliness as not the least of her dowry, and all fear of any immediate antagonism from that quarter was at an end.

By the alliance with the kings of France, the Norman dukes had been greatly helped to gain their present eminence, and to the Norman dukes the French kings, in their turn, owed their stability upon their own thrones; they had fought for each other and stood by each other again and again. Now, there was a rift between them that grew wider and wider—a rift that came from jealousy and fear of the Normans' wealth and enormous growth in strength. They were masters of the Breton country, and had close ties of relationship, moreover, with not only Brittany, but with Flanders and the smaller county of Ponthieu, which lay between them and the Flemings. Normandy stretched her huge bulk and strength between France and the sea; she commanded the French rivers, the French borders; she was too much to be feared; if ever her pride were to be brought down, and the old vassalage insisted upon, it could not be too soon. Henry forgot all that he owed to the Normans' protection, and provoked them by incessant hostilities—secret and open treacheries,—and the fox waged war upon the lion, until a spirit of enmity was roused that hardly slept again for five hundred years.

There were other princes ready enough to satisfy their fear and jealousy. The lands of the conspirators stretched from Burgundy to the

Pyrenees. Burgundy, Blois, Ponthieu, Aquitaine, and Poictiers all joined in the chase for this William the Bastard, the chief of the hated pirates. All the old gibes and taunts, and contemptuous animosity were revived; now was the time to put an end to the Norman's outrageous greed of power and insolence of possession, and the great allied army divided itself in two parts, and marched away to Normandy.

King Henry's brother, Odo, turned his forces toward Rouen, and the king himself took a more southerly direction, by the way of Lisieux to the sea. They meant, at any rate, to pen the duke into his old Danish region of the Côtentin and Bessin districts; all his eastern lands, the grant from Charles the Simple, with the rest, were to be seized upon and taken back by their original owners.

Things had changed since the battle of Val-ès-dunes. There was no division now among the Norman lords, and as the word to arm against France was passed from one feudal chieftan to another, there was a great mustering of horse and foot. So the king had made up his mind to punish them, and to behave as if he had a right to take back the gift that was unwillingly wrung from Charles the Simple. Normandy is our own, not Henry's, was the angry answer; and Ralph of Tesson, and the soldiers of Falaise, the Lord of Mortain, the men of Bessin, and the barons of the Côtentin were ready to take the field, and stand shoulder to shoulder. There had been a change indeed, in Normandy; and from one end of it to the other there was a cry of shame and treachery upon Henry, the faithless ally and overlord. They had learned to know William as a man not against their interests but with them, and for them and the glory of Normandy; and they had not so soon forgotten the day of Val-ès-dunes and their bitter mistake.

The king's force had come into the country by the frontier city of Aumale, and had been doing every sort of damage that human ingenuity could invent between conqueror and vanquished. It was complained by those who escaped that the French were worse than Saracens. Old people, women, and children were abused or quickly butchered; men were taken prisoners; churches and houses were burnt or pulled to pieces. There was a town called Mortemer which had the ill-luck to be chosen for the French head-quarters, because it was then a good place for getting supplies and lodging, though now there is nothing left of it but the remains of an ancient tower and a few dwellings and gardens. Here the feasting and revelry went on as if Normandy were already fallen. All day there were raids in the neighboring country, and bringing in of captives, and plunder; and William's spies came to Mortemer, and went home to tell the duke the whole story of the hateful scene. There was a huge army collected there fearless of surprise; this was the place to strike a blow, and the duke and his captains made a rapid march by night so that they reached Mortemer before daylight.

There was no weapon more cherished by the pirates' grandchildren than a blazing fire-brand, and the army stole through the town while their enemies still slept, stupid with eating and drinking, or weary from the previous day's harrying. They waked to find their houses in flames, the roofs crackling, a horrid glare of light, a bewilderment of smoke and shouts; the Normans ready to kill, to burn, to pen them back by sturdy guards at the streets' ends. There was a courageous resistance to this onslaught, but from early morning until the day was well spent the fight went on, and most of the invaders were cut to pieces. The dead men lay thick in the streets, and scattered everywhere about the adjacent fields. "Only those were spared who were worth sparing for the sake of their ransom. Many a Norman soldier, down to the meanest serving-man in the ranks, carried off his French prisoner; many a one carried off his two or three goodly steeds with their rich harness. In all Normandy there was not a prison that was not full of Frenchmen." All this was done with scarcely any loss to the Normans, at least so we are told, and the news came to William that same evening, and made him thank God with great rejoicing. It would seem as if only a God of battles could be a very near and welcome sovereign to this soldier-lord of Normandy.

The victor had still another foe to meet. The king's command was still to be vanquished, and perhaps it might be done with even less bloodshed. The night had fallen, and he chose Ralph of Toesny, son of that Roger who sought the Spanish kingdom, the enemy of his own ill-championed childhood, to go as messenger to the king's tent. The two chieftains cannot have been encamped very far apart, for it was still dark when Ralph rode fast on his errand. He crept close to where the king lay in the darkness and in the glimmer of dawn he gave a doleful shout: "Wake, wake, you Frenchmen! You sleep too long; go and bury your friends who lie dead at Mortemer"; then he stole away again unseen, while the startled king and his followers whispered together of such a terrible omen. Ill news travels apace; they were not long in doubt; a panic seized the whole host. Not for Rouen now, or the Norman cities, but for Paris the king marched as fast as he could go; and nobody gave him chase, so that before long he and his counts were safe at home again with the thought of their folly for company. Craft is not so fine a grace as courage; but craft served the Normans many a good turn; and this was not the least glorious of William's victories, though no blood was spilt, though the king was driven away and no sword lifted to punish him. The Normans loved a bit of fun; we can imagine how well they liked to tell the story of spoiling half an army with hardly a scratch for themselves, and making the other half take to its heels at the sound of Ralph de Toesny's gloomy voice in the night. There were frequent hostilities after this along the borders, but no more leagues of the French counts; there was a castle of Breteuil built to stand guard against the king's castle of Tillières, and William Fitz-Osbern was made commander of it; there was an expedition of the Count of Maine, aided by Geoffrey Martel and a somewhat unwilling Breton prince, against the southern castle of Ambrières. But when William hastened to its relief the besiegers took to flight, except the Lord of Maine, who was captured and put into prison until he was willing to acknowledge himself the duke's vassal; and after this there were three years of peace in Normandy.

It had grown to be a most orderly country. William's famous curfew bell was proved to be an efficient police force. Every household's fire was out at eight o'clock in winter, and sunset in summer, and its lights extinguished; every man was in his own dwelling-place then under dire penalty; he was a strict governor, but in the main a just one this son of the lawless Robert. He upheld the rights of the poor landholders and widows, and while he was feared he was respected. It was now that he gave so much thought to the rights of the Church, or the following out of his own dislike, in the dismissal of his Uncle Mauger, the primate of the duchy.

There is still another battle to be recorded in this chapter,—one which for real importance is classed with the two famous days of Val-ès-dunes and Hastings,—the battle fought at Varaville, against the French king and his Angevine ally, who took it into their silly heads to go a-plundering on the duke's domain.

Bayeux and Caen were to be sacked, and all the surrounding country; besides this, the allies were going to march to the sea to show the Bastard that he could not lock them up in their inland country and shake the key in their faces. William watched them as a cat watches a mouse and lets the poor thing play and feast itself in fancied security. He had the patience to let the invaders rob and burn, and spoil the crops; to let them live in his towns, and the French king himself hold a temporary court in a fine new abbey of the Bessin, until everybody thought he was afraid of this mouse, and that all the Normans were cowards; then the quick, fierce paw struck out, and the blow fell. It is a piteous story of war, that battle of Varaville!

There was a ford where the French, laden with their weight of spoils, meant to cross the river Dive into the district of Auge. On the Varaville side the land is marshy; across the river, and at no great distance, there is a range of hills which lie between the bank of the Dive and the rich country of Lisieux. The French had meant to go to Lisieux when they started out on their other enterprise. But William had waited for this moment; part of the army under the king's command had crossed over, and were even beginning to climb the hills. The rear-guard with the great baggage trains were on the other bank, when there was a deplorable surprise. William, with a body of trained troops, had come out from Falaise; he had recruited his army with all the peasants of the district; armed with every rude weapon that could be gathered in such haste, they were only too ready to fall upon the French mercilessly.

The tide was flowing in with disastrous haste, and the Frenchmen had not counted upon this awful foe. Their army was cut in two; the king looked down in misery from the height he had thoughtlessly gained. Now we hear almost for the first time of that deadly shower of Norman arrows, famous enough since in history. Down they came with their sharp talons; the poor French were huddling together at the river's brink; there was no shelter; the bowmen shot at them; the peasants beat them with flails and scythes; into the rushing water they went, and floated away writhing. There was not a man left alive in troop after troop, and there were men enough of the Normans who knew the puzzling, marshy ground to chase and capture those other troopers who tried to run away. Alas for the lilies of France! how they were trailed in the mire of that riverside at Varaville! It was a massacre rather than a battle, and Henry's spirit was humbled. "Heavy-hearted, he never held spear or shield again," says the chronicle. There were no more expeditions against Normandy in his time; he sued for a truce, and paid as the price for it, the castle of Tillières, and so that stronghold came back to its rightful lords again. Within two years he died, being an old man, and we can well believe a disappointed one. Geoffrey Martel died too, that year, the most troublesome of the Bastard's great neighbors. This was 1060; and it was in that year that Harold of England first came over to Normandy—an unlucky visit enough, as time proved. His object was partly to take a look at the political state of Gaul; but if he meant to sound the hearts of the duke's neighbors in regard to him, as some people have thought, he could not have chosen a more unlucky time. If he meant to speak for support in case William proved to be England's enemy in days to come, he was too late; those who would have been most ready to listen were beyond the reach of human intrigues, and their deaths had the effect of favoring William's supremacy, not disputing it.

There is no record of the great earl's meeting the Norman duke at all on this first journey. If we had a better account of it, we might solve many vexed questions. Some scholars think that it was during this visit that Harold was inveigled into taking oath to uphold William's claim to the English crown, but the records nearly all belong to the religious character of the expedition. Harold followed King Cnut's example in going on a pilgrimage to Rome, and brought back various treasures for his abbey of Waltham, the most favored religious house of his earldom. He has suffered much misrepresentation, no doubt, at the hands of the monkish writers, for he neglected their claims in proportion as he favored their secular brethren, for whom the abbey was designed. A monk retired from the world for the benefit of his own soul, but a priest gave his life in teaching and preaching to his fellow-men. We are told that Harold had no prejudice against even a married priest, and this was rank heresy and ecclesiastical treason in the minds of many cloistered brethren.

XIII. HAROLD THE ENGLISHMAN.

"The languid pulse of England starts

And bounds beneath your words of power."

—Whittier.

JUST here we might well stop to consider the true causes and effects of war. Seen in the largest way possible, from this side of life, certain forces of development are enabled to assert themselves only by outgrowing, outnumbering, outfighting their opposers. War is the conflict between ideas that are going to live and ideas that have passed their maturity and are going to die. Men possess themselves of a new truth, a clearer perception of the affairs of humanity; progress itself is made possible with its larger share of freedom for the individual or for nations only by a relentless overthrowing of outgrown opinions. It is only by new combinations of races, new assertions of the old unconquerable forces, that the spiritual kingdom gains or rather shows its power. When men claim that humanity can only move round in a circle, that the world has lost many things, that the experience of humanity is like the succession of the seasons, and that there is reproduction but not progression, it is well to take a closer look, to see how by combination, by stimulus of example, and power of spiritual forces and God's great purposes, this whole world is nearer every year to the highest level any fortunate part of it has ever gained. Wars may appear to delay, but in due time they surely raise whole nations of men to higher levels, whether by preparing for new growths or by mixing the new and old. Generals of battalions and unreckoned camp-followers alike are effects of some great change, not causes of it. And no war was ever fought that was not an evidence that one element in it had outgrown the other and was bound to get itself manifested and better understood. The first effect of war is incidental and temporary; the secondary effect makes a link in the grand chain of the spiritual education and development of the world.

We grow confused in trying to find our way through the intricate tangle of stories about the relation of Harold and William to each other, with their promises and oaths and understanding of each other's position in regard to the throne of England. Of course, William knew that Harold had a hope of succeeding the Confessor. There was nobody so fit for it in some respects as he—nobody who knew and loved England any better, or was more important to her welfare. He had fought for her; he was his father's son, and the eyes of many southern Englishmen would turn toward him if the question of the succession were publicly put in the Witanagemôt. He might have defamers and enviers, but the Earl of the West Saxons was the foremost man in England. He had a right to expect recognition from his countrymen. The kingship was not hereditary, and Eadward had no heirs, if it had been. Eadward trusted him; perhaps he had let fall a hint that he meant to recommend his wise earl as successor, even though it were a repetition of another promise made to William when Harold was a banished man and the house of Godwine serving its term of disgrace and exile.

It appears that Eadward had undergone an intermediate season of distrusting either of these two prominent candidates for succession. But the memory of Eadward Ironside was fondly cherished in England, and his son, Eadward the Outlaw, the lawful heir of the crown, was summoned back to his inheritance from Hungary. There was great rejoicing, and the Atheling's wife and his three beautiful children, a son and two daughters, were for a time great favorites and kindled an instant loyalty all too soon to fade. Alas! that Eadward should have returned from his long banishment to sicken and die in London just as life held out such fair promises; and again the Confessor's mind was troubled by the doubtful future of his kingdom.

On the other hand, if we trust to the Norman records now,—not always unconfirmed by the early English historians,—we must take into account many objections to, as well as admissions of, Harold's claim. Eadward's inclination seems often to swerve toward his Norman cousin, who alone seemed able to govern England properly or to hold her jealous forces well in hand. The great English earls were in fact nearly the same as kings of their provinces. There was much opposition and lack of agreement between them; there was a good deal of animosity along the borders in certain sections, and a deep race prejudice between the Danes of Northumberland and the men of the south. The Danes from oversea were scheming to regain the realm that had belonged to their own great ruler Cnut, and so there was a prospect of civil war or foreign invasion which needed a strong hand. Harold's desire to make himself king was not in accordance with the English customs. He was not of the royal house; he was only one of the English earls, and held on certain grounds no better right to pre-eminence than they. Leofric and Siward would have looked upon him as an undeserving interloper, who had no right to rule over them. "The grandsons of Leofric, who ruled half England," says one historian, "would scarcely submit to the dominion of an equal. . . . No individual who was not of an ancient royal house had ever been able to maintain himself upon an Anglo-Saxon throne."

Before we yield too much to our natural sentiment over the story of this unfortunate "last of the Saxon kings," it is well to remember the bad and hindering result to England if Harold had conquered instead of fallen on the battle-field of Hastings. The weakness of England was in her lack of unity and her existing system of local government.

There are two or three plausible stories about Harold's purpose in going to Normandy. It is sometimes impossible in tracing this portion of history through both English and Norman chronicles to find even the same incidents mentioned. Each historian has such a different proof and end in view, and it is only by the closest study, and a good deal of guesswork beside, that a reasonable account of Harold's second visit, and the effects of it, can be made out. We may listen for a moment to the story of his being sent by Eadward to announce that the English crown was to be given to the Norman duke by Eadward's own recommendation to the council, or we may puzzle our way through an improbable tale that Godwine's son, Wolfnoth, and grandson, Hakon, were still held by William as hostages between Eadward and Godwine, though Godwine's family had long since been formally reinstated and re-endowed. Harold is supposed to have gone over to demand their release, though Eadward mournfully warned him of danger and treachery.

The most probable explanation is that Harold was bound on a pleasure excursion with some of his family either to Flanders or some part of his own country, and was shipwrecked and cast ashore on the coast of Ponthieu. All accounts agree about this, though they differ so much about the port he meant to make and his secret purpose.

In those days wrecking was a sadly common practice, and the more illustrious a rescued man might be, the larger ransom was demanded. When we reflect that much of the brutal and lawless custom of wrecking survived almost if not quite to our own time in England, we cannot expect much from the leniency of the Count of Ponthieu's subjects, or indeed much clemency from that petty sovereign himself. Harold was thrown into prison and suffered many things there before the Duke of Normandy could receive his message and come to his relief.

We might imagine for ourselves now a fine historical picture of William the Conqueror seated in his palace at Rouen, busy with affairs of church and state. He has grown stouter, and his face shows marks of thought and care which were not all there when he went to England. His hair is worn thin by his helmet, and the frank, courteous look of his youth has given place to sternness and insistance, though his smile is ready to be summoned when occasion demands. He is a man who could still be mild with the gentle, and pleasantry was a weapon and tool if it were not an unconscious habit. Greater in state and less in soul, says one historian, who writes of him from an English standpoint at this hour in his career. A Norman gentleman lived delicately in those days; he was a worthy successor of a Roman gentleman in the luxurious days of the empire, but not yet enfeebled and belittled by ease and extravagance—though we do listen with amusement to a rumor that the elegant successors of Rolf the Ganger were very dependent upon warm baths, and a good sousing with cold water was a much dreaded punishment and penance. The reign of the valet had become better assured than the reign (in England) of the offspring of Woden and the house of Cerdic.

But we forget to watch the great Duke of the Normans as he sits in his royal chamber and listens to a messenger from the prisoned Earl of the West Saxons. It is a moment of tremendous significance, for by the assistance of winds and waves Harold has fallen into his power. He must tread carefully now and use his best cleverness of strategy and treacherous artifice. How the bystanders must have watched his face, and listened with eager expectation for his answer. The messenger pleads Harold's grievous condition; hints of famine, torture, and death itself have been known to escape this brutal Count of Ponthieu who keeps the great Englishman in his dungeon as if he were a robber. Perhaps he only wishes to gain a greater ransom, perhaps he acts in traitorous defiance of his Lord of Normandy's known friendship for England.

William replies at last with stern courtesy. He is deeply grieved, we can hear him say, for the earl's misfortune, but he can only deal in the matter as prince with prince. It is true that Guy of Ponthieu is his vassal and man, but Guy is governor of his coast, and makes his own laws. It will cost great treasure to ransom this noble captive, but the matter must be carefully arranged, for Guy is hot-tempered and might easily be provoked into sending Harold's head to Rouen without his body. Yet half the Norman duchy shall be spent if need be for such a cause as the English earl's release.

Fitz-Osbern, the duke's seneschal and Malet de Graville, and the noble attendants of the palace murmur a pleased assent as the half-satisfied messenger is kindly dismissed. They detect an intrigue worthy of the best Norman ability, and know by William's face that he has unexpectedly gained a welcome control over events.

The liberation of Harold was effected after much manœuvring, necessary or feigned, and when he appeared before William it was as a grateful man who was in debt not only for his release from danger and discomfort, but for a great sum of money and a tract of valuable landed property.

It is impossible not to suspect that Guy of Ponthieu and William were in league with each other, and when the ransom was paid, the wrecker-count became very amiable, and even insisted upon riding with a gay company of knights to the place where the Norman duke came with a splendid retinue to meet his distinguished guest. William laid aside the cumbrous forms of court etiquette and hurried to the gates of the Chateau d'Eu to help Harold to dismount, and greeted him with cordial affection, as friend with friend. Harold may well have been dazzled by his reception at the most powerful court in that part of the world. To have a welcome that befitted a king may well have pleased him into at least a temporary acknowledgment of his entertainer's majestic power and rights. No doubt, during that unlucky visit it seemed dignity enough to be paraded everywhere as the great duke's chosen companion and honored friend and guest. At any rate, Harold's visit seems to have given occupation to the court, and we catch many interesting glimpses of the stately Norman life, as well as the humble, almost brutal, condition of the lower classes, awed into quietness and acquiescence by the sternness and exactness of William's rule. It must be acknowledged that if the laws were severe they prevented much disorder that had smouldered in other times in the lower strata of society; men had less power and opportunity to harm each other or to enfeeble the state.

No greater piece of good luck could have befallen the duke than to win the post of Harold's benefactor, and he played the part gallantly. Not only the duke but the duchess treated their guest with uncommon courtesy, and he was admitted to the closest intimacy with the household. If Harold had been wise he would have gone back to England as fast as sails could carry him, but instead of that he lingered on, equally ready to applaud the Norman exploits in camp and court, and to show his entertainers what English valor could achieve. He went with the duke on some petty expedition against the rebellious Britons, but it is hard to make out a straight story of that enterprise. But there is a characteristic story of Harold's strength in the form of a tradition that when the Norman army was crossing the deep river Coesnon, which pours into the sea under the wall of Mount St. Michel, some of the troops were being swept away by the waves, when Harold rescued them, taking them with great ease, at arm's length, out of the water.

There is a sober announcement in one of the old chronicles, that the lands of Brittany were included in Charles the Simple's grant to Rolf, because Rolf had so devastated Normandy that there was little there to live upon. At the time of William's expedition, Brittany itself was evidently taking its turn at such vigorous shearing and pruning of the life of its fertile hills and valleys. The Bretons liked nothing so well as warfare, and when they did not unite against a foreign enemy, they spent their time in plundering and slaughtering one another. Count Conan, the present aggressor, was the son of Alan of Brittany, William's guardian. Some of the Bretons were loyal to the Norman authority, and Dôl, an ancient city renowned for its ill luck, and Dinan were successively vacated by the rebels. Dinan was besieged by fire, a favorite weapon in the hands of the Normans; but later we find that both the cities remained Breton, and the Norman allies go back to their own country. There is a hint somewhere of the appearance of an army from Anjou, to take the Bretons' part, but the Norman chroniclers ignore it as far as they can.

It is impossible to fix the date of this campaign; indeed there may have been more than one expedition against Brittany. Still more difficult is it to learn any thing that is undisputed about the famous oath that Harold gave to William, and was afterward so completely punished for breaking. Yet, while we do not know exactly what the oath was, Harold's most steadfast upholders have never been able to deny that there was an oath, and there is no contradiction, on the English side, of the whole affair. His best friends have been silent about it. The most familiar account is this, if we listen to the Norman stories: Harold entered into an engagement to marry one of William's daughters, who must have been very young at the time of the visit or visits to Normandy, and some writers claim that the whole cause of the quarrel lay in his refusal to keep his promise. There is a list beside of what appears to us unlikely concessions on the part of the English earl. Harold did homage to the duke, and formally became his man, and even promised to acknowledge his claim to the throne of England at the death of the Confessor. More than this, he promised to look after William's interest in England, and to put him at once into possession of the Castle of Dover, with the right of establishing a Norman garrison there. William, in return, agreed to hold his new vassal in highest honor, giving him by and by even the half of his prospective kingdom. When this surprising oath was taken, Harold was entrapped into swearing upon the holiest relic of Norman saints which had been concealed in a chest for the express purpose. With the superstitious awe that men of his time felt toward such emblems, this not very respectable act on William's part is made to reflect darkly upon Harold. Master Wace says that "his hand trembled and his flesh quivered when he touched the chest, though he did not know what was in it, and how much more distressed he was when he found by what an awful vow he had unwittingly bound his soul."

So Harold returned to England the duke's vassal and future son-in-law, according to the chronicles, but who can help being suspicious, after knowing how Harold was indebted to the duke and bound with cunningly contrived chains until he found himself a prisoner? William of Poitiers, a chronicler who wrote in the Conqueror's day, says that Harold was a man to whom imprisonment was more odious than shipwreck. It would be no wonder if he had made use of a piece of strategy, and was willing to make any sort of promise simply to gain his liberty.

The plot of the relic-business put a different face upon the whole matter, and yet, even if Harold was dazzled for the time being by William's power and splendor, one must doubt whether he would have given up all his ambition of reigning in England. He was already too great a man at home to play the subject and flatterer with much sincerity, even though his master were the high and mighty Duke of the Normans, and he had come from a ruder country to the fascination and elegance of the Norman court. Whatever the oath may have been that Harold gave at Bayeux, it is certain that he broke it afterward, and that his enemies made his failure not only an affair of state, but of church, and waged a bitter war that brought him to his sad end.

Now, the Norman knights might well look to it that their armor was strong and the Norman soldiers provide themselves with arrows and well-seasoned bows. It was likely that Harold's promise was no secret, and that some echo of it reached from one end of the dukedom to the other. There were great enterprises on foot, and at night in the firelight there was eager discussion of possible campaigns, for though the great Duke William, their soldier of soldiers, had bent the strength of his resistless force upon a new kingdom across the Channel and had won himself such a valuable ally, it was not likely that England would be ready to fall into his hand like a ripe apple from the bough. There was sure to be fighting, but there was something worth fighting for; the petty sorties against the provincial neighbors of Normandy were hardly worth the notice of her army. Men like the duke's soldiers were fit for something better than such police duty. Besides, a deep provocation had not been forgiven by those gentlemen who were hustled out of England by Godwine and his party, and many an old score would now stand a chance of repayment.

Not many months were passed before the news came from London that the holy king Eadward was soon to leave this world for a better. He was already renowned as a worker of miracles and a seer of visions, and the story was whispered reverently that he had given his ring to a beggar who appeared before him to ask alms in the middle of a crowd assembled at the dedication of a church. The beggar disappeared, but that very night some English pilgrims on their way to Jerusalem are shelterless and in danger near the holy city. Suddenly a company of shining acolytes approach through the wilderness, carrying two tapers before an old man, as if he were out on some errand of the church. He stops to ask the wondering pilgrims whence they come and whither they are going, and guides them to a city and a comfortable lodging, and next morning tells them that he is Saint John the Evangelist. More than this, he gives them the Confessor's ring, with a message to carry back to England. Within six months Eadward will be admitted to paradise as a reward for his pure and pious life. The message is carried to the king by miraculous agency that same night, and ever since he prays and fasts more than ever, and is hurrying the builders of his great Westminster, so that he may see that holy monument of his piety dedicated to the service of God before he dies.

The Norman lords and gentlemen who listened to this tale must have crossed themselves, one fancies, and craved a blessing on the saintly king, but the next minute we fancy also that they gave one another a glance that betokened a lively expectation of what might follow the news of Eadward's translation.

Twice in the year, at Easter and Christmas, the English king wore his crown in the great Witanagemôt and held court among his noblemen. In this year the midwinter Gemôt was held at the king's court at Westminster, instead of at Gloucester, to hallow the Church of St. Peter, the new shrine to which so much more of the Confessor's thought had gone than to the ruling of his kingdom.

But in the triumphant days to which he had long looked forward, his strength failed faster and faster, and his queen, Edith, the daughter of Godwine, had to take his place at the ceremonies. The histories of that day are filled with accounts of the grand building that Eadward's piety had reared. He had given a tenth part of all his income to it for many years, and with a proud remembrance of the Norman churches with which he was familiar in his early days, had made Westminster a noble rival of them and the finest church in England. The new year was hardly begun, the Witan had not scattered to their homes, before Eadward the Confessor was carried to his tomb—the last of the sons of

Woden. He had reigned for three and twenty years, and was already a worn old man.

> "Now, in the falling autumn, while the winds
> Of winter blew across his scanty days
> He gathered up life's embers——"

But as he lay dying in the royal palace at Westminster everybody was less anxious about the king, than about the country's uncertain future. Harold had been a sort of under-king for several years, and had taken upon himself many of the practical duties of government. He had done great deeds against the Welsh, and was a better general and war-man than Eadward had ever been. Nobody had any hope of the Confessor's recovery, and any hour might find the nation kingless. The Atheling's young son was a feeble, incompetent person, and wholly a foreigner; only the most romantic and senseless citizen could dream of making him Lord of England in such a time as that. There were a thousand rumors afloat; every man had his theory and his prejudice, and at last there must have been a general feeling of relief when the news was told that the saint-king was dead in his palace and had named Harold as his successor. The people clung eagerly to such a nomination; now that Eadward was dead he was saint indeed, and there was a funeral and a coronation that same day in the minster on the Isle of Thorney; his last word to the people was made law.

No more whispering that Harold was the Duke of the Normans' man, and might betray England again into the hands of those greedy favorites whom the holy king had cherished in his bosom like serpents. No more fears of Harold's jealous enemies among the earls; there was a short-sighted joy that the great step of the succession had been made and settled fast in the consent of the Witan, who still lingered; to be dispersed, when these famous days were at an end, by another king of England than he who had called them together.

The king had prophesied in his last hours; he had seen visions and dreamed dreams; he had said that great sorrows were to fall upon England for her sins, and that her earls and bishops and abbots were but ministers of the fiend in the eye of God; that within a year and a day the whole land would be harried from one end to another with fire and slaughter. Yet, almost with the same breath, he recommends his Norman friends, "those whom in his simplicity he spoke of as men who had left their native land for love of him," to Harold's care, and does not seem to suspect their remotest agency in the future harrying. True enough some of the Norman officers were loyal to him and to England. This death-bed scene is sad and solemn. Norman Robert the Staller was there, and Stigand, the illegal archbishop; Harold, the hope of England, and his sister, the queen, who mourns now and is very tender to her royal husband, who has given her a sorry lot with his cold-heartedness toward her and the dismal exile and estrangement he has made her suffer. He loves her and trusts her now in this last day of life, and her woman's heart forgets the days that were dark between them. He even commends her to Harold's care, and directs that she must not lose the honors which have been hers as queen.

There is a tradition that when Eadward lay dying he said that he was passing from the land of the dead to the land of the living, and the chronicle adds: "Saint Peter, his friend, opened to him the gates of Paradise, and Saint John, his own dear one, led him before the Divine Majesty." The walls that Eadward built are replaced by others; there is not much of his abbey left now but some of the foundation and an archway or two. But his tomb stands in a sacred spot, and the prayers and hymns he loved so devoutly are said and sung yet in his own Westminster, the burying-place of many another king since the Confessor's time.

XIV. NEWS FROM ENGLAND.

"Great men have reaching hands."

—SHAKESPEARE.

So Harold was crowned king of England. Our business is chiefly with what the Normans thought about that event, and while London is divided between praises of the old king and hopes of the new one, and there are fears of what may follow from Earl Tostig's enmity; while the Witan are dispersing to their homes, and the exciting news travels faster than they do the length and breadth of the country, we must leave it all and imagine ourselves in Normandy.

Duke William was at his park of Quevilly, near Rouen, and was on his way to the chase. He had been bending his bow—the famous bow that was too strong for other men's hands—and just as he gave it to the page who waited to carry it after him, a man-at-arms came straight to his side; they went apart together to speak secretly, while the bystanders watched them curiously and whispered that the eager messenger was an Englishman.

"Eadward the king is dead," the duke was told, but that not unexpected news was only half the message. "Earl Harold is raised to the kingdom."

There came an angry look into the duke's eyes, and the herald left him. William forgot his plans for the hunt; he strode by his retainers; he tied and untied his mantle absent-mindedly, and presently went down to the bank of the Seine again and crossed over in a boat to his castle hall. He entered silently, and nobody dared ask what misfortune had befallen him. His companions followed him and found him sitting on a bench, moving restlessly to and fro. Then he became quieter; he leaned his head against the great stone pillar and covered his face with his mantle. Long before, in the old Norse halls, where all the vikings lived together, if a man were sick or sorry or wished for any reason to be undisturbed, he sat on his own bench and covered his head with his cloak; there was no room where he could be alone; and after the old custom, in these later days, the knights of William's court left him to his thoughts. Then William Fitz-Osbern, the "bold-hearted," came into the quiet hall humming a tune. The awe-struck people who were clustered there asked him what was the matter; then the duke looked up.

"It is in vain for you to try to hide the news," said the Seneschal. "It is blazing through the streets of Rouen. The Confessor is dead, and Harold holds the English kingdom."

The duke answered gravely that he sorrowed both for the death of Eadward and for the faithlessness of Harold.

"Arise and be doing," urges Fitz-Osbern. "There is no need for mourning. Cross the sea and snatch the kingdom out of the usurper's hand," and in this way stern thought and dire purpose were thrown into the duke's holiday. The messenger had brought a lighted torch in his hand that was equal to kindling great plans that winter day in Normandy.

William and all his men, from the least soldier to the greatest, knew that if they wished for England the only way to get it was to fight for it. There had never been such a proof of their mettle as this would be. The Normans who went to Italy had no such opponents as Harold and the rest of the Englishmen fighting on their own ground for their homes and their honor; but Norman courage shone brightest in these days. This is one of the places where we must least of all follow the duke's personal fortunes too closely, or forget that the best of the Normans were looking eagerly forward to the possession of new territory. Many of their cleverest men, too, were more than ready to punish the English for ejecting them from comfortable positions under Godwine's rule, and were anxious to reinstate themselves securely. There was no such perilous journey before the army as the followers of the Hautevilles had known, while their amazing stories of gain and glory incited the Normans at home to win themselves new fortunes. It is a proof that civilization and the arts of diplomacy were advancing, when we listen (and the adventurers listened too) while excuse after excuse was tendered for the great expedition. The news of Harold's accession was simply a welcome signal for action, but the heir of Rolf the Ganger was a politician, an astute wielder of public opinion, and his state-craft was now directed toward giving his desire to conquer England and reign over it a proper aspect in the eyes of other nations.

The right of heritage was fast displacing everywhere the people's right to choose their kings. The feudal system was close and strong in its links, but while Harold had broken his oath of homage to William, that alone was not sufficient crime. Such obligations were not always unbreakable, and were too much a matter of formality and temporary expediency to warrant such an appeal to the common law of nations as William meant to make. As nearly as we can get at the truth of the matter, the chief argument against Harold the Usurper was on religious grounds—on William's real or assumed promise of the succession from Eadward, and Harold's vow upon the holy relics of the saints at Rouen. This at least was most criminal blasphemy. The Normans gloried in their own allegiance to the church. Their duke was blameless in private life and a sworn defender and upholder of the faith, and by this means a most formidable ally was easily won, in the character of Lanfranc the great archbishop.

Lanfranc and William governed Normandy hand in hand. In tracing the history of this time the priest seems as familiar with secular affairs, with the course of the state and the army and foreign relations, as the duke was diligent in attending ecclesiastical synods and church services. It was a time of great rivalry and uncertainty for the papal crown; there was a pope and an anti-pope just then who were violent antagonists, but Archdeacon Hildebrand was already the guide and authority of the Holy See. Later he became the Pope famous in history as Gregory VII. We are startled to find that the expedition against England was made to take the shape of a crusade, even though England was building her own churches, and sending pilgrims to the Holy Land, and pouring wealth most generously into the church's coffers. "Priests and prelates were subject to the law like other men," that was the trouble; and "a land where the king and his Witan gave and took away the staff of the bishop was a land which, in the eyes of Rome, was more dangerous than a land of Jews or Saracens." "It was a policy worthy of William to send to the threshold of the apostles to crave their blessing on his intended work of reducing the rebellious land, and it was a policy worthy of one greater than William himself, to make even William, for once in his life, the instrument of purposes yet more daring, yet more far-sighted, than his own. On the steps of the papal chair, and there alone, had William and Lanfranc to cope with an intellect loftier and more subtle than even theirs."

William sent an embassy to Harold probably very soon after the receipt of the news of his coronation. The full account of both the demand and its reply have been forgotten, but it is certain that whatever the duke's commands were they were promptly disobeyed, and certain too that this was the result that William expected and even desired. He could add another grievance to his list of Harold's wrongdoings, and now, beside the original disloyalty, William could complain that his vassal had formally refused to keep his formal promise and obligation. Then he called a council of Norman nobles at Lillebonne and laid his plans before them.

It was a famous company of counsellors and made up of the duke's oldest friends. There were William Fitz-Osbern, and the duke's brother Odo of Bayeux, whose priesthood was no hindrance to his good soldiery; Richard of Evreux, the grandson of Richard the Fearless; Roger of Beaumont and the three heroes of Mortemer; Walter Giffard; Hugh de Montfort and William of Warren; the Count of Mortain and Roger Montgomery and Count Robert of Eu. All these names we know, and familiar as they were in Normandy, they were, most of them, to strike deeper root in their new domain of England. We do not find that they objected now to William's plans, but urged only that they had no right to speak for the whole country, and that all the Norman barons ought to be called together to speak for themselves.

This was a return to the fashions of Rolf's day, when the adventurers boasted on the banks of the Seine that they had no king to rule over them, and were all equal; that they only asked for what they could win with their swords. We do not find any other record of a parliament in Normandy; perhaps nothing had ever happened of late which so closely concerned every armed man within the Norman borders. The feudal barons had a right to speak now for themselves and their dependants, and in the great ducal hall of the castle at Lillebonne William duke told them his story and called upon them for help. He had a great wish to revenge Harold's treatment of him by force of arms, and asked the noble company of barons what aid they would render; with how many men and how many ships and with what a sum of money they would follow him and uphold the weighty and difficult enterprise.

Now we find many of the barons almost unwilling; even doubtful of the possibility of conquering such a kingdom as England. After insisting that they had longed to go plundering across the Channel, and that the old love for fighting burned with as hot a fire as ever within their breasts, the chronicles say that this Norman parliament asked for time to talk things over in secret before the duke should have any answer. We are given a picture of them grouped around this and that pleader for or against the duke, and are told that they demurred, that they objected to crossing the sea to wage war, and that they feared the English. For a moment it appears as if the whole mind of the assembly were opposed to the undertaking. They even feared if they promised unusual supplies of men and treasure that William would forever keep them up to such a difficult standard of generosity. I must say that all this does not ring true or match at all with the Norman character of that time. It would not be strange if there were objectors among them, but it does not seem possible when they were so ready to go adventuring before and after this time; when they were after all separated by so short a time from Rolf the Ganger's piracies, that many could have been so seriously daunted by the prospect of such limited seafaring as crossing the Channel. It appears like an ingenious method of magnifying the greatness and splendor of the Norman victory, and the valiant leadership of the duke and his most trusted aids.

William Fitz-Osbern was chosen to plead with the barons, and persuade them to follow the duke's banner. He reminded them that they were William's vassals, and that it would be unwise to disappoint him. William was a stern man and fearful as an enemy. If any among them loved their ease, and wished to avoid their lawful tribute of service, let them reflect that they were in the power of such a mighty lord and master. What was their money worth to them if the duke branded them as faithless cowards, and why did they wish to disgrace their names and take no part in this just and holy war against the usurper?

These were the arguments we can fancy brave Fitz-Osbern giving them one by one if indeed they hung back and were close-fisted or afraid. They commissioned him at last to speak for them at the next hearing, and when he boldly promised for each man double his regular fee and allotment—for the lord of twenty knights forty knights, and "for himself, of his love and zeal, sixty ships armed and equipped and filled with fighting men," the barons shouted at first "No, no!" and the hall at Lillebonne echoed with the noise.

But it was all settled finally, and we are told that the duke himself talked with his barons one by one, and that at last they were as eager as he. The whole objection seems to have been made for fear that their doubled and extraordinary tribute should be made a precedent, but the duke promptly gave his word of honor that it should not be so, and their estates should not be permanently weighted beyond their ability. The scribes took down the record of the knights and soldiers that each baron had promised, and from this time there was a hum and stir of war-making in Normandy, and that spring there were more women than men in the fields tending the growing crops.

The duke set himself seriously to work. All the barons of his duchy and all their men were not enough to depend upon for the overthrowing of England. William must appeal to his neighbors for help, and in this he was aided by the Pope's approval, and the blessing that was promised to those who would punish Harold and his countrymen, traitors to the Holy Church. The spoils of England were promised to all who would win a share in them, and adventurers flocked from east, north, and south to enroll themselves in the Norman ranks. Alan of Brittany was ready to command his forces in person and to come to William's assistance, and so was Eustace of Boulogne, but the French nobles who gathered about their young King Philip, still under Baldwin of Flanders's guardianship, were by no means willing to help forward any thing that would make their Norman rivals any more powerful than they were already. From Flanders there were plenty of adventurers, and some high noblemen who needed little urging to join their fortunes to such an expedition, and William sent embassies to more distant countries still, with better or worse results. There is a tradition that even the Normans of Sicily came northward in great numbers.

The most important thing, next to carrying a sufficient force into England, was to leave the Norman borders secure from invasion. If they were repulsed in England and returned to find they had lost part of Normandy, that would be a sorry fate indeed, and the duke exerted himself in every way to leave his territory secure.

The most powerful alliance was that with the papal court at Rome. Here Lanfranc could serve his adopted country to good effect. Hildebrand's power was making itself felt more and more, and it was he who most ardently desired and fostered the claim of the Church to a mastery of all the crowns of Christendom. "The decree went forth, which declared Harold to be a usurper and William to be the lawful claimant of the English crown. It would even seem that it declared the English king and all his followers to be cut off from the communion of the faithful. William was sent forth as an avenger to chastise the wrong and perjury of his faithless vassal. But he was also sent forth as a missionary, to guide the erring English into the true path, to teach them due obedience to Christ's vicar, and to secure a more punctual payment of the temporal dues of his apostle. The cause of the invasion was blessed, and precious gifts were sent as the visible exponents of the blessing. A costly ring was sent, containing a relic, holier, it may be, than any on which Harold had sworn—a hair of the prince of the apostles. And with the ring came a consecrated banner." These were, after all, more formidable weapons than the Norman arrows. They inspired not only courage, but a sense of duty and of righteous service of God. Alas for poor humanity that lends itself so readily to wrongdoing, and even hopes to win heaven by making this earth a place of bloodshed and treachery. Now, William had something besides English lands and high places for knight and priest alike on conquered soil—he could give security and eminence in the world to come. Heaven itself had been premised by its chief representative on earth to those who would fight for the Duke of Normandy against England. Hildebrand had made a last appeal to the holy assembly of cardinals when he told the story of the profaned relics and Harold's broken oath, and had urged the willing fathers of the church to consider how pious and benevolent it would be to Christianize the barbarous and heathen Saxons. Nobody took pains to remember that the priesthood of England owned a third of the English lands, and ruled them with a rod of iron. So long as England would not bend the knee to Rome, what did all that matter?

One significant thing happened at this time. Who should make his appearance at the duke's court but Tostig, the son of Godwine, eager, no doubt, to plot against Harold, and to take a sufficient revenge for the banishment and defeat by means of which he was then an outcast. He did not linger long, for the busy duke sent him quickly away, not uncommissioned for the war that was almost ready to begin.

Harold also had set himself at work to gather his forces and to be in readiness for an attack which was sure to come. Another enemy was first in the field, for in the spring Tostig appeared in the Isle of Wight, the captain of a fleet of ships that were manned by Flemish and Norman men. He had received aid from William, and proceeded to wreak his vengeance upon the Kent and Sussex villages over which his father had once ruled. He does not appear to have gained any English allies, except at the seaport of Sandwich, where he probably hired some sailors; then he went northward from there with sixty ships and attacked the coast of Godwine's earldom. He made great havoc in the shore towns, but Eadwine and Morkere of Northumberland hurried to meet him with their troops and drove him away, so that with only twelve ships left he went to Scotland, where Malcolm, the Scottish king received him with a hearty welcome, and entertained him politely the rest of the summer. They had lately been sworn enemies, but now that Tostig was fighting against England, Malcolm put aside all bygone prejudice.

In the summer of that eventful year, Tostig first proposed to the king of Denmark that he should come to England and help him to recover his earldom. Swegen had the good sense to refuse, and then the outlaw went on to Norway to make further proposals to Harold Hardrada, who also listened incredulously, but when Tostig suggested that Harold should be king of England, and that he would only ask to be under-king of the northern territory, that he would do homage to Harold and serve him loyally, the great Norwegian chieftain consented to make ready for an expedition. He seems to have been much like Rolf the Ganger, and a true, valiant viking at heart. The old saga whence the story comes makes us forget the plottings and claims of Rome and the glories of Norman court life; the accounts of Harold Hardrada's expedition are like a breath of cold wind from the Northern shores, and the sight of a shining dragon-ship stealing away between the high shores of a fiord, outward-bound for a bout of plundering. But the saga records also the fame and prowess of that other Harold, the son of Godwine, and magnifies the power of such an enemy.

Perhaps the English king trusted at first in the ability of the northern earls to take care of their own territory, and only tried to stand guard over the southern coast.

He gathered an army and kept it together all the latter part of the summer, a most unprecedented and difficult thing in those days; and with help from the local forces, or what we should call the militia, his soldiers kept guard along the shores of Sussex and Kent. We cannot estimate what a troublesome step forward in the art of warfare this was for Englishmen, who were used to quick forced marches and decisive battles, and a welcome dispersion after the cessation of whatever exciting cause or sudden summons had gathered them.

Harold's ships patrolled the Channel and the foot-soldiers paced the downs, but food, always hard to obtain, became at last impossible, and in September the army broke ranks. Harold himself went back to London, whither the fleet was also sent, but on the way it met with disaster, and many of the ships were lost and many more began to leak and were reluctantly judged unseaworthy. The whole southern coast was left undefended; it was neither the king's fault nor the subjects' fault. Both had done their best, but the crops must be gathered then or not at all, and at any rate, the army was weakened by famine and a growing belief in the uncertainty of attack.

Alas for Harold's peace of mind! In those very days William the Norman's host was clustering and gathering like bees just ready to swarm, on the coast of Normandy, and from the mouth of the Bergen fiord came Harold Hardrada with a great company, with a huge mass of treasure, such as had not for years and years floated away from a Northern haven. It seems as if he had determined to migrate, to crush the English usurper, and then to establish himself as Cnut had done in the richer southern kingdom. There must have been some knowledge in Norway of the state of things in England and Normandy, but this famous old adventurer was ready to fight whoever he met, and the Black Raven was flying at his masthead. Bad omens cast their shadows over this great expedition of the last of the sea-kings, but away he sailed to the Shetland Islands and left his wife and daughters there, while he gained new allies; and still farther south, Tostig came to meet him with a new army which he had gathered in Flanders. An Irish chieftain and a great lord from Iceland were there too, and down they all came upon the defenceless country that was marked as their prey, burning and destroying church and castle and humble homestead, daring the Englishmen to come out and fight and drive them away again. We have no time to trace their lawless campaign. The two northern earls summoned their vassals, but in a few days after the Northmen had landed they had taken, without much trouble it appears to us, the city of York, and news was hurriedly sent to the king of England.

What a grievous message! Harold, the son of Godwine, was ill, his southern coast was undefended, still he could not forget the message that William had sent to him late in the summer by a spy who had crossed to Normandy, that the Normans would soon come and teach him how many they were and what they could do. But a holy abbot consoled the king by telling him that Eadward the Confessor had shown himself in a vision and assured his successor of certain victory.

The prophecy was proved to be true; the king summoned his strength and his soldiers and marched to York. There King Harold was to set up his new kingdom; he had not the desire for revenge that filled Tostig's breast, and was anxious to prove himself a generous and wise ruler. As he came toward the walls which had been so easily won, the rival Harold's army comes in sight first a great cloud of dust like a whirlwind, and next the shining spears prick through and glitter ominously. A little later Harold of England sends a message to his brother Tostig. He shall have again his kingdom of Northumberland if he will be loyal; and Tostig sends back a message in his turn to ask what shall be the portion of Harold Hardrada. "Seven feet of English ground for his grave," says the other Harold, and the fight begins.

Alas for the tall Northman, the winner of eighty castles from the Saracens, the scourge of Moslem and robber in Palestine; the ally of Sicily, of Russia, and the Greeks! Alas for the kingdom he had lightly lost in Norway! Alas for the wife and daughters who were watching all through those shortening September days in the Orkneys for the triumphant return of the fleet—for Harold the sagaman and sea-king, who built his hopes too high. He may be fierce with the old rage of the Berserkers, and lay sturdily about him with his heavy two-handed sword; he may mow down great swaths of Englishmen like grain, but the moment comes when an arrow flies with its sharp whistle straight at his throat, and he falls dead, and his best fighters fall in heaps above him; the flag of the Black Raven of Norway is taken. Tostig is dead, and Harold of England is winner of that great day at Stamford Bridge, the last great victory that he and his men would ever win, the last fight of England before the Conquest. Out of the crowd of ships that had come from the North only four and twenty sailed away again, and Harold made peace with the Orkney-men and the Icelanders and the rest. Since that day there has been peace between England and the countries of the Northern Seas. Harold's last victory was with the past, one might say, with the Northmen of another age and time, as if the last tie of his country were broken with the old warfare and earlier enemies. New relationships were established, the final struggle for mastery was decided. The battle of Stamford Bridge might have been called a deadly game at jousting, and the English knight receives the prize and rides home the victor of the tournament. Yet that very day of triumph saw the approach of a new foe—the Norman ships full of horses and men are ready to put out for the English shore. Harold must fight another battle and lose it, and a new order of things must begin in Britain. The Northmen and the Normans; it is a long step between the two, and yet England's past and her future meet; the swordsmen's arms that ache from one battle must try their strength again in another; but the Normans bring great gifts at the point of their arrows—without them "England would have been mechanical, not artistic; brave, not chivalrous; the home of learning, not of thought."

Three days after the fight Harold sits at a splendid banquet among his friends, and a breathless messenger comes in fleet-footed with bad news. Muster your axemen and lances, Harold, King of the English; the Normans have come like a flight of locusts and are landing on the coast of Kent.

XV. THE BATTLE OF HASTINGS.

"I see thy glory, like a shooting star,

Fall to the base earth from the firmament!

Thy sun sets weeping in the lowly west."

—Shakespeare.

EARLY in the summer there was a sound of wood-chopping and a crash of falling trees in the forests of Normandy, and along her shores in the shipyards the noise of shipwrights' mallets began, and the forging of bolts and chains. The hemp-fields enlarge their borders, and catch the eye quickly with their brilliant green leafage. There is no better trade now than that of the armorer's, and many a Norman knight sees to it that the links of his chain-mail jerkin and helmet are strongly sewn, and that he is likely to be well defended by the clanking habit that he must buckle on. Horses and men are drilling in the castle yards, and every baron gathers his troop, and is stern in his orders and authority. The churches are crowded, the priests are urging the holy cause, and war is in everybody's mind. The cherry blossoms whiten and fall, the apple-trees are covered with rosy snow, mid-summer sees the young fruit greaten on the boughs, the sun rides high in the sky, and the soldiers' mail weighs heavy; through the country-lanes go troops of footmen and horsemen. You can see the tips of their unstrung bows moving above the hedges, and their furled banners with heraldic device or pious seal. They are all going toward the sea, toward the mouth of the river Dive. The peasant women and children stand in their cottage doors and watch the straggling processions on their way. It is indeed a cause to aid with one's prayers, this war against the heathen English.

All summer long, armed men were collecting at William's headquarters from every part of Normandy, or wherever his summons had wakened a favorable response. If we can believe the chroniclers, the army was well paid and well fed and kept in good order. It became a question which army would hold its ground longest; Harold's, on the

Sussex downs, or William's, by the Dive. At last, news was brought that the Englishmen were disbanded, then the Frenchmen—as we begin to hear our Normans called,—the Frenchmen begin to make ready for their expedition. There may have been skirmishes by sea in the hot weather, but it was not until early autumn that William gave orders to embark. There are different stories about the magnitude of the force. The defeated party would have us believe that they were enormously overpowered, and so set the numbers very high; the conquerors, on the other hand, insist that they had not quantity so much as quality to serve them in the fight, and that it was not the size of their army but the valor of it that won the day. We are told that there were six hundred and ninety-six ships and fourteen thousand men; we are told also that there were more than three thousand ships and sixty thousand men, all told; and other accounts range between these two extremes.

For a month the Norman army waited at the mouth of the Dive for a south wind, but no south wind blew, while an adverse storm scattered them and strewed the shore with Norman bodies. At last, the duke took advantage of a westerly breeze and set sail for St. Valery, off the coast of Ponthieu, from whence he hoped to go more easily over to England. At the famous abbey of St. Valery he was saying his prayers and watching the weather-cocks for fifteen days, and he and his captains made generous offerings at the holy shrines. The monks came out at last in solemn procession bearing their sacred relics, and the Norman host knelt devoutly and did homage. At Caen, in June, the two great minsters had been dedicated, and William and Matilda had given their young daughter Cecily to the service of God, together with rich offerings of lands and money. In their own churches, therefore, and at many another Norman altar beside, prayer and praise never ceased in those days while Harold was marching to Stamford Bridge.

At last, on Wednesday, the twenty-seventh of September, the wind went round to the southward, and the great fleet sailed. The soldiers believed that their prayers had been answered, and that they were the favorites of heaven. They crowded on board the transport-ships, and were heedless of every thing save that they were not left behind, and had their armor and weapons ready for use. The trumpets were playing, their voices cried loud above the music that echoed back in eager strains from the shore. The horsemen shouted at their horses, and the open ships were plainer copies of the dragonships of old; they carried gayly dressed gentlemen, and shining gonfanons, and thickets of glittering spears. The shields were rich with heraldic blazoning, and the golden ship, Mora, that the Duchess Matilda had given to the duke, shone splendid on the gray water, as just at evening William himself set sail and turned the gilded figure of a boy blowing an ivory trumpet, like some herald of certain victory, toward the shore of Kent. The Pope's sacred banner was given to the welcome breeze, and William's own standard, figured with the three lions of Normandy, fluttered and spread itself wide. The colored sails looked gay, the soldiers sang and cheered, and away they went without a fear, these blessed Normans of the year 1066. On the Mora's masthead blazed a great lantern when the darkness fell. It was a cloudy night.

In the early morning, the Mora being lighter-laden than the rest, found herself alone on the sea, out of sight of either land or ships, but presently the loitering forest of masts rose into view. At nine o'clock William had landed at Pevensey on the Sussex shore. As he set foot for the second time on English soil, he tripped and fell, and the bystanders gave a woful groan at such a disastrous omen. "By the splendor of God," cried the duke, in his favorite oath, "I have taken seizin of my kingdom; see the earth of England in my two hands! "at which ready turn of wit a soldier pulled a handful of thatch from a cottage roof and gave it to his master for a further token of proprietorship. This also was seizin of all that England herself embraced.

There was nobody to hinder the Normans from landing or going where they pleased. At Pevensey they stayed only one day for lack of supplies, and then set out eastward toward Hastings. In the Bayeux tapestry, perhaps the most reliable authority so far as it goes, there is an appealing bit of work that pictures a burning house with a woman and little child making their escape. The only places of safety, we are told elsewhere, were the churchyards and the churches. William's piety could hardly let him destroy even an enemy's sacred places of worship.

The next few days were filled with uncertainty and excited expectancy. Clearly there was no army in the immediate neighborhood of Hastings; the Normans had that part of the world to themselves apparently, and hours and days went by leaving them undisturbed. Many a voice urged that they might march farther into the country, but their wary leader possessed his soul in patience, and at last came the news of the great battle in the north, of Harold's occupation of York, and the terrible disaster that had befallen the multitude of Harold Hardrada and Tostig, with their allies. Now, too, came a message to the duke from Norman Robert the Staller, who had stood by the Confessor's deathbed, and who kept a warm heart for the country of his birth, though he had become a loyal Englishman in his later years. Twenty thousand men have been slain in the north, he sends word to William; the English were mad with pride and rejoicing. The Normans were not strong enough nor many enough to risk a battle; they would be like dogs among wolves, and would be worse than overthrown. But William was scornful of such advice—he had come to fight Harold, and he would meet him face to face—he would risk the battle if he had only a sixth part as many men as followed him, eager as himself for his rights.

Harold had bestirred his feasting and idle army, and held council of his captains at York. Normans and French and the men of Brittany had landed at Pevensey in numbers like the sand of the sea and the stars of heaven. If only the south wind had blown before, so that he might have met these invaders with his valiant army, too soon dispersed! To have beaten back William and then have marched north to Stamford Bridge, that, indeed, would have been a noble record. Now the Normans were burning and destroying unhindered in the south; what should be done? And every captain-baron of the English gave his word that he would call no man king but Harold the son of Godwine; and with little rest from the battle just fought, they made ready to march to London. They knew well enough what this new invasion meant; a prophetic dread filled their hearts, for it was not alone out of loyalty to Harold, but for love of England, that these men of different speech and instincts must be pushed off the soil to which they had no lawful claim.

The fame of the northern victory brought crowds of recruits to the two banners, the Dragon of Wessex and Harold's own standard, the Fighting Man, as they were carried south again. Nothing succeeds like success; if Harold could conquer the great Hardrada, it were surely not impossible to defeat the Norman duke. So the thanes and churchmen alike rallied to the Fighting Man. The earls of the north half promised to follow, but they never kept their word; perhaps complete independence might follow now their half-resented southern vassalage. At least they did not mean to fight the battles of Wessex until there was no chance for evasion. But while Harold waited at London, men flocked together from the west and south, and he spent some days in his royal house at Westminster, heavy-hearted and full of care in his great extremity. He was too good a general, he had seen too much of the Norman soldiery already to underrate their prowess in battle; he shook his head gloomily when his officers spoke with scorn of their foes. One day he went on a pilgrimage to his own abbey at Waltham, and the monks' records say that, while he prayed there before the altar and confessed his sins and vowed his fealty to God, who reigns over all the kingdoms of the earth; while he lay face downward on the sacred pavement, the figure of Christ upon the cross bowed its head, as if to say again, "It is finished." Thurkill, the sacristan, saw this miracle, and knew that all hope must be put aside, and that Harold's cause was already lost.

Next, the Norman duke sent a message to Westminster by a monk from the abbey of Fécamp, and there was parleying to and fro about Harold's and William's rival claims to the English crown. It was only a formal challenging and a final provocation to the Englishmen to come and fight for their leader, there where the invaders had securely entrenched and established themselves. "Come and drive us home if you dare, if you can!" the Normans seemed to say tauntingly, and Harold saw that he must make haste lest the duke should be strengthened by reinforcements or have time to make himself harder to dislodge. William's demand that he should come down from the throne had been put into insolent words, and the Kentish people were being pitifully distressed and brought to beggary by the host of foreigners. Yet Gyrth, the son of Godwine, begged his royal brother to stay in London; to let him go and fight the Normans; and the people begged Harold, at the last moment, to listen to such good counsel. But Harold refused; he could never play coward's part, or let a man who loved him fight a battle in his stead; and so when six days were spent he marched away to the fight where the two greatest generals the world held must match their strength one against the other, hand to hand. The King of England had a famous kingdom to lose, the Duke of Normandy had a famous kingdom to win.

On the night before the fourteenth of October, the armies stood before each other near Hastings, on the field of Senlac, now called Battle. They made their camps hastily; for hosts of them the rude shelters were a last earthly dwelling-place and habitation of earthly hopes or fears. Through the Norman encampment went bands of priests, and the Normans prayed and confessed their sins. The Bishop of Coutances and Duke William's half-brother Odo, Bishop of Bayeux, both these high officials of the Church were there to stay the hands of their parishioners, and uphold the devout fighters in this crusade. Odo made the soldiers promise that whoever survived the morrow's battle would never again eat meat on Saturday; by such petty means he hoped to gain success at the hands of God who rules battles on a larger scope, and who, through the quarrels and jealousies of men, brings slowly near the day when justice shall be done on earth as it is in heaven. They sang hymns; the watch-fires flickered and faded; the gray morning dawned, and there in the dim light stood the English on a hillside that jutted like a promontory into the marshy plain. A woodland lay behind them, as if the very trees of the English soil had mustered with the men; in the thickest of the ranks was Harold's royal banner, the Fighting Man, and Harold himself stood close beside it with his brothers. The awful battle-axes, stained yet with the blood of those who died at Stamford Bridge, were in every man's hand, and every man was sheltered by his shield and kept silence. The Normans saw their foes stand waiting all together shoulder to shoulder, yet there was silence— an awful stillness in which to see so vast a host of men, and yet not hear them speak. The English had feasted that night, and sung their songs, and told the story of the northern fight. How their battle-axes looked gray and cold as the light dawned more and more! The Normans knew that they might feel the bitter edges and the cleaving steel of them ere the day was spent.

Archers first, behind them the lancers, and behind all, the horsemen; so the Normans were placed, high-hearted and bold with their great errand. To gain is better than to keep; by night this England might be theirs in spite of the battle-axes. While the day was yet young, Taillefer, the minstrel, went riding boldly out from the ranks singing the song of Roland and Charlemagne at Roncesvalles, tossing his sword lightly and fast into the air and catching it deftly as he galloped to the English lines. There sat the duke on his horse that was a present from the king of Spain. His most holy relics were hung about his neck; as he glanced from Taillefer along his army front he could see the Côtentin men, led by Neal of Saint Saviour, and his thoughts may have gone back quickly to the battle of his early youth at Val-ès-dunes. What a mighty host had gathered at his summons! All his Norman enemies were his followers now; he had won great championship, and if this day's fortune did not turn against him, the favor of the Holy Mother Church at Rome, the church of the apostles and martyrs, was won indeed; and no gift in Christendom would be more proudly honored than this kingdom of England made loyal to the papal crown. William the Bastard, the dishonored, insulted grandson of a Falaise tanner,—William, the Duke of proud Normandy, at the head of a host, knocking at the gates of

England; nay, let us set the contrast wider yet, and show Rolf the Ganger, wet by salt spray on the deck of his dragon-ship, steering boldly southward, and William, Duke of the Normans, rich and great, a master of masters, and soon to be king of a wide and noble land, and winner of a great battle, if the saints whom he worshipped would fight upon his side.

Taillefer has killed his two men, and been killed in his turn; his song has ended, and his sword has dropped from his hand. The Normans cry "*Dex aide! Dex aide! Ha Rou!*" and rush boldly up the hill to Harold's palisades. The arrows flew in showers, but the English stand solid and hew at the horsemen and footmen from behind their shields. Every man, even the king, was on foot; they shouted "Out! out!" as the Normans came near; they cried "God Almighty!" and "Holy Cross!" and at this sound Harold must have sadly remembered how the crucifix had bowed its head as he lay prone before it. And the fight grew hotter and hotter, the Normans were beaten back, and returned again fiercely to the charge, down the hill, now up the hill over the palisades, like a pouring river of men, dealing stinging sword-thrusts—dropping in clumsy heaps of javelin-pricked and axe-smitten lifelessness; from swift, bright-eyed men becoming a bloody mass to stumble over, or feebly crying for mercy at the feet that trampled them; so the fight went on. Harold sent his captains to right and left, and William matched his captains against them valiantly. The Norman arrows were falling blunted and harmless from the English shields, and he told the archers to shoot higher and aim so that the arrows might fall from above into the Englishmen's faces. There was no sound of guns or smoke of powder in that day, only a fearful wrangling and chopping, and a whir of arrow and lance and twang of bowstring. Yes, and a dolorous groaning as closer and closer the armies grappled with each other, hand to hand.

Hour after hour the day spent itself, and the fight would never be done. There was a cry that the duke was dead, and he pulled off his helmet and hurried along the lines to put new courage into his men. The arrows were dropping like a deadly rain, the axemen and lancers were twisted and twined together like melted rock that burns and writhes its way through widening crack and crevice. The hot flood of Normans in chain-mail and pointed helmets sweeps this way, and the English with their leathern caps and their sturdy shoulders mailed like their enemies, swinging their long-handled weapons, pour back again, and so the day draws near its end, while the races mix in symbolic fashion in the fight as they must mix in government, in blood, in brotherhood, and in ownership of England while England stands.

Harold has fallen, the gleaming banner of the Fighting Man, with its golden thread and jewelry, is stained with blood and mire. An arrow has gone deep into the king's eye and brain; he has fallen, and his foes strike needless blows at his poor body, lest so valiant a spirit cannot be quieted by simple death. The English have lost the fight, there is a cry that they are flying, and the Normans hear it and gather their courage once more; they rally and give chase. All at once there is a shout that thrills them through and through—a glorious moment when they discover that the day is won. William the Bastard is William the Conqueror, a sad word for many English ears in days to come; to us the sign of great gain that was and is England's—of the further advance of a kingdom already noble and strong. The English are strongest, but the Normans are quickest. The battle has been given to Progress, and the Norman, not the Saxon, had the right to lead the way.

But the field of Senlac makes a sad and sorry sight as the light of the short October day is fading and the pale stars shine dimly through the chilly mist that gathers in from the sea. It is not like the bright Norman weather; the slow breeze carries a faint, heavy odor of fallen leaves, and the very birds give awesome cries as they fly over the battle-field. There are many of the victors who think of the spoils of England, but some better men remember that it is in truth a mighty thing to have conquered such a country. What will it mean in very truth that England is theirs?

Later, William the Conqueror and his knights am resting and feasting and bragging of their deeds, there where Harold's standards were overthrown and the banner of the Three Lions of Normandy waves in the cool night wind. The living men look like butchers from the shambles, and the dead lie in heavy heaps; here and there a white face catches a ray of light and appeals for pity in its dumb loneliness. There are groans growing ever fainter, and cries for help now and then, from a soldier whose wits have come back to him, though he lay stunned and maimed among those who are forever silent. There go weeping men and women with litters—they cannot find the king, and they must lead the woman who loved him best of all the earth, Edith the Swanthroated, through this terrible harvest-field to discover his wounded body among the heaps of slain. He must be buried on the sea-shore, the Norman duke gives command to William Malet, and so guard forever the coast he tried to defend.

The heralds of victory set sail exultantly across the brown water of the Channel; the messengers of defeat go mourning to London and through the sorrowful English towns. Harold the son of Godwine, and his brother, Gyrth the Good—yes, and the flower of all Southern England; no man of Harold's own noble following lived to tell the story and to bewail this great defeat. There were some who lived to talk about it in after days;—and there was one good joy in saying that as the Normans pursued them after the day was lost, they hid in ambush in the fens and routed their pursuers with deadly, unexpected blows. But the country side looked on with dismay while William fought his way to London, not without much toil and opposition, but at last the humbled earldoms willingly or unwillingly received their new lord. Since Eadgar the underwitted Atheling was not fit for the throne, and the house of Godwine had fallen, William the Norman was made monarch of England, and there was a king-crowning in Westminster at Christmas-tide.

XVI. WILLIAM THE CONQUEROR.

"Then in his house of wood with flaxen sails

She floats, a queen, across the fateful seas."

—A. F.

RATHER than follow in detail the twenty-one years of William's English reign, we must content ourselves with a glance at the main features of it. We cannot too often remind ourselves of the resemblance between the life and growth of a nation and the life and growth of an individual; but while William the Conqueror is in so many ways typical of Normandy, and it is most interesting to follow his personal fortunes, there are many developments of Norman character in general which we must not overlook. William was about forty years old when the battle of Hastings was fought and won; Normandy, too, was in her best vigor and full development of strength. The years of decadence must soon begin for both; the time was not far distant when the story of Normandy ends, and it is only in the history of France and of England that the familiar Norman characteristics can be traced. Foremost in vitalizing force and power of centralization and individuality, while so much of Europe was unsettled and misdirected toward petty ends, this duchy of Rolf the Ganger seems, in later years, like a wild-flower that has scattered its seed to every wind, and plants for unceasing harvests, but must die itself in the first frost of outward assailment and inward weakness.

The march to London had been any thing but a triumphant progress, and the subjects of the new king were very sullen and vindictive. England was disheartened, her pride was humbled to the dust, and many of her leaders had fallen. In the dark winter weather there was sorrow and murmuring; the later law of the curfew bell, a most wise police regulation, made the whole country a prison.

A great deal of harrying had been thought necessary before the people were ready to come to William and ask him to accept the crown. William had a great gift for biding his time, and in the end the crown was proffered, not demanded. We learn that the folk thought better of their conqueror at last, that Cnut was remembered kindly, and the word went from mouth to mouth that England might do worse than take this famous Christian prince to rule over her. Harold had appealed to heaven when the fight began at Senlac, but heaven had given the victory to other hands. The northern earls had forsaken them, and at any rate the Norman devastations must be stopped. If William would do for England what he had done for his own duchy and make it feared for valor and respected for its prosperity like Normandy, who could ask more? So the duke called a formal council of his high noblemen and, after careful consideration, made known his acceptance! There was a strange scene at the coronation in Westminster. Norman horsemen guarded the neighboring streets, a great crowd of spectators filled the church, and when the question was put to this crowd, whether they would accept William for their king, there was an eager shout of "Yea! yea! King William!" Perhaps the Normans had never heard such a noisy outcry at a solemn service. Again the shout was heard, this time the same question had been repeated in the French tongue, and again the answer was "Yea! yea!"

The guards outside thought there was some treachery within, and feared that harm might come to their leader, so, by way of antidote or revenge, they set fire to the buildings near the minster walls. Out rushed the congregation to save their goods or, it might be, their lives, while the ceremony went on within, and the duke himself trembled with apprehension as he took the solemn oath of an English king, to do justice and mercy to all his people. There was a new crown to be put on, what had become of the Confessor's?—but at last the rite was finished and William, king of the English, with his priests and knights, came out to find a scene of ruin and disorder; it was all strangely typical—the makeshift splendors, the new order of church and state, the burning hatred and suspicions of that Christmastide. Peace on earth, good-will to men! alas, it was any thing but that in the later years of William's reign.

No doubt he built high hopes and made deep plans for good governance and England's glory. He had tamed Normandy to his guiding as one tames a wild and fiery horse, and there seemed to be no reason why he could not tame England. In the beginning he attempted to prove himself lenient and kind, but such efforts failed; it was too plain that the Normans had captured England and meant to enjoy the spoils. The estates belonging to the dead thanes and ealdormen, who fought with Harold, were confiscated and divided among the Normans: this was the fortune of war, but it was a bitter grievance and injustice. O, for another Godwine! cried many a man and woman in those days. O, for another Godwine to swoop down upon these foreign vultures who are tearing at England's heart! But even in the Confessor's time there was little security for private property. We have even seen the Confessor's own wife banished from his side without the rich dowry she had brought him, and Godwine's estates had been seized and refunded again, as had many another man's in the reign of that pious king whom everybody was ready to canonize and deplore.

After the king had given orders to his army to stop plundering and burning, there was a good deal of irregular depredation for which he was hardly responsible. He was really king of a very small part of England. The army must not be disbanded, it must be kept together for possible defence, but the presence of such a body of rapacious men, who needed food and lodging, and who were not content unless they had some personal gain from the rich country they had helped to win, could not help being disastrous. Yet there is one certain thing—the duke meant to be master of his new possessions, and could use Englishmen to keep his Norman followers in check, while he could indulge his own countrymen in their love of power and aggrandizement at England's expense. There are touching pictures of his royal progress through the country in the early part of his reign; the widows of thanes and the best of the churls would come out with their little children, to crave mercy and the restitution of even a small part of their old estates to save them from beggary. Poor women! it was upon them that the heaviest burden fell; the women of a war-stricken country suffer by far the most from change and loss; not the heroes who die in battle, or the heroes who live to tell the story of the fight, and who have been either victors or vanquished. Men are more reasonable; they have had the recompense of taking part in the struggle. If they have been in the wrong or in the right, great truths have come home to them as they stood sword in hand.

The Norman barons, who had followed their leader beyond the Channel, had been won by promises, and these promises must be kept. They were made rich with the conquered lands, and given authority, one would think, to their heart's content. They were made the king's magistrates and counsellors, and as years went by there was more and more resentment of all this on the part of the English. They hated their Norman lords; they hated the taxes which the king claimed. The strong point of the Saxon civilization was local self-government and self-dependence; but the weak point was the lack of unity and want of proper centralization and superintendence. William was wise in overcoming this; instead of giving feudalism its full sway and making his Norman barons petty monarchs with right of coinage and full authority over their own dominion, he claimed the homage and loyalty, the absolute allegiance of his subjects. But for his foresight in making such laws, England might have been such a kingdom as Charles the Simple's or Hugh Capet's, and hampered with feudal lords greater than their monarch in every thing but name.

In England, at last, every man held his land directly from the king and was responsible to him. The Witanagemôt was continued, but turned into a sort of feudal court in which the officials of the kingdom, the feudal lords, had places. The Witan became continually a smaller body of men, who were joined with those officers of the royal power higher than they. It must be remembered that the Conqueror did not make his claim to the throne because he had won his right by the sword. He always insisted that he was the lawful successor to Eadward, and the name of Harold the Usurper was omitted from the list of

English kings. Following this belief or pretence he was always careful to respect the nationality of the country, and made himself as nearly as possible an Englishman. His plans for supplanting the weakness and insularity of many English institutions by certain Continental fashions, wrought a tremendous change, and put the undeveloped and self-centred kingdom that he had won, on a footing with other European powers. The very taxes which were wrung from the unwilling citizens, no doubt, forced them to wider enterprise and the expansion of their powers of resource. Much of England's later growth has sprung from seed that was planted in these years—this early springtime of her prosperity, when William's stern hands swept from field and forest the vestiges of earlier harvests, and cleared the garden grounds into leafless deserts, only to make them ready for future crops.

The very lowest classes were more fortunate under William's rule than they had been in earlier times. Their rights and liberties were extended, and they could claim legal defence against the tyrannies of their masters. But the upper ranks of people were much more dissatisfied and unhappy. . The spirit of the laws was changed; the language of the court was a foreign language; and the modified feudalism of the king put foreigners in all high places, who could hold the confiscated estates, and laugh at the former masters now made poor and resourceless. The folk-land had become *Terra Regis;* England was only a part of Normandy, and the king was often away, busier with the affairs of his duchy than of his kingdom. Yet, as had often happened before in this growing nation's lifetime, a sure process of amalgamation was going on, and though the fire of discontent was burning hot, the gold that was England's and the gold that was Normandy's were being melted together and growing into a greater Treasure than either had been alone. We can best understand the individuality and vital force of the Norman people by seeing the difference their coming to England has made in the English character. We cannot remind ourselves of this too often. The Norman of the Conqueror's day was already a man of the world. The hindering conditions of English life were localism and lack of unity. We can see almost a tribal aspect in the jealousies of the earldoms, the lack of sympathy or brotherhood between the different quarters of the island. William's earls were only set over single shires, and the growth of independence was rendered impossible; and his greatest benefaction to his new domain was a thoroughly organized system of law. As we linger over the accounts of his reign, harsh and cruel and unlovable as he appears, it is rather the cruelty of the surgeon than of a torturer or of a cut-throat. The presence of the Normans among the nations of the earth must have seemed particularly irritating and inflammatory, but we can understand, now that so many centuries have smoothed away the scars they left, that the stimulus of their energy and their hot ambition helped the rest of the world to take many steps forward.

While we account for the deeds of the fighting Normans, and their later effects, we must not forget their praying brethren who stood side by side with them, lording it over the English lands and reaching out willing hands for part of the spoils. We must thank them for their piety and their scholarship, and for the great churches they founded, even while we laugh at the greed and wordliness under their monkish cloaks. Lanfranc was made bishop of Canterbury, and wherever the Conqueror's standard was planted, wherever he gained foothold, as the tide of his military rule ebbed and flowed, he planted churches and monasteries. Especially he watched over his high-towered Battle Abbey, which marked the spot where the banner of the Fighting Man was defeated and the banner of the Three Lions of Normandy was set up in its place.

Before we go further we must follow the king back to his duchy in the spring after that first winter in England. Three Englishmen were chosen to attend his royal highness, and although they might easily guess that there was something more than mere compliment in this flattering invitation, these northern earls, Eadwine, Morkere, and Waltheof (the Bear's great-grandson), were not anxious to hurry forward the open quarrel which William himself was anxious to avoid.

Nothing could have been more unsafe in the unsettled condition of England than to have left these unruly leaders to plot and connive during his absence; besides, it would be a good thing to show such rough islanders the splendours of the Norman court.

The Norman chroniclers are not often willing to admit that England was in any respect equal to their own duchy, but when they have to describe William's triumphant return, they forget their prudence and give glowing accounts of the treasure of gold and silver that he brings with him, and even the magnificent embroideries, tapestries and hangings, and clerical vestments,—though they have so lately tried to impress upon their readers that heathen squalor of social life across the Channel which the Christian had sought to remedy. Church after church was richly endowed with these spoils, and the Conqueror's own Church of St. Stephen at Caen fared best of all. Beside the English wealth we must not forget the goods of Harold Hardrada, which had been brought with such mistaken confidence for the plenishing of his desired kingdom. There is a tradition of a mighty ingot of gold won in his Eastern adventures, so great that twelve strong youths could scarcely carry it. Eadwine and Morkere of Northumberland must have looked at that with regretful eyes.

Whatever the English prejudice might have been, the Normans had every reason to be proud of their seventh duke. He had advanced their fortunes in most amazing fashion, and they were proud of him indeed on the day when he again set his foot on Norman ground. The time of year was Lent. Spring was not yet come, but it might have been a summer festival, if one judged by the way that the people crowded from the farthest boundaries of the country to the towns through which William was to pass. It was like the glorious holidays of the Roman Empire. The grateful peasants fought and pushed for a sight of their leader. The world is never slow to do honor to its great soldiers and conquerors. The duke met his wife at Rouen, and that was the best moment of all; Matilda had ruled Normandy wisely and ably during his five or six months' absence, with old Roger de Beaumont for her chief counsellor.

The royal procession trailed its gorgeous length from church to church and from city to city about the duchy; the spoils of England seemed inexhaustible to the wondering spectators, and those who had made excuse to lag behind when their bows and lances were needed, were ready enough now to clutch their hands greedily in their empty pockets and follow their valiant countrymen. William himself was not slow in letting the value of his new domain be known; the more men the better in that England which might be a slippery prize to hold. He had many a secret conference with Lanfranc, who had been chief adviser and upholder of the invasion. The priest-statesman seems almost a greater man than the soldier-statesman; many a famous deed of that age was Lanfranc's suggestion, but nobody knew better than these two that the conquest of England was hardly more than begun, and long and deep their councils must have been when the noise of shouting in the streets had ended, and the stars were shining above Caen.

No city of Normandy seems more closely connected with those days than Caen. As one walks along its streets, beneath the high church towers and gabled roofs of the houses, it is easy to fancy that more famous elder generation of Normans alive again, to people Caen with knights and priests and minstrels of that earlier day. The Duchess Matilda might be alive yet and busy with her abbey church of Holy Trinity and her favorite household of nuns; the people shout her praises admiringly, and gaze at her lovingly as she passes through the street with her troop of attendants. Caen is prosperous and gay. "Large, strong, full of draperies and all sorts of merchandise; rich citizens, noble dames, damsels, and fine churches," says Froissart years afterwards. Even this very year one is tempted to believe that one sees the same fields and gardens, the same houses, and hears the same bells that William the Conqueror saw and heard in that summer after he had become king of England.

And in Bayeux, too, great portions of the ancient city still remain. There where the Northmen made their chief habitation, or in Rouen or Falaise, we can almost make history come to life. Perhaps the great tapestry was begun that very summer in Bayeux; perhaps the company of English guests, some of those noble dames well-skilled in "English work" of crewel and canvas, were enticed by Bishop Odo into beginning that "document in worsted" which more than any thing else has preserved the true history of the Conquest of England. Odo meant to adorn his new church with it, and to preserve the account of his own part in the great battle and its preliminaries, with the story of Harold's oath and disloyalty, and William's right to the crown. There is an Italian fashion of drawing in it—the figures are hardly like Englishmen or Normans in the way they stand or make gestures to each other in the rude pictures. Later history has associated the working of these more than fifteen hundred figures with Matilda and her maidens, as a tribute to the Conqueror's valor, but there are many evidences to the contrary. The old idea that the duchess and her women worked at the tapestry, and said their prayers while the army had gone to England, seems improbable the more one studies the work itself.

Yet tradition sometimes keeps the grain of truth in its accumulation of chaff. There is no early record of it, and its historical value was rediscovered only in 1724 by a French antiquary. The bright worsteds of it still keep their colors on the twenty-inches wide strip of linen, more than two hundred feet in length. Odo is said to have given it to his chapter at Bayeux, and it has suffered astonishingly little from the ravages of time.

But we must return to Norman affairs in England. Odo himself and William Fitz-Osbern had been made earls of the Counties Palatine of Kent and Hereford, and were put in command in William's absence. The rapacity of these Norman gentlemen was more than their new subjects could bear. The bishop at least is pretty certain to have covered his own greedy injustice by a plea that he was following out the king's orders. Revolt after revolt troubled the peace of England. Harold's two sons were ready to make war from their vantage-ground in Ireland; the Danes and Scots were also conspiring against the new lord of the English. At last some of the Normans themselves were traitorous and troublesome, but William was fully equal to such minor emergencies as these. He went back to England late in 1067, after spending the summer and autumn in Normandy, and soon found himself busy enough in the snarl of revolt and disagreement. One trouble followed another as the winter wore away. The siege of Exeter was the most conspicuous event, but here too William was conqueror, and Southwestern England was forced to submit to his rule. At Easter-tide a stately embassy was sent to bring over the Duchess Matilda from Normandy, and when it returned she was hallowed as Queen by Ealdred the archbishop. Let us hope that, surrounded by her own kindred and people, she did not see the sorrowful English faces of those women who had lost husband and home together, and who had been bereft of all their treasures that strangers might be enriched.

There is a curious tradition that a little while after this, much woe was wrought because those other Norman ladies, whose lords had come over to England to fight and remained to plunder, refused to join them, because they were not fond of the sea, and thought that they were not likely to find better fare and lodging. Very likely the queen's residence in her new possessions had a good effect, but some of the Norman men were obliged to return altogether, their wives having threatened to find new partners if they were left alone any longer. It may have been an excuse or a jest, because so many naturally desired to see their own country again.

Both Saxons and Normans paid great deference to the instinctive opinions of women. When such serious matters as going to war were before them, a woman's unreasoning prejudice or favor of the enterprise was often taken into account. They seem to have almost taken the place of the ancient auguries! However, it is not pleasant to feminine conceit to be told directly that great respect was also paid to the neighing of horses!

Henry, the king's youngest son, was born not long after the queen's arrival, and born too in Northern England the latest and hardest won at that time of the out-lying provinces. The very name that was given to the child shows a desire for some degree of identification with new interests. William and Matilda certainly had England's welfare at heart, for England's welfare was directly or indirectly their own, and this name was a sign of recognition of the hereditary alliance with Germany; with the reigning king and his more famous father. There is nothing more striking than the traditional slander and prejudice which history preserves from age to age. Seen by clearer light, many reported injustices are explained away. If there was in England then, any thing like the present difficulty of influencing public opinion to quick foresight and new decisions, the Conqueror and Baldwin of Flanders' daughter had any thing but an easy path to tread. Selfish they both may have been, and bigoted and even cruel, but they represented a better degree of social refinement and education and enlightenment. Progress was really what the English of that day bewailed and set their faces against, though they did not know it. William and Matilda had to insist upon the putting aside of worn-out opinions, and on coming to England had made the strange discovery that they must either take a long step backward or force their subjects forward. They were not conscious reformers; they were not infallibly wise missionaries of new truth, who tried actually to give these belated souls a wider outlook upon life, but let us stop to recognize the fact that no task is more thankless than his who is trying to go in advance of his time. Men have been burnt and hanged and disgraced and sneered at for no greater crime; in fact, there is nothing that average humanity so much resents as the power to look ahead and to warn others of pitfalls into which ignorant shortsightedness is likely to tumble. Nothing has been so resented and assailed as the thorough survey of England, and the record of its lands and resources in the Domesday Book. Yet nothing was so necessary for any sort of good government and steady oversight of the nation's affairs. We only wonder now that it was not made sooner. The machinery of government was of necessity much ruder then. No doubt William's tyranny swept its course to and fro like some Juggernaut car regardless of its victims, yet for England a unified and concentrated force of government was the one thing to be insisted upon; Harold and his rival earls might have been hindering, ineffectual rulers of the country's divided strength and jealous partisanship.

Yet the future right direction and prosperity of England was poor consolation to the aching hearts of the women of that time, or the landless lords who had to stand by and see new masters of the soil take their places. What was won by William's sword must be held by his sword, and the more sullen and rebellious the English grew, the more heavily they were taxed and the faster the land was rid of them. They were chased into the fens, and pursued with fire and bloodshed. "England was made a great grave," says Dickens, "and men and beasts lay dead together." The immediate result of the Conqueror's rule was like fire and plough and harrow in a piece of new land.

It was a sad and tiresome lifetime, that of the Conqueror; just or unjust toward his new subjects, they hated him bitterly; his far-sighted plans for the country's growth and development gave as much displeasure as the smallest of his personal prejudices or selfish whims. Every man's hand was against him, and hardly an eye but flashed angrily at the sight of the king. Eadward the Confessor, pious ascetic, and relic-worshipper, had loved the chase as well as this warlike successor of his ever loved it, and had been very careful of his royal hunting-grounds, but nobody raised an outcry against his unsaintly love of slaughtering defenceless wild creatures, or thought him the less a meek and gentle soul, beloved by angels and taught by them in visions. But ever since, the Conqueror's love of hunting has been an accusation against him as if he were the only man guilty of it, and his confiscation of the Hampshire lands to make new forest seemed the last stroke that could be borne. The peasants' cottages were swept away and the land laid waste. Norman was master and Englishman was servant. The royal train of horses and dogs and merry huntsmen in gay apparel clattered through the wood, and from hiding-places under the fern men watched them and muttered curses upon their cruel heads. There were already sixty-eight royal forests in different parts of the kingdom before New Forest was begun. Everybody thought that England had never seen such dark days, but so everybody thought when the Angles and Saxons and Jutes came, and even so vigorous a pruning and digging at the roots as this made England grow the better.

Large tracts of the hunting-grounds had been unfit for human habitation, and it was better to leave them to the hares and deer. Wide regions of the country, too, were occupied by the lowest class of humanity, who lived almost in beastly fashion, without chance of enlightenment or uplifting. They were outlaws of the worst sort who could not be brought into decent order or relationship with respectable society, and it was better for these to be chased from their lairs and forced to accept the companionship of townsfolk. With these, however, there were many who suffered undeserved. Among the rank weeds of England there were plucked many blooming things and useful growths of simple, long-established home-life and domestic affection. When fire was leaping high at the city gates it is impossible not to regret its enmity against dear and noble structures of the past, even though it cleared the way for loftier minsters and fairer dwelling-places. In criticising and resenting such a reign as William the Norman's over England, we must avoid a danger of not seeing the hand of God in it, and the evidences of an overruling Providence, which works in and through the works of men and sees the end of things from the beginning as men cannot. There may be overstatement in William of Malmesbury's account of the bad condition of the country at the time of the Conquest, but the outlines of it cannot be far from right. "In process of time," he says, "the desire after literature and religion had decayed for several years before the arrival of the Normans. The clergy, contented with a very slight degree of learning, could scarcely stammer out the words of the sacraments, and a person who understood grammar was an object of wonder and astonishment. The nobility were given up to luxury and wantonness. The commonalty, left unprotected, became a prey to the most powerful, who amassed fortunes by either seizing on their property or selling their persons into foreign countries; although it be an innate quality of this people to be more inclined to revelling than to the accumulation of wealth. Drinking was a universal practice, in which they passed whole nights, as well as days. They consumed their whole substance in mean, despicable houses, unlike Normans and French, who, in noble and splendid mansions, lived with frugality." "There cannot be a doubt," says Mr. Bruce in his interesting book about the Bayeux tapestry, "that by the introduction of the refinements of life the condition of the people was improved, and that a check was given to the grosser sensualities of our nature. Certain it is that learning received a powerful stimulus by the Conquest. At the period of the Norman invasion a great intellectual movement had commenced in the schools on the Continent. Normandy had beyond most other parts profited by it. William brought with him to England some of the most distinguished ornaments of the school of his native duchy; the consequence of this was that England henceforward took a higher walk in literature than she had ever done before." One great step was the freeing of the lower classes; there was one rank of serfs, the churls, who were attached to the land, and were transferred with it, without any power of choosing their employer or taking any steps to improve their condition. Another large class, the thews, were the absolute property of their owners. William's law that every slave who had lived unchallenged a year and a day in any city or walled town in the kingdom should be free forever, was, indeed, "a door of hope to many," besides the actual good effects of town life, the natural rivalry and promotion of knowledge, the stimulus given to the cultivation and refinements of social life. He protected the early growth of a public sentiment, which was finally strong enough to venture to assert its rights and to claim recognition. He relentlessly overthrew the flourishing slave-trade of the town of Bristol and no doubt made many enemies by such an act.

Whatever may have been the king's better nature and earlier purposes in regard to his kingdom and duchy, as he grew older one finds his reputation growing steadily worse. He must have found the ruling of men a thankless task, and he apparently cared less and less to soften or control the harshness of his underrulers and officers. His domestic relations had always been a bright spot in his stern, hard life, but at length even his beloved wife Matilda no longer held him first, and grieved him by favoring their troublesome son Robert, who was her darling of all their children. Robert and his mother had been the nominal governors of Normandy when he was still a child and his father was away in England. They seem to have been in league ever afterward, for when Robert grew up he demanded Normandy outright, which made his father angry, and the instant refusal provoked Master Curt-hose to such an extent that he went about from court to court in Europe bewailing the injustice that had been shown him. He was very fond of music and dancing, and spent a great deal of money, which the queen appears to have been always ready to send him. He was gifted with a power of making people fond of him, though he was not good for very much else.

After a while William discovered that there was a secret messenger who carried forbidden supplies to the rebellious prince, and the messenger happily had time to betake himself to a convenient convent and put on the dress and give, let us hope, heart-felt vows of monkhood. This is what Orderic Vitalis reports of a meeting between the king and queen: "Who in the world," sighs the king, "can expect to find a faithful and devoted wife? The woman whom I loved in my soul, and to whom I entrusted my kingdom and my treasures, supports my enemies; she enriches them with my property; she secretly arms them against my honor perhaps my life." And Matilda answered: "Do not be surprised, I pray you, because I love my eldest born. Were Robert dead and seven feet below the sod, and my blood could raise him to life, it should surely flow. How can I take pleasure in luxury when my son is in want? Far from my heart be such hardness! Your power cannot deaden the love of a mother's heart." The king did not punish the queen, we are assured gravely; and Robert quarrelled with his brothers, and defied his father, and won his mother's sympathy and forbearance to the end. He found the king of France ready to uphold his cause by reason of the old jealousy of William's power, and while he was ensconced in the castle of Gerberoi, and sallying out at his convenience to harry the country, William marched to attack him, and the father and son fought hand to hand without knowing each other until the king was thrown from his horse. Whereupon Robert professed great contrition, and some time afterward, the barons having interceded and Matilda having prayed and wept, William consented to a reconciliation, and even made his son his lieutenant over Normandy and Brittany.

In 1083 the queen died, and there was nobody to lift a voice against her prudence and rare virtue, or her simple piety. There was no better woman in any convent cell of Normandy, than the woman who had borne the heavy weight of the Norman crown, and who had finished the sorry task as best she could, of reigning over an alien, conquered people. The king's sorrow was piteous to behold, and not long afterward their second son, Richard, was killed in the New Forest, a place of misfortune to the royal household. Another trouble quickly followed, which not only hurt the king's feelings, but made him desperately angry.

William had been very kind to all his kinsfolk on his mother's side, and especially to his half-brother, Odo, the Bishop of Bayeux. He had loaded him with honors, and given him, long ago, vice-regal authority in England. Even this was not enough for such an aspiring ecclesiastic, and, under the pretence of gathering tax-money (no doubt insisting that it was to serve the miserliness and greed of the king), he carried on a flourishing system of plundering. After a while it was discovered that he had an ambition to make himself Pope of Rome, and was using his money for bribing cardinals and ingratiating himself with the Italian nobles. He bought himself a palace in Rome and furnished it magnificently, and began to fit out a fleet of treasure-ships at the Isle of Wight. One day when they were nearly ready to set sail, and the disloyal gentlemen who were also bound on this adventure were collected into a comfortable group on shore, who should appear among them but William himself. The king sternly related what must have been a familiar series of circumstances to his audience: Odo's disloyalty when he had been entirely trusted, his oppression of England, his despoiling of the churches and the confiscation of their lands and treasures, lastly that he had even won away these knights to go to Rome with him; men who were sworn to repulse the enemies of the kingdom.

After Odo's sins were related in detail, he was seized, but loudly lamented thereat, declaring that he was a clerk and a minister of the Most High, and that no bishop could be condemned without the judgment of the Pope. The people who stood by murmured anxiously, for nobody knew what might be going to happen to them also. Crafty William answered that he was seizing neither clerk, nor prelate, nor Bishop of Bayeux, only his Earl of Kent, his temporal lieutenant, who must account to him for such bad vice-regal administration, and for four years after that Odo was obliged to content himself with close imprisonment in the old tower of Rouen.

Those four years were in fact all that remained of the Conqueror's earthly lifetime, and dreary years they were. In 1087 William returned to Normandy for the last time. The French king was making trouble; some say that the quarrel began between the younger members of the family, others that Philip demanded that William should do homage for England. Ordericus Vitalis, the most truthful of the Norman historians, declares that the dispute was about the proprietorship of the French districts of the Vexin.

The Conqueror was an old man now, older than his years; he had never quite recovered from his fall when Robert unhorsed him at the castle of Gerberoi; besides he had suffered from other illness, and had grown very stout, and the doctors at Rouen were taking him in charge. The king of France joked insolently about his illness, and at the end of July William started furiously on his last campaign, and no doubt took vast pleasure in burning the city of Mantes. When the fire was down he rode through the conquered town, his horse stepped among some smouldering firebrands and reared, throwing his clumsy rider suddenly forward against the high pommel of the saddle, a death-blow from which he was never to recover. He was carried back to Rouen a worse case for the doctors' skill than ever, and presently fever set in, and torture followed torture for six long weeks. The burning fever, the midsummer heat, the flattery or neglect of his paid attendants; how they all reminded him and made him confess at last his new understanding and sorrow for the misery he had caused to many another human being! Yet we can but listen forgivingly as he says: "At the time my father went of his own will into exile, leaving to me the Duchy of Normandy, I was a mere child of eight years, and from that day to this I have always borne the weight of arms."

The three sons, Rufus William, Robert Curt-hose, and Henry Beauclerc, were all eager to claim their inheritance, but the king sends for Anselm, the holy abbot, and puts them aside while he makes confession of his sins and bravely meets the prospect of speedy death. He gives directions concerning the affairs of England and Normandy, gives money and treasure to poor people and the churches; he even says that he wishes to rebuild the churches which were so lately burnt at Mantes. Then he summons his sons to his bedside and directs those barons and knights who were present to be seated, when, if we may believe Ordericus the Chronicler, the Conqueror made an eloquent address, reviewing his life and achievements and the career of many of his companions. The chronicle writers had a habit of putting extremely pious and proper long speeches into the mouths of dying kings, and as we read these remarks in particular we cannot help a suspicion that the old monk sat down in his cell some time afterward and quietly composed a systematic summary of what William would have said, or ought to have said if he could. Yet we may believe in the truth of many sentences. We do not care for what he expressed concerning Mauger or King Henry, the battle of Mortemer or Val-ès-dunes, but when he speaks of his loyalty to the Church and his friendship with Lanfranc, and Gerbert, and Anselm, of his having built seventeen monasteries and six nunneries, "spiritual fortresses in which mortals learn to combat the demons and lusts of the flesh"; when he tells his sons to attach themselves to men of worth and wisdom and to follow their advice, to follow justice in all things and spare no effort to avoid wickedness, to assist the poor, infirm, and honest, to curb and punish the proud and selfish, to prevent them from injuring their neighbors, devoutly to attend holy church, to prefer the worship of God to worldly wealth;—when he says these things we listen, and believe that he was truly sorry at last for the starving homeless Englishmen who owed him their death, for even the bitter resentment he showed for the slaughter of a thousand of his brave knights within the walls of Durham. He dares not give the ill-gotten kingdom of England to anybody save to God, but if it be God's will he hopes that William Rufus may be his successor. Robert may rule Normandy. Henry may take five thousand pounds' weight of silver from the treasury. It is true that he has no land to dwell in, but let him rest in patience and be willing that his brothers should precede him. By and by he will be heir of everything.

At last the king unwillingly gives permission for Odo's release along with other prisoners of state. He prophesies that Odo will again disturb the peace and cause the death of thousands, and adds that the bishop does not conduct himself with that chastity and modesty which become a minister of God. For a last act of clemency he gives back to Baudri, the son of Nicolas, all his lands, "because without permission he quitted my service and passed over into Spain. I now restore them to him for the love of God; I do not believe that there is a better knight under arms than he, but he is changeable and prodigal, and fond of roving into foreign countries."

On the morning of the eighth of September the great soul took its flight. The king was lying in restless, half-breathless sleep or stupor when the cathedral bells began to ring, and he opened his eyes and asked what time it was. They told him it was the hour of prime. "Then he called upon God as far as his strength sufficed, and on our holy lady, the blessed Mary, and so departed while yet speaking, without any loss of his senses or change of speech."

"At the time when the king departed this world, many of his servants were to be seen running up and down, some going in, others coming out, carrying off the rich hangings and the tapestry, and whatever they could lay their hands upon. A whole day passed before the corpse was laid upon its bier, for they who were wont before to fear him now left him lying alone. But when the news spread much people gathered together, and bishops and barons came in long procession. The body was well tended and carried to Caen as he had before commanded. There was no bishop in the province, nor abbot, nor noble prince, who did not go to the burying if he could, and there were besides many monks, priests, and clerks."

So writes Master Wace in his long rhyme of the Conquest; but the rhyme does not end as befits the Conqueror's fame. The chanting monks had hardly set the body down within the church, at the end of its last journey, when there was a cry of fire without, and all the people ran away and left the church empty save for the few monks who stayed beside the bier. When the crowd returned the service went on again, but just as the grave was ready a vavasour named Ascelin, the son of Arthur, pushed his way among the bishops and barons, and mounted a stone to make himself the better heard "Listen to me, ye lords and clerks!" he cries; "ye shall not bury William in this spot. This church of St. Stephen is built on land that he seized from me and my house. By force he took it from me, and I claim judgment. I appeal to him by name that he do me right."

"After he had said this he came down. Forthwith arose great clamor in the church, and there was such tumult that no one could hear the other speak. Some went, others came; and all marvelled that this great king, who had conquered so much and won so many cities and so many castles, could not call so much land his own as his body might be covered in after death."

We cannot do better than end with reading the Saxon chronicle, which is less likely to be flattering than the Norman records.

"Alas, how false and unresting is this earth's weal! He that erst was a rich king, and lord of many lands; had then of all his lands but seven feet space; and he that was once clad with gold and gems, lay overspread with mold! If any one wish to know what manner of man he was, or what worship he had, or of how many lands he was the lord, then will we write of him as we have known him; for we looked on him and somewhile dwelt in his herd.

"This King William that we speak about was a very wise man and very rich; more worshipped, and stronger than any of his foregangers were. He was mild to the good men that loved God, and beyond all metes stark to those who with said his will. On that same ground where God gave him that he should win England, he reared a noble minster and set monks there and well endowed it.

"Eke he was very worshipful. Thrice he wore his king-helm (crown), every year as oft as he was in England. At Easter he wore it at Winchester; at Pentecost at Westminster; at midwinter at Gloucester, and then were with him all the rich men over all England: archbishops and diocesan bishops; abbots and earls; thanes and knights. Truly he was so stark a man and wroth that no man durst do any thing against his will. He had earls in his bonds who had done against his will. Bishops he set off their bishoprics, and abbots off their abbacies, and thanes in prison. And at last he did not spare his brother Odo; him he set in prison. Betwixt other things we must not forget the good peace that he made in this land, so that a man that was worth aught might travel over the kingdom unhurt with his bosom full of gold. And no man durst slay another man though he had suffered never so mickle evil from the other.

"He ruled over England, and by his cunning he had so thoroughly surveyed it, that there was never a hide of land in England that he wist not both who had it and what its worth was, and he set it down in his writ. Wales was under his weald, and therein he wrought castles; and he wielded Manncynn withal. Scotland he subdued by his mickle strength. Normandy was his by kin—and over the earldom that is called Mans he ruled. And if he might have lived yet two years he had won Ireland, and without any armament.

"Truly in his time men had mickle taxing and many hardships. He let castles be built, and poor men were sorely taxed. The king" (we might in justice read oftener the king's officers)—"The king was so very stark, and he took from his subjects many marks of gold and many hundred pounds of silver, and that he took of his people some by right and some by mickle unright, for little need. He was fallen into covetousness, and greediness he loved withal.

"The king and the head men loved much, and over much, the getting in of gold and silver, arid recked not how sinfully it was got so it but came to them. . . .

"He set many deer-friths and he made laws therewith, that whosoever should slay hart or hind, him man should blind. And as he kept to himself the slaying of the harts, so eke did he the boars. He loved the high deer as much as if he were their father. Eke he set as to the hares that they should go free. His rich men bemoaned, and his poor men murmured, but he recked not the hatred of them all, and they must follow the king's will if they would have lands or goods or his favor.

"Wa-la-wa! that any man should be so moody, so to upheave himself and think himself above all other men! May God Almighty have mild-heartedness on his soul and give him forgiveness of his sins! These things we have written of him both good and evil, that men may choose the good after their goodness, and withal flee from evil, and go on the way that leadeth all to heaven's kingdom."

XVII. KINGDOM AND DUKEDOM.

"Yes, while on earth a thousand discords ring,

Man's senseless uproar mingling with his toil,

Still do thy quiet ministers move on."

—MATTHEW ARNOLD.

WILLIAM RUFUS hurried away to claim the kingdom of England before his father died. Robert was at Abbeville, some say, with his singers and jesters, making merry over the prospect of getting the dukedom. Henry had put his five thousand pounds of silver into a strong box and gone his ways likewise. Normandy was in the confusion that always befell a country in those days while one master had put off his crown and the next had not put it on. There were masses being said in the Norman churches for the good of the Conqueror's soul, and presently, as the autumn days flew by and grew shorter and shorter, news was received that the English had received William Rufus and made him king with great rejoicing. There was always much to hope from the accession of a new monarch; he was sure to make many promises, and nobody knew that he would not keep every one of them.

But neither in England nor Normandy did the outlook promise great security. Robert was made duke, and Robert had plenty of friends, whose love and favor were sure to last as long as his money held out. He had a better heart than his brothers, but he was not fit for a governor. "Robert, my eldest-born, shall have Normandy and Maine," the Conqueror had told his barons on his death-bed. "He shall serve the king of France for the same. There are many brave men in Normandy; I know none equal to them. They are noble and valiant knights, conquering in all lands whither they go. If they have a good captain, a company of them is made to be dreaded, but if they have not a lord whom they fear, and who governs them severely, the service they render will soon be but poor. The Normans are worth little without strict justice; they must be bent and bowed to their ruler's will, and whoso holds them always under his foot and curbs them tightly, may get his business well done by them. Haughty are they and proud, boastful and arrogant; difficult to govern, and needing to be at all times kept under, so that Robert will have much to do and to provide in order to manage such a people."

The dying king may have smiled grimly at the thought that Robert's ambition knew not what it asked. The gay gentleman had given his father trouble enough, but the weight of Normandy should be his to carry. The red prince, William, had been a dutiful son, and he wished him joy of England. He was order-loving, and had a head for governing. "Poor lads!" the old father may have sighed more than once. It was all very well to be princes and knights and gay riders and courtiers, but the man who has a kingdom to govern must wend his ways alone, with much hindrance and little help.

The two courts bore little likeness to the Conqueror's as time went on, and there was endless dissension among the knights. In England the Normans complained greatly of the division of the kingdom and the duchy. Odo, who had regained his earldom of Kent, was full of mischievous, treacherous plans, and had no trouble in persuading other men that they stood no chance of holding their lands or keeping their rights under Rufus; it would be much better to overthrow him and to do homage to Robert of Normandy in the old fashion. Robert was careless and easy, and William was strong and self-willed. Robert was ready to favor this party at once, and after a while William discovered what was going on, and found the rebels under Odo were fortifying their castles and winning troops of followers to their side—in fact, England was all ready for civil war. The king besieged Odo forthwith in the city of Rochester, and there was a terrible end to the revolt. Robert had been too lazy or too inefficient to keep his promise of coming to the aid of his allies, and disease broke out in the garrison and raged until Odo sent messengers to ask forgiveness, and to promise all manner of loyalty and penitence. The king was in a state of fury, and meant to hang the leaders of the insurrection and put the rest to death by the most ingenious tortures that could be invented. At last, however, his own barons and officers made piteous pleas for the lives of their friends and relatives, and in the end they were driven out and deprived of their English estates, and Odo was altogether banished from the country. No longer an earl, he went back much humbled to his bishopric of Bayeux, which Robert had been foolish enough to restore to him. But the intrigues went on. The Norman barons in England were separated from their hereditary possessions in Normandy, and William Rufus owed the safety of his crown to the upholding of the English. Presently he went over to Normandy, where things were getting worse and worse under Robert's rule, and announced his intention of seizing the silly duke's dominions. Robert had already sold the Côtentin to Henry for a part of the five thousand pounds in the strong box, and after a good deal of dissension, and a prospect of a long and bloody war, which the nobles on both sides did every thing they could to prevent, the brothers made up their quarrel. They signed an agreement that the one who outlived the other should inherit all the lands and wealth, and then they made a league to go and fight Henry Beauclerc, who was living peaceably enough on his honestly-got Côtentin possessions. They chased him out of the country to the French Vexin, where he spent a forlorn year or two; but he could afford to wait for his inheritance, as the Conqueror had told him long before.

William Rufus went back to England, and in the course of time there was a war with the Scotch, who were defeated again and again and finally made quiet. Then the Welsh rebelled in their turn and were much harder to subdue. Robert got the king of France to join forces with him soon afterward, and that war was only avoided by the payment to France by Rufus of an enormous sum of money.

All this time William Rufus was doing some good things for his kingdom and a great many more bad ones that there is not time to describe. After Lanfranc's death the king grew worse and worse; he was apparently without any religious principle, and there was always a quarrel between him and the priests about the church money, which both of them wanted. When bishops and abbots died the king would not appoint their successors, and took all the tithes for himself. His chief favorite was a low-born, crafty, wicked man named Ralph Flambard, and the two were well matched. William Rufus had little of the gift for business that made his father such a practical statesman and organizer, and, in fact, his boisterous, lawless, indecent manner of living shocked even the less orderly of his subjects. He had the lower and less respectable of the Norman qualities, and something of the rudeness of the worst of his more remote ancestry crops out in his conduct. Once when he was very ill and was afraid that he was going to die with all his sins on his head, he sent for Anselm, the holy prior, his father's friend and counsellor, and appointed him to the archbishopric of Canterbury, which had been vacant ever since Lanfranc's death four years before. Rufus' guilty conscience was quieted, and the people of England were deeply thankful for such a prelate, but before long the king and Anselm naturally did not find each other harmonious, and after a brave fight for what he believed to be the right, Anselm appealed to Rome and left England with orders never to return.

Robert was the same careless man that he had been in his youth; through war and peace, danger and security, he lived as if there were no to-morrow to provide for and no future to be dreaded. I have sketched the course of affairs as briefly as possible in both England and Normandy, as if the only men within their borders were these two incompetent brothers who so ill became the Conqueror's "kingly helm," as Master Wace loves to call the crown. But the church builders were still at work like ants busy with their grains of sand, towers were rising, knights were fighting and parading, ladies were ordering their households, the country men and women were tilling the green fields of both countries and gathering in their harvests year by year. There had been trouble now and then, as we have just seen, between the kingdom and the duchy, between both of them and their border foes, but almost ten years went by, and the children who had played with their toys and sighed over their horn books the summer that William the Conqueror died were now men and women grown. It would not seem like the old Normandy if the news of some new great enterprise did not run like wildfire through the towns and country lanes. The blood of the Northmen was kindled with the blood of all Christendom at the story of the Turks' capture of the Holy Sepulchre and the blessed city of Jerusalem. The knights of Sicily were already on their journey by sea and shore; the mother church at Rome called to her children in every land to defend her holiest shrines against the insolence of the heathen.

Duke Robert was most zealous. To go on pilgrimage had been many a knight's ambition, but this was the greatest pilgrimage of all. Robert, as usual, had no money, but to his joy he succeeded in making a bargain with his more thrifty English brother, and pledged Normandy to William Rufus for five years for the sum of something less than seven thousand pounds. Away he went with his lords and gentlemen; they wore white crosses on their right shoulders, and sang hymns as they marched along. Not only lords and gentlemen made up this huge procession of thousands and thousands, but men of every station—from the poor cottages and stately halls alike. If any better persuasion had been needed than the simple announcement that the Turks had taken Jerusalem, it had come by way of Peter the Hermit's preaching. This had created a religious frenzy that the world had never known; from town to town the great preacher had gone with an inexhaustible living stream of persuasive eloquence always at his lips. Women wept and prayed and gave their jewels and rich garments, and men set their teeth and clenched their hands, armed themselves and followed him.

England did not listen at first, and William Rufus chuckled over his good bargain, and taxed his unwilling subjects more heavily than ever to get the money to pay his crusader brother. England would listen by and by, but in this first crusade she took little part, while the Normans and Frenchmen and all their neighbors spent three years of fearful suffering and hardship in the strange countries of the East; at last they won the Holy Sepulchre. The Turks were still fighting to win it back again; they were dangerous enemies, and the Christian host was dwindling fast. The cry was sent again through Europe for more soldiers of the Holy Cross.

Here we come face to face again with the old viking spirit: under all the fast-increasing luxury that threatened to sap and dull the life of Normandy, the love of adventure and fierce energy of character were only sleeping. The most sentimental and pleasure-loving of Robert's knights could lightly throw off his ribbons and gay trappings, and buckle on his armor when the summons came. Quickly they marched and fiercely they fought in the holy wars, and so it came about that the Norman banners were planted at the gates of Jerusalem and Antioch, and new kingdoms were planted in the East. This is not the place to follow the Crusaders' fortunes, or the part that the Norman Sicilians played in the great enterprise of the Middle Ages. At least it must make but an incident in my scheme of the Story of the Normans.

There is a familiar modern sound in the bewailings of our old chroniclers over their taxes. Resentment and pathos were blended then as they are now in such complaints, but though William Rufus was not the least of such extortionate offenders, he gave much of the money back in fine buildings; the famous Great Hall of Westminster was built in his day, and the stout wall that surrounded his father's Tower of London, besides a noble bridge across the Thames.

When people expected un failing generosity and gold thrown to the crowd oftener than in these days, it is difficult to see how the king could satisfy popular expectation without preliminary taxation. Yet the wails of the chroniclers go up like the chirp of the grasshopper. There was one mistaken scheme of benevolence in the endowment of charities, which have borne bitter fruit of pauperism ever since, for which taxation might well have been spared.

William Rufus died in the year 1100, in the New Forest. The peasants believed that it was enchanted and accursed, and that evil spirits flew about among the trees on dark and stormy nights. There was a superstition that it was a fated place to those who belonged to the

Conqueror's line. Another prince had been killed there, named Richard, too—the son of Duke Robert of Normandy.

The last year of the Red King's reign had been peaceful. The Witan gathered to meet him at Westminster and Winchester and Gloucester, and he reigned unchallenged from Scotland to Maine, and there was truce with the French king at Paris. One August morning he went out to the chase after a jolly night at one of the royal hunting-lodges. The party scattered in different directions, and the king and Sir Walter Tyrrel, a famous sportsman, were seen riding away together, and their dogs after them. That night a poor forester, a lime-burner, was going through the forest with his clumsy cart, and stumbled over the king's body, which lay among the ferns with an arrow deep in the breast. He lifted it into the cart and carried it to Winchester, where it was buried next day with little sorrow. There were few bells tolled and few prayers said, for the priests owed little to any friendliness of William Rufus.

There were many stories told about his death. Tyrrel said that the arrow was shot by an unknown hand, and that he had run away for fear that people should accuse him of the murder, which they certainly did! Others said that Tyrrel shot at a stag and the arrow glanced aside from an oak, but nobody knows now, and in those days too many people were glad that the king was dead, to ask many questions or to try to punish any one.

Robert might have claimed the kingdom now because of the old agreement, but he was still in the East fighting for Jerusalem. Henry Beauclerc had been one of the huntsmen that fatal morning, so he hurried to Winchester and claimed the crown. He made more good promises than any of his predecessors, and the people liked him because he was English-born, and so they made another Norman king. Henry Beauclerc reigned over England thirty-five years, and won himself another name of the Lion of Justice. He did not treat his brother Robert justly, however he may have deserved his title in other ways; but he had a zoological garden and brought wild beasts from different quarters of the earth, and he fostered a famous love of learning, and put Ralph

Flambard in the Tower as soon as he possibly could, and more than all, chose an excellent woman for his wife, Maud, the good daughter of the Scottish King Malcolm. He was an untruthful man, but a great man for all that, and made a better king than some that England had already endured. In many ways his reign was a gain to England. There was a distinct advance in national life, and while the English groaned under his tyranny they could not help seeing that he sought for quietness and order and was their best champion against the worse tyranny of the nobles. Mr. Freeman believes that the Saxon element was the permanent one in English history, and that the Norman conquest simply modified it somewhat and was a temporary influence brought to bear for its improvement. It is useless to argue the question with such odds of learning and thought as his against one, but the second invasion of Northmen by the roundabout way of Normandy, seems as marked a change as the succession of the Celts to the Britons, or the Saxons to the Danes. The Normans had so distinctly made a great gain in ideas and civilization, that they were as much foreigners as any Europeans could have been to the Anglo-Saxons of that eleventh century, and their coining had a permanent effect, besides a most compelling power. It seems to me that England would have disintegrated without them, not solidified, and a warring handful of petty states have been the result.

Yet undoubtedly through many centuries of history writing the English of the Conqueror's day have been made to take too low a place in the scale of civilization. As a nation, they surely responded readily to the Norman stimulus, but the Normans had never found so good a chance to work out their own ideas of life and achievement as on English soil in the first hundred years after the Conquest. In many respects the Saxon race possesses greater and more reliable qualities than any other race; stability, perseverance, self-government, industry are all theirs. Yet the Normans excelled them in their genius for great enterprises and their love of fitness and elegance in social life and in the arts. Indeed we cannot do better than to repeat here what has been quoted once already. "Without them England would have been mechanical, not artistic; brave, not chivalrous; the home of learning, not of thought."

It has also been the fashion to ignore the influence of five hundred years' contact between Roman civilization and the Saxon inhabitants of Great Britain. Surely great influences have been brought to bear upon the Anglo-Saxon race. That the making of England was more significant to the world and more valuable than any manifestation of Norman ability, is in one way true, but let us never forget that much that has been best in English national life has come from the Norman elements of it rather than the Saxon. England the colonizer, England the country of intellectual and social progress, England the fosterer of ideas and chivalrous humanity, is Norman England, and the Saxon influence has oftener held her back in dogged satisfaction and stubbornness than urged her forward to higher levels. The power of holding, back is necessary to the stability of a kingdom, but not so necessary as the

"Glory of going on and still to be——"

The conjunction of Norman and Saxon elements has made England the great nation that she is.

It is too easy as we draw near the end of this story of the Normans to wander into talk about the lessons of Norman history and to fall into endless generalizations. Let us look a little longer at Henry Beauclerc's time while Robert, under the shadow of his name of duke, spends enough dreary blinded years in prison to give him space to remember again and again the misspent years of his youth and his freedom; while Henry plots and plans carefully for the continuance of his family upon the throne of England and Normandy, only to be disappointed at every turn. His son is coming from France with a gay company and is lost in the White Ship with all his lords and ladies, and the people who hear the news do not dare to tell the king, and at last send a weeping little lad into the royal presence to falter out the story of the shipwreck. What a touch of humanity is there! The king never smiled afterward, but he plotted on and went his kingly ways, "the last of those great Norman kings who, with all their vices, their cruelty, and their lust, displayed great talents of organization and adaptation, guided England with a wise, if a strong, hand through the days of her youth, and by their instinctive, though selfish, love of order paved the way for the ultimate rise of a more stable, yet a freer government."

The last Norman Duke of Normandy was really that young Prince William, who was drowned in the White Ship off the port of Barfleur, whom Henry had invested with the duchy and to whom the nobility had just done homage. After his death, the son of Robert made claim to the succession, and the greater proportion of the Normans upheld his claim, and the king of France openly favored him, but he died of a wound received in battle, and again Henry, rid of this competitor, built an elaborate scheme upon the succession of his daughter Matilda, whom he married to Geoffrey Plantagenet, son of the Count of Anjou. But for all this, after the king's death, the law of succession was too unsettled to give his daughter an unquestioned claim. Hereditary title was not independent yet of election by the nobles, and Matilda's claims were by many people set aside. There were wars and disorders too intricate and dreary to repeat. Stephen, Count of Boulogne, son of that Count Stephen of Blois who married the Conqueror's daughter Adela, usurped the throne of England, and there was a miserable time of anarchy in both England and Normandy. And as the government passed away in this apparently profitless interregnum to the houses of Blois and of Anjou, so Normandy seems like Normandy no longer. Her vitality is turned into different channels, and it is in the history of England and of France and of the Low Countries that we must trace the further effect of Norman influence.

XVIII.   CONCLUSION.

"I looked: aside the dust-cloud rolled,—

The Waster seemed the Builder too;

Upspringing from the ruined Old

I saw the New."

—WHITTIER.

IT will be clearly seen that there is great apparent disproportion between certain parts of this sketch of the rise and growth of the Norman people. I have not set aside the truth that Normandy was not reunited to France until 1204, and I do not forget that many years lie between that date and the time when I close my account of the famous duchy. But the story of the growth of the Normans gives one the key to any later part of their history, and I have contented myself with describing the characters of the first seven dukes and Eadward the Confessor, who were men typical of their time and representative of the various types of national character. Of the complex questions in civic and legal history I am not competent to speak, nor does it seem to me that they properly enter into such a book as this. With Mr. Freeman's learned and exhaustive work at hand as a book of reference, the readers of this story of Normandy will find all their puzzles solved.

But I hope that I have made others see the Normans as I have seen them, and grow as interested in their fortunes as I have been. They were the foremost people of their time, being most thoroughly alive and quickest to see where advances might be made in government, in architecture, in social life. They were gifted with sentiment and with good taste, together with fine physical strength and intellectual cleverness. In the first hundred years of the duchy they made perhaps as rapid progress in every way, and had as signal influence among their contemporaries, as any people of any age,—unless it is ourselves, the people of the young republic of the United States, who might be called the Normans of modern times. For with many of the gifts and many of the weaknesses (and dangers, too) of our viking ancestry, we have repeated the rapid increase of power which was a characteristic of our Norman kindred; we have conquered in many fights with the natural forces of the universe where they fought, humanity against humanity. Much of what marked the Northman and the Norman marks us still.

The secret of Normandy's success was energetic self-development and apprehension of truth; the secret of Normandy's failures was the secret of all failures—blindness to the inevitable effects of certain causes, and unwillingness to listen to her best and most far-seeing teachers. Carlyle said once to a friend: "There has never been a nation yet that did any thing great that was not deeply religious." The things that are easy and near are chosen, instead of the things that make for righteousness. When luxury becomes not the means, but the end of life, humanity's best weapons grow rusty, and humanity's best intelligence is dulled and threatens to disappear. The church forgets her purpose and invites worshippers of the church instead of worshippers of God. The state is no longer an impersonated administrator of justice and order, but a reservoir from which to plunder and by which to serve private ends.

I am not able to speak of the influence of the Normans upon the later kingdom of France, the France of our day, as I confess the writer of such a book as this should have been, but there is one point which has been of great interest as the southward course of the Northmen has been eagerly followed.

It has been the common impression that there was a marked growth of refinement and courtliness, of dignified bearing and imaginative literature connected with the development of the French men and women of early times, to the gradual widening of which the modern world had been indebted for much of its best social attainment.

I think that a single glance at the France of the ninth and tenth centuries will do away with any belief in its having been the sole inspirer or benefactor. The Franks were products of German development, and were not at that time pre-eminent for social culture. They were a ruder people by far than the Italians or even the people of Spain, less developed spiritually, and wanting in the finer attributes of human instinct or perception. Great as they already were, no one can claim that quickness of tact or special intolerance of ill-breeding came from their direction. Dante speaks, a little later than this, of the "guzzling Germans," and though we must make allowance for considerable race prejudice, there was truth, too, in his phrase. Not from the Franks, therefore, but from among the very rocks and chasms of the viking nature, sprang a growth of delicate refinement that made the yellow-haired jarls and the "sea-kings' daughters" bring a true, poetical, and lovely spirit to Normandy, where they gave a soul to the body of art and letters that awaited them. Each nation had something to give to the other, it is true, but it was the Northern spirit that made the gifts of both available and fruitful to humanity.

It may rightly be suggested that the standard of behavior was low everywhere in the tenth century, according to our present standards, but it is true that there was a re-kindling of light in the North, which may be traced in its continued reflections through Norway to Normandy, and thence to France and England and the world. We have only to remind ourselves of the development of literature in Iceland and the building of governmental and social strength and dignified individuality, to see that the Northmen by no means owed every thing to the influence of French superiority and precedence. We have only to compare the tenth century with the eleventh, to see what an impulse had been given. The saga-lovers and the clear-eyed people of the North were gifted with a spark of grace peculiarly their own.

There is a pretty story told by an English traveller in Norway, who met a young woman leading an old blind beggar through the street of a poor, plain village. She was descended from one of the noble families of ancient times; it was her pleasure and duty to serve the friendless old man. But the traveller insists that never, among the best people he has met, has he found such dignity and grace as this provincial woman wore, who knew nothing of courts or the world's elegance. There was a natural nobility in her speech and manner which the courtliest might envy, and which might adorn the noblest palace and be its most charming decoration. It is easy to write these words with sympathy, and perhaps the traveller's half-forgotten story has been embellished unconsciously with the memory in my mind of kindred experiences in that country of the North. Plainness and poverty make gentle blood seem more gracious still, and the green mountain-sides and fresh air of old Norway have not yet ceased to inspire simple, unperverted souls, from whose life a better and higher generation seems more than possible.

The impulses that make toward social development are intermittent. There is the succession of growing time and brooding time, of summer and winter, in the great ages of the world. If we look at the Normans as creatures of a famous spring where Europe made a bold and profitable advance in every way, I think that we shall not be far from right.

In telling their story in this imperfect way I have not been unmindful of the dark side of their character, but what they were is permanent, while what they were not was temporary. The gaps they left were to be filled up by other means—by the slow processes by which God in nature and humanity evolves the best that is possible for the present with something that forestalls the future. The stones that make part of a cathedral wall are shaped also with relation to the very dome.

Here, at the beginning of the Norman absorption into England, I shall end my story of the founding and growth of the Norman people. The mingling of their brighter, fiercer, more enthusiastic, and visionary nature with the stolid, dogged, prudent, and resolute Anglo-Saxons belongs more properly to the history of England. Indeed, the difficulty would lie in not knowing where to stop, for one may tell the two races apart even now, after centuries of association and affiliation. There are Saxon landholders, and farmers, and statesmen in England yet—unconquered, unpersuaded, and un-Normanized. But the effect on civilization of the welding of the two great natures cannot be told fairly in this or any other book we are too close to it and we ourselves make too intimate a part of it to judge impartially. If we are of English descent we are pretty sure to be members of one party or the other. Saxon yet or Norman yet, and even the confusion of the two forces renders us not more able to judge of either, but less so. We must sometimes look at England as a later Normandy; and yet, none the less, as the great leader and personified power that she is and has been these many hundred years, drawing her strength from the best of the Northern races, and presenting the world with great men and women as typical of these races and as grandly endowed to stand for the representatives of their time in days to come, as the men and women of Greece were typical, and live yet in our literature and song. In the courts and stately halls of England, in the market-places, and among followers of the sea or of the drum, we have seen the best triumphs and glories of modern humanity, no less than the degradations, the treacheries, and the mistakes. In the great pageant of history we can see a nation rise, and greaten, and dwindle, and disappear like the varying lifetime of a single man, but the force of our mother England is not yet spent, though great changes threaten her, and the process of growth needs winter as well as summer. Her life is not the life of a harborless country, her fortunes are the fortunes of her generosity. But whether the Norman spirit leads her to be self-confident or headstrong and wilful, or the Saxon spirit holds her back into slowness and dulness, and lack of proper perception in emergencies or epochs of necessary change, still she follows the right direction and leads the way. It is the Norman graft upon the sturdy old Saxon tree that has borne best fruit among the nations—that has made the England of history, the England of great scholars and soldiers and sailors, the England of great men and women, of books and ships and gardens and pictures and songs! There is many a gray old English house standing among its trees and fields, that has sheltered and nurtured many a generation of loyal and tender and brave and gentle souls. We shall find there men and women who, in their cleverness and courtliness, their grace and true pride and beauty, make us understand the old Norman beauty and grace, and seem to make the days of chivalry alive again.

But we may go back farther still, and discover in the lonely mountain valleys and fiord-sides of Norway even a simpler, courtlier, and nobler dignity. In the country of the sagamen and the rough sea-kings, beside the steep-shored harbors of the viking dragon-ships, linger the constantly repeated types of an earlier ancestry, and the flower of the sagas blooms as fair as ever. Among the red roofs and gray walls of the Norman towns, or the faint, bright colors of its country landscapes, among the green hedgerows and golden wheat-fields of England, the same flowers grow in more luxuriant fashion, but old Norway and Denmark sent out the seed that has flourished in richer soil. To-day the Northman, the Norman, and the Englishman, and a young nation on this western shore of the Atlantic are all kindred who, possessing a rich inheritance, should own the closest of kindred ties.

Printed in Germany
by Amazon Distribution
GmbH, Leipzig